Beyond "1984": The Future of Library Technical Services

Beyond "1984": The Future of Library Technical Services

Peter Gellatly
Editor

The Haworth Press
New York

Beyond "1984": The Future of Library Technical Services has also been published as *Technical Services Quarterly,* Volume 1, Numbers 1/2, Fall/Winter 1983.

The Haworth Press, Inc., 28 East 22 Street, New York, NY 10010

Library of Congress Cataloging in Publication Data
Main entry under title:

Beyond ''1984'' : the future of library technical services.

''Has also been published as Technical services quarterly, volume 1, numbers 1/2, fall 1983''—T.p. verso.
  Includes bibliographical references.
  1. Processing (Libraries)—Addresses, essays, lectures, 2. Libraries—Automation—Addresses, essays, lectures. 3. Library science—Data processing—Addresses, essays, lectures. I. Gellatly, Peter.
Z688.5.B49 1983 025'.02'02854 83-17166
ISBN 0-86656-275-3

Beyond "1984": The Future of Library Technical Services

Technical Services Quarterly
Volume 1, Numbers 1/2

CONTENTS

Beyond "1984": The Future of Library Technical Services

INTRODUCTION

About *Technical Services Quarterly*

In an essay in this opening issue of *TSQ*, Norman Stevens projects that by the year 2019 the technical services operation will be a thing of the past and the people associated with it, if not long since departed, working in other capacities elsewhere. We agree that the face of librarianship and information science in general will have changed considerably by that distant time, but assert with a bravado at least the equal of Stevens' own that, in spite of inevitable changes, the work of the technical services specialist will by then have become not less but more important.

Whatever else may be said, it is clear that libraries are more concerned now than ever before with making their collections accessible to the user. They realize, as Anaya says in his admirable essay, *The Magic of Words,* that their collections, 10,000 volumes in size or 1,000,000, hold an infinitude of riches, and that it is up to them as a bounden duty to provide the appropriate bibliographical apparatus to define and control these riches.

Activity in the technical services area has over the past twenty years attained a height and intensity that places it among the most phenomenal library happenings of all time. Electronic data processing revolutionizes everything it touches, and the changes it has brought and continues to bring to librarianship and its allied sciences are as great certainly as those that mandated the replacing 100 years ago of the ledger catalog with the three-by-five catalog we all grew up with. If indeed, as Naisbitt postulates in *Megatrends,* the world has left the industrial era and proceeded into the information era, the changes that lie ahead in technical services, far from reducing the area to one of vast obsolescence will surely bring it even greater volatility and life than are found there at present. The online catalog is a reality even now, and other monumental changes will follow quickly. An enthusiastic library school teacher of our acquaintance declares everything to be new and exciting. That suggestion is clearly on the mark.

TSQ's mission is to keep track of the changes and to comment on them in theme issues, like the present, and in others that deal in true journalistic fashion with a variety of topics. *TSQ* aims, moreover, to provide its special family of readers with a forum for voicing opinions and sharing experiences that have to do with any aspect of the new librarianship, and invites your participation in this venture.

Peter Gellatly
Editor

What Is Ahead in Technical Services

The book is not dead. . . , Tom Surprenant in the *Wilson Library Bulletin*

Goodbye, written word. Jack Nicholson as David Stabler in *The King of Marvin Gardens*

It is easy to be sanguine about the future or gloomy to the point of projecting upon it a doomsday scenario of stultifyingly chilling proportions. Nineteen eighty-four is of course, here, but whether gloom and doom or excited optimism is a proper response to this event depends in a real sense upon our constitutional makeup and the way in which we regard the world and what is happening in it.

However this may be, one thing is certain, and that is that walking backwards into the Twenty-First Century is not a procedure that most of us can recommend. In this inaugural issue of *TSQ* the changes taking place in technical services now, and those that can be expected later are described, and their impact on library services in general is examined.

A friend suggested as this project began that she was looking forward with interest to the ''bold predictions and cogent insights'' that the project would produce. And while some of the things our authors say do indeed partake of that abstract perfection that is both undeniable and unprovable, it remains true that predictions, however fully rounded and elegant, can be as far off-course as any errant Challenger satellite. Everything is of course hypothesis. Hard and irrefutable fact is rare at any time, and no claim is made in our study to absolute or even relative prescience. We hope nevertheless that our findings will prove diverting and useful.

We live in an unsettling world, one in which high government officials speak of ''hardware kill capacity'' and questionable slogans like ''Peace through Strength'' seem to have appeal. Yet we manage most of the time to look forward gladly enough to what lies ahead. Change, we know, is inevitable, a great constant, and we would not resist it if we could, realizing, as somebody has said, that resistance does not retard it but instead leaves the resisters disadvantaged and often stranded. Yet, as any weatherperson will concede, the issuing of statements about anticipated change is a procedure fraught with difficulty. Consequently, if the changes forecast by those of us with the temerity to make forecasts give the impression, in McHarg's term, that earth will soon be nothing more than a trail of dust in the stratosphere, a kind of super El Chichón extrusion, the possibility remains of a far less apocalyptic future than this. We prefer to think that while there will be changes, and many of them far-reaching, their effect will in general be benign and acceptable.

Robert Benchley once remarked, "Tell us your phobias, and we will tell you what you are afraid of." Phobias are one thing, anxieties another; and if the first can be dismissed as excessive and beside the point, anxieties are less easily dealt with. Our lives are full of these—they adrenalize and impart a hyper quality to simple, everyday occurrences—and there is no escape from them.

One anxiety that afflicts us all derives from the incursion into our lives of high technology influences. The incursion may manifest itself in relatively mild form as a case of CRT euphoria, a condition in which the victim is mesmerized into inactivity by the flickering of a CRT screen, or in more insidious form as the Pac-Man syndrome. In this, compulsions are played out with disastrous consequences. An instance is described in the movie, *The Producers.* Here the protagonist, Zero Mostel, crazed by whatever whirrings and clickings the computer age gives forth, determines that the world will be a better place without authors in it, and sets out to dispatch as many in his immediate vicinity as he can.

For most of us, fortunately, high technology influences are less deadly. We feel an uneasiness about certain happenings, but are able to cope decently enough, despite Toffler, with our uneasiness. Librarians are certainly no longer afraid of the computer, if indeed they ever were. Few of us, in fact, would now feel at ease in a library without computers. We have entered what Tonkery refers to as a period of "console librarianship," and a return to pre-computer days becomes for us increasingly unthinkable.

If we want to know what the Twenty-First Century will really be like, then its arrival must be attended. In the meantime, of course, speculation suggests all sorts of splendid—and sometimes not so splendid—possibilities. At one end of the scale is the reductionist notion that the printed word will be available only on TV screens and that, as a corollary, libraries will be relegated to a minor and unrecognizable role in some vast electronic network of information agencies. At the other end is the proposition that nothing much will have changed—that we may be using AACR3 or −4, but MARC will still exist, and so will the printed book. In between these extremes lie a myriad of suggestions, both cautious and intrepid, that, if they do nothing more, make abundantly clear that library matters will be characterized in coming years by a volatility unlike any that has occurred heretofore in implication and transforming impact.

We can in truth expect a crescendo of change. How much confidence is to be placed in predictions as to the nature and extent of the change remains, of course, a question. The transition from horse and buggy transportation to space travel and from water and wind power to nuclear, changes more or less foreseen in the last century, did take place, although in ways and with consequences not apparent at the time. Thus, if it is possible to imagine in outline what lies ahead, that is all that can be done. Time will fill in the details.

What follows are a number of perceptions—some categorical, some impressionistic—about the future and what it portends:

As the reality of 1984 fails to match the full bleakness of Orwell's age of Newspeak and doublethink, so the year 2000 will be a smaller disaster than much present opinion infers.

Saul Kent predicts in *The Life-Extension Revolution* (Morrow, 1980) that findings in pituitary research will permit the reversal of the ageing process. By the end of the century, he says, ordinary people, and not just those sturdy yak-herds in the Caucasus, can expect to live for 150 years, and look at 150 as though they were fifty or sixty.

Cryogenic breakthroughs will occur, according to Rodney Gorney, author of *The Human Agenda* (University of California Press, 1982), but misgivings will accompany them, as, for one thing, the hazards of returning from suspended animation are not properly understood. What ship's captain, Gorney asks, would want to return to a world in which there were no ships. Or, he might have added, what librarian to a world without libraries.

Wayne Boucher of the University of Southern California's

Center for Futures Research, says that flex-time and the compressed workweek will before long be observed everywhere. It is unlikely, he adds, that the traditional forty-hour weekly stint will change. People will do their work when they choose to do it, but work no less hard than at present.

Boucher says also that millionaire status will hold little cachet by the year 2000. One in 10,000 Americans was a millionaire in 1960; today the ratio is about one to 2500; by 2000 inflation will have eroded the dollar to the point at which nearly everybody has become a millionaire.

John Naisbitt indicates in *Megatrends* (Warner, 1982) that 60-70% of Americans are now engaged in some form of information processing. By the end of the century, he contends, the percentage will have risen to 80.

Power points out that 5% of librarians are self-employed now and that by 2000 half will be. For the most part, she says, these will earn their living as independent information specialists. Others will serve as management and computer consultants, booksellers and subscription agents.

The computer will play an increasingly large role in libraries. As a result, libraries will gradually cease being paper-intensive organizations, as Marcum and Boss describe them. Their paper files will disappear, replaced by online files of various descriptions, and disappearing along with the paper files will be what McClure and Coy call the librarian's 3 × 5 mentality.

Lancaster says that the computer is changing the way in which things are done, and will soon determine what is done.

Librarians will have an intimate acquaintance with FORTRAN, COBOL, BASIC and their numerous successors, and will think nothing of tossing off a complicated program during their coffee-break.

Computer adaptations will, according to Upham, bring word- and time-crunching procedures; and these, she says will allow information to be greatly compressed and compiled at astronomic speed.

Computer jargon will swamp the world. Word-processors, if *Doonesbury* can be credited, will become "consumer-compatible lifeware," and other such grotesqueries will flourish. Language will undergo a complete metamorphosis by the year 2000, when today's version of it will seem not merely quaint, but totally antiquated. Vocabulary, syntax, idiom and phonetic structure will evolve into as yet unforeseen forms and patterns. The new language will have the click and bite of the computer, and will be as strange to the ear as the sound of Middle Earth or outer space.

Computers, which even now can talk, will become much more articulate than they are at present. And they will learn foreign languages.

Computer to computer links—interconnection—will become commonplace before the present decade is out.

Androbots will invade the library during the '90s. These will be used in fetching items from the stacks—books perhaps or their surrogates—and in returning them to the shelf afterwards. (And if the androbot checking books at the door looks suspiciously like Darth Vader, no one should be too surprised.)

Technical services will be decentralized, i.e., the distinctions drawn between technical and public work will disappear. Everybody will become his or her own cataloger, and work at the public desk will be shared by all alike.

According to McKinley, post-1984 processing will be carried out through use of interconnected online arrangements of various sorts. (Both McKinley and Thompson postulate the creation of a new cottage industry that will provide many of the products now issued by library technical units.)

The online updating and correcting of records will be accelerated to such a degree by the end of the century that an operation now requiring twenty minutes of attention will complete itself in a matter of seconds. Processing backlogs, in consequence will become a thing of the past.

By the year 2000 cross-references will be plentiful, authorities will never be in dispute, a content analysis will be thoroughgoing and incisive, and there will be access to everything by class numbers, ISBNs and ISSNs and other identifiers.

OPACs (online public access catalogs) will be used in libraries of all sorts and sizes. The card catalog will gradually be phased out, and by the end of the century will be as obsolete as the ledger catalog.

Random access computer memory will, according to Micciche, be generally available to libraries and their users within the next few years' time.

All cataloging, Bloss says, will become union or distributed cataloging, i.e., it will be produced and shared on a nationwide, if not worldwide, basis.

UBC and UAP (universal bibliographical control and universal availability of publications) will be realized early in the new century.

Before long, Lancaster says, print-on-paper publications will all as a matter of course have their electronic counterparts, as the *Index Medicus* does today.

Electronic books, i.e., books that have no print equivalent and that are accessed rather than distributed, will be common by the early part of the next century.

Because the printed book is convenient, portable, attractive and relatively inexpensive (Katz would add to this list the fact that it provides a pleasant tactile experience), the printed book will survive. At the same time, many items, like the *American Academic Encyclopedia*, a prototype electronic publication, will be available in online fashion only.

The general interest magazine, which has been in decline for the past twenty years or so, will continue to lose ground as VCRs and pay TV compete for the country's entertainment dollar.

The online journal will have made such headway by the turn of the century that it will be as common then as the online index is right now.

Bloss suggests that a national periodicals center will be established before the new century is very old. Electronic copies of materials in its collection will be made available to borrowers at a fee that depends upon the size of the item and the distance over which it must be transmitted.

The NPC will maintain an online union list of serials that is thoroughly inclusive and up-to-date.

Hardcopy collections will become largely retrospective in nature, according to Bloss.

Farrington points out that hardcopy collections will shrink in physical size, as books and other print items are replaced by media of great storage density such as the videodisc, videotex and teletext.

New wave formats like the laser-read optical digital recording will by the end of the century occupy as much shelf-space in libraries as print items do now.

Microfilm as a storage medium will give way within the next decade to storage on optical discs. Deteriorating materials will likewise be transferred for conservation purposes to optical discs.

Facsimile transmission will be perfected before the end of the century. Color transmission will by then be effective and inexpensive.

Commercial networks operated by booksellers, subscription agencies, and sometimes governmental offices will relieve libraries of much of their day-to-day processing activity.

Present-day examples of this kind of network are LINX, PERLINE, and Artemis.

The great American utilities, OCLC, RLIN and WLN, will join forces by the end of the century, and together be able to provide their clients with bibliographical services of all possible descriptions.

Galsworthy says that if no thought is given to the future, no future is possible. This is stern, but perhaps in light of present world conditions, it bears heeding. Libraries, in examining trends and happenings in their own area, are setting the stage for a future that will be both productive and worthwhile.

PG

Technical Services in Ten Years

Neal L. Edgar

ABSTRACT. A capsule history of library information control is presented, and the role of the computer in this function is explored. Some thoughts are then presented on advances being made in library activities of various sorts.

In an address of welcome to the first A.L.A. Conference in 1876, John William Wallace asked:

> Will it be practicable to continue through another century the formation of libraries, which shall contain all books upon every subject? Will not such libraries if continued and formed tumble to pieces by their own weight, and when the subjects into which their infinite volumes are divided have all grown sufficiently large, break up and resolve themselves into their primordial elements?[11]

Perhaps any library can have any item it wishes, but no library can have everything. None does now, and none ever will.

The same is true for total information control. In a science fiction setting, Hal Draper[2] predicted information control through notched electrons. But the system of indexes, files, and catalogs, each raised to many powers, finally collapsed. The result? All information was apparently lost, and everyone had to start over, building indexes, files, and catalogs.

Twenty-five years after Wallace, Charles P. Steinmetz wondered about the future of electricity:

> On a subject like this it obviously is not possible to make any definite statements. We do not know what the future will

Neal L. Edgar was Associate Curator, Special Collections Division, Kent State University Libraries, Kent, OH 44242 (mailing: c/o Susanna Edgar, 1378 Athena Drive, Kent, OH 44240).

bring. A single year's development may reverse the trend of progress and turn it into an entirely different direction.[10]

The same is true, I think, about the future of technical services; but we can at least ponder the question a bit and toss out a few ideas. I would certainly hope, incidentally, that we are not headed in the same direction as Star Trek which had a librarian, Mr. Spock, but no books at all.

One assumption about the future of technical services is that an increased use of computers is a certainty. Another assumption is that technical processing is largely repetitive and can be done in robot fashion. This second assumption is often refined by attempting to show that robotic operations, controlled by relatively simplistic computer programs, can control most technical service operations. The most important fact that should influence thinking in this area is that each item, even copies of the same monograph, is different from all other items. The differences may be small or minor, but in a strict sense, no item is exactly congruent with any other. This observation alone implies that computer programs, written to feed computer operations, have to confront a very large set of complex variables, and that once a combination has been met, the programs may never see that particular set again. There is also an implication that the programs have to be written to deal with combinations which have not yet been encountered.

One syllogism might be: computers are found in an increasing number of places carrying out more and more operations; libraries are a part of society, and incorporate a wide variety of activities; therefore, computers will have an increasing role in libraries. That reasoning may be both logical and true. I will admit that computers are more and more important in libraries, but that is not necessarily the syllogism for technical services.

Another bit or reasoning is also logical and will be recognized as being true insofar as technical services in libraries are concerned: computers, while increasing their roles in society, cannot yet carry out all activities, such as those requiring abstract reasoning; libraries incorporate many activities which require abstract reasoning and decision making, such as interpreting reference questions, selecting among available publications, and synthesizing bibliographic details needed in library acquisitions and cataloging; therefore, libraries include, and will continue to include, activities which computers cannot carry out and will not be able to perform at any time in the immediate future.

In early 1983, at least three of the four major networks (or utilities or whatever may be the proper designation) appear to be in trouble of one sort or another—mechanical, financial, contractual, data base size and access, membership cohesiveness, and so on. The literature of librarianship, and sometimes the more publicly available press, contain references to this situation. In many cases, these facilities are unable to fulfill promises, and the reasons often seem to be a failure to understand the technical problems of bibliographic control that surface for millions of items, each different, if only in minute ways, one from another.

But it is not just the conglomerates. Several systems, some designed for the "total" operation of one library, are also unable to work well, or at least with promised performance. This is often true for the library for which the system was designed. And when attempts are made to transfer single-library systems to other libraries, the failure rate seems to be higher. It is necessary to go through the argument that promises of fulfillment are no more than rhetoric? Even wandering through the exhibit booths at an A.L.A. annual conference leaves the impression that many snake oil salesmen are still lurking around.

Tom Alexander wrote three articles examining the concepts involved with the problem of "endowing a computer with genuine intelligence." One of these[1] uses the common example of a chess-playing computer program. Such a program would have to calculate moves and countermoves in an order of magnitude numbering beyond the total of atoms in the universe. Obviously, this is impractical, partly because such a computer program would be unable to disregard unreasonable combinations. If that is a valid observation for chess games, it probably is also valid for a wholly computerized technical processing system designed for use in libraries.

In the developing world of using computers for an increasing number of human activities, a term often encountered is "artificial intelligence"—a phrase which, to my nineteenth-century way of thinking, is an obvious oxymoron. Understanding analogies, recognizing generalizations, drawing inferences, and other intellectual activities often associated with thought still seem, to me, to be beyond the capacity of computers. Indeed, computers are very fast in making calculations, and printing devices which operate in terms of many hundreds of lines per minute are also impressive. But I am reminded that quantity has no correlation with quality. What is commonly seen in advertising about computer systems is almost pure "hype." The implications are that the answers are already here, but with only a little exposure it becomes obvious that this is not the case. Computers have not yet learned to think, and my belief is that this will not happen for some years to come. One frightening aspect of this problem is the proliferation of computer "game parlors." Here, people are mesmerizing themselves at the expense of many things, not the least of which is reading. First we dispense with thinking, and then we do away with reading?

Leonard Shatzkin recently examined the publishing industry to discover trends and to suggest some future possibilities. Among the cogent statements he makes is:

> People who read books, even trivial books, are, on the average, more educated, more sophisticated, more affluent, more influential, and more concerned than those who do not. This attracts to books the writer who feels he has something to say to such people.[9]

Note that Shatzkin says, ". . .read books. . .," not squint at computer screens. He is speaking about printed materials. This also implies that those who do not read are, on the other hand, less educated, sophisticated, etc., etc. Despite some possible post hoc reasoning involved here, experience with books and reading tends to support the notion that intellectual growth and reading are symbiotic. If this is so, it is difficult to imagine continued intellectual development without the necessary tool of the printed page. It may be that computers are fast and can, under severe limits, handle vast amounts of information. But it is also true that printed materials are both convenient and practical, to use Shatzkin's words, in ways that computers clearly are not. Simply put, printed materials will remain the principal method of information exchange into the distant future.

Sheila Intner's recent study of public access to media makes two important points: first, she believes that ". . .media cataloging is entering a period of great progress with AACR 2." Her data apparently support the basic principles for which the code's new edition was formulated. At the same time, Intner points out that most public libraries continue to have manual catalogs:

> Is the card catalog disappearing in public libraries? Not yet, according to the responses to this study. More than 85% of the public catalogs are in card form, followed by computer-output-microform (COM) (9%) and book catalogs (2%).[3]

Colman McCarthy, not a librarian, but an observer of the current social scene, observed that:

> Eighty-two percent of the nation's libraries are in towns with populations under 25,000. In one survey, 14% of the responding libraries in towns under 2,500 said they were without phones. Rural libraries average collections of only 16,000 books, well below the 40,000 new titles published each year by American publishers.[5]

What demographic evidence exists that this will change dramatically during the next decade? The majority of libraries are small, and it is quite likely that these, and other libraries, won't even see issues of *Technical Services Quarterly* and have the advantage of the advice which will be found in its issues. These libraries are concerned with processing small numbers of books; and computer-assisted systems, especially for libraries without telephones, are neither available to them nor appropriate to their needs and budgets. Computer systems will not be found, in the near future, in all libraries, let alone the majority of them. They may have small, "personal" computers for game playing and similar substitutes for thinking; but they will not depend on computers for processing materials and providing information from national data banks.

Carlton Rochell hits on an important aspect of futuristics which may apply to libraries and technical services, namely the tendency to use new tools to do old work.[7] He discusses information availability, video applications, and telematics. He also discusses text availability, pointing out that magazines and other printed material will be in data banks, instantly available, in whole or in part, to anyone. (This is true now in such systems as LEXUS and NEXUS.) Rochell also argues that public libraries will lose patrons to "private sector information providers." This development does assume something about costs being carried by the consumers, but he does not provide an answer to that. The problem of getting all this information into data banks is also not discussed. However, new tools, not yet developed, may deal with this process.

Both electronic newspapers and encyclopedias are discussed in some current, non-library literature.[6,8] These articles tend to make such statements as this by Rossman: "The technology of the information age is drawing together all of today's reference books and research materials into one system." All? Nonsense. A start is being made, but only a small part of information is available through the use of data banks. Petroski mentions electronic commands "to search for stories containing key words and phrases." Wonderful. The success of such indexing wholly depends on the quality of the people who identify subject matter and the strength of the thesauri used. This will improve in time, but it will not replace an individual's approach to information based on complex reasoning processes.

Over 200 titles, available in the World Future Society's catalog, are divided into about twenty areas, including "Communications" and "Futuristics."[12] Both introduce books on computers of various kinds and purposes, and topics such as microelectronics and artificial intelligence. Many of the titles are not new, some dating before the mid-1970s. And from reading the descriptions, none has a library, or even what might be called information processing, focus.

To me, this is significant. The World Future Society seems to consider many human activities as important. Many are discussed in publications provided by the society. But the library operations are apparently not a part of their interest. Probably this is because most non-librarians do not comprehend library operations. Part of this is because predicting just what will work in library operations is so difficult.

Nonetheless, we are headed in the right direction in the development of information available in machines and in the indexing of that material. Clerical procedures are changing drastically.[4] Some processes used by libraries lend themselves to computer use. For example, filing rules as used in card catalogs have changed to accommodate new techniques. The "old" L. C. filing rules would probably have needed computer programs well beyond any reasonable construction. The new rules issued by both A. L. A. and L. C. essentially have two rules: one for numbers, and one for everything else which puts things in order "as is," not, as is often the case with older rules, "as if." Both sets of rules are designed for the computer manipulation of information.

Searching in data bases does have some conveniences, but many drawbacks also exist. Librarians still are evaluating, selecting, ordering, receiving, and processing materials. And many of these activities remain "manual." Libraries which have "approval" or "blanket order" plans have, to some degree, surrendered the selection of some materials to computer programs and to processing done by untrained people at large jobbers. Librarians and other professionals, such as subject-trained faculty members, need to be involved with collection development, and trained bibliographers and catalogers are still needed to carry out collection management. This will not change quickly.

Technical services operations will increasingly use computers for such operations as: correspondence, accounting, notification, the flow of materials, and some steps in bibliographic control. These uses of computers are welcome, and mean improvements in service and efficiencies. In the process of accepting these changes, the organization of technical services work may well have to change in order to use the developments fully. Jobs and work organization will have to change. New tools will have to be developed.

What will not change in the near future will be the need to make intellectual choices. An example of this is dealing with changes in titles or other bibliographic details involved with serials. These will have to be made by trained people who understand the processes involved, who physically handle the material, and who make decisions based on a large number of subtle variables. The intervention of the mind will continue to control technical services in libraries.

What does the future mean for library technical services? More use of computers; more sophistication in information manipulation; an increase in the number of details available; probably faster processing; and techniques not yet envisioned or developed—all these are coming. But in the future, librarians will also be carrying out intellectual activities interrelating people and books, and these activities will continue to be manual. And they will continue to be manual in all libraries. Only a small percentage of libraries will be using machines for computer operations because only a small number of libraries will have the necessary funds. I do not see dramatic change for the most part in technical service operations in the next decade. Some things will improve around the edges, yes; but the intellectual operations will remain the same and will continue to be carried out by trained librarians and other thinking people.

BIBLIOGRAPHY

1. Alexander, Tom. "Teaching Computers the Art of Reason." *Fortune.* 105 (May 17, 1982), 82-92.

2. Draper, Hal. "MS FND IN A LBRY." in: *17 × Infinity.* Edited by Graff Conklin. N.Y.: Dell, 1963. p. 52-58.

3. Intner, Sheila S. "A Survey Explores: Equality of Cataloging in the Age of AACR 2." *American Libraries*. 14 (February 1983), 102-103.

4. Kornbluh, Marvin. "The Electronic Office: How It Will Change the Way You Work." *The Futurist*. 16 (June 1982), 37-42.

5. McCarthy, Colman. "Commentary: Boy's Love of Books Wins Him a Library." *The Plain Dealer*. Cleveland, Ohio. August 1, 1982.

6. Petroski, Henry. "The Electronic Newspaper: An Easy Route to 1984?" *The Futurist*. 16 (August 1982), 59-60.

7. Rochell, Carlton. "Telematics—2001 AD." *Library Journal*. 107 (October 1, 1982), 1809-1815.

8. Rossman, Parker. "The Coming Great Electronic Encyclopedia." *The Futurist*. 16 (August 1982), 53-58.

9. Shatzkin, Leonard. *In Cold Type: Overcoming the Book Crisis*. Boston, Mass.: Houghton Mifflin, 1982.

10. Steinmetz, Charles P. *The Future of Electricity*. N.Y.: Electrical School. [1900?].

11. Wallace, John William. *An Address of Welcome*. Philadelphia, Penn.: Sherman & Co., 1876.

12. World Future Society. "Book Catalog Spring 1983." *The Futurist*. 17 (February 1983), 33-52.

Technical Services:
The Decade Ahead

Theodore C. W. Grams, BA, MSLS

ABSTRACT. Traces future direction of technical services, and explains that automation progress may be slowed by increased costs. Anticipates interconnection of major bibliographic utilities, access to Library of Congress authority files on line, automated serials control, wide use of on-line library catalogs, and a common inquiry language. States that while publication formats may change, the book will remain a principal information element. Predicts upgrading of clerical staff to handle complex automated procedures, and describes related changes in acquisitions, cataloging, and serials. Notes problems posed by curtailment of the individual's access to information and the abridgment of his right to privacy.

It would appear well established that the activities common to technical services in a majority of college and university libraries include the acquisition of monographs, serials, and other library materials, by exchange, gift, and purchase; their organization for use by cataloging, other processing, and special indexing; binding and shelf preparation; and more recently, collection conservation and restoration.[1] These functions may be expected to remain through the next decade, although the amount of time allocated to each may vary because of changes in the mission of the parent institution and the availability of resources.

In the public sector, intense competition for funds and concern for cost containment seem destined to remain throughout the next decade, and to continue to have an impact on college and university library programs. University libraries will continue to acquire books throughout this period, despite the predictions to the contrary of Jenkins,[2,3,4] chiefly because the book will remain a highly efficient

Theodore C. W. Grams, Professor, Head of Processing Services, Portland State University Library, P. O. Box 1151, Portland, OR 97207.

19

self-contained unit for information transfer, teaching, and research, usable in a wide variety of situations without the employment of costly peripheral equipment. It will share its place with products of the new technology—the on-line catalogs and data bases, optical image storage discs, videodiscs, and cable and consumer systems—at the time and to the extent that each is able to supply reader-acceptable copy or text in addition to citations, at truly affordable prices.[5,6]

Despite some reduction in the labor-intensive character of technical services operations as a result of automation, expenses for personal services have been perceived as part of a continuously rising curve. However, increases already occurring in the costs of the new technology are reported in a recent study by the Public Policy Research Organization, University of California, Irvine, quoted by Rochell in part as follows:

> The costs of computing are higher than generally estimated and they are rising: the cost of decentralized computer configurations are rising faster than the already rising costs of computing generally; and the benefits of computing are difficult to assess. . .especially in highly sophisticated and complicated systems. . .[7]

Perhaps, therefore, for all but the exceptionally well endowed, change involving a substantial use of the new technology in technical services will occur more slowly than before, and then only in applications where carefully designed and applied studies show a positive cost-benefit ratio.[8]

At the national level, projects presently under development or nearing completion, may be expected to impact technical services operations by the end of the decade in the following ways:

— Interconnection of the major bibliographic utilities (OCLC, RLIN, and WLN) will permit access to each data base by all participants.
— On-line access through the major bibliographic utilities to the Library of Congress name, series, and subject authority files will be possible.
— Substantial progress will have occurred in the development of the technical standards which affect information science and libraries, thereby facilitating intersystems communications, bib-

liographic data display in languages using non-Roman alphabets, and other enhancements.[8]

— Retrospective conversion of card catalogs will be facilitated by access to enlarged data bases of the major bibliographic networks, and through availability of special procedures and controls.

— A new edition of the cataloging rules, more useful and acceptable to the library community, will replace AACR-2.

— Cataloging standards review centers will be maintained by all of the major bibliographic utilities in cooperation with the Library of Congress to facilitate the maintenance of quality control.

— Conservation and restoration activities will increase substantially, and regional centers will be established to provide for widespread conversion of deteriorating materials to optical-disc storage.

— An improved set of machine filing rules will be developed to improve COM catalog user access.

— Changes in publication techniques derived from the new technology will result in the publication of some monographic and serial material on optical image storage discs, videodiscs, and on tape; the latter also may be made available for sale to individuals for copying into personal computers.

Certain aspects of the acquisitions, cataloging, and serials activities already automated will be further developed. In acquisitions, the following changes may be expected in the next decade:

— On-line availability of a common inquiry language and protocols will permit on-line access to *Books in Print* and other national bibliographies by a wide variety of users.

— On-line access to major dealer and publisher inventory files will be available.

— On-line order transmission to major dealers and publishers, and others with electronic mail facilities will be possible, as will receipt of billings and funds transfer.

Libraries will continue to receive announcements, blurbs, and catalogs from various publishers. While use will be made of the electronic media by a number of major publishers, the resources of other vendors for insertion of advertising and related material in data bases available to all libraries and the book trade will remain limited. The acceptability of on-line data of this kind for use in book selection and collection development will be enhanced through the availability of more user-friendly equipment, such as the table top viewing screen. Other traditional acquisitions procedures will continue to be needed to obtain material from certain overseas and third world countries, and from other sources too specialized to be represented in the data bases.

In cataloging, the following changes may be expected in the next decade:

— More highly trained staff will be required to replace those less skilled, to handle special problems, complex exceptions, and related matters associated with the expanded machine-readable bibliographic data bases and authority files.
— Enhancements to cataloging input screens will provide more user-supportive procedures, although the entry of original cataloging records will remain complex.
— With general availability of bar-code or similar systems for circulation control, shelf preparation will require less time.
— The metallic strip security system will be replaced by one more effective and reasonably priced.

In serials, the following changes may be expected in the next decade:

— Computer-based check in systems will become available for use at reasonable cost by large- and medium-sized libraries. Similar systems for serials budget control, order placement, invoice payment, and binding management also will be provided as a joint venture by the major bibliographic utilities and serial subscription agencies.
— Regional and national union lists of serials will be created automatically through on-line systems provided by the major bibliographic utilities, and will be available to all participants on line.

Among the questions involving use of the new technology which remain to be answered are the following: Who shall benefit? Who may suffer? The access to information by all citizens at reasonable cost, and the right of the individual to privacy, long have been considered critical to the existence of a free society. It seems possible that both may be compromised hereafter through the action of the marketplace alone. In the decade ahead, these and similar issues will merit our special attention.

REFERENCES

1. Howard P. Lowell. "Sources of Conservation Information for the Librarian," *Collection Management*, 4 (Fall 1982): 1-18.

2. John H. Jenkins. "A Regional Publisher Looks at the Future," *AB Bookman's Weekly*, 71 (14 February 1983): 1087, 1090, 1092, 1094, 1096-1099.

3. Elie A. Shneour. "A Look into the Book of the Future," *Publishers Weekly*, 223 (21 January 1983): 48.

4. Sharon M. Edge. "Options in Technology: Academic Libraries," *Library Acquisitions: Practice and Theory*, 6 (1982): 271-288.

5. Tom Surprenant. "Future Libraries," *Wilson Library Bulletin*, 57 (October 1982): 152-159.

6. Stephen K. Stoan. "Computer Searching, a Primer for the Uninformed Scholar," *Academe*, 68 (November-December 1982): 10-15.

7. Carlton Rochell. "Telematics—2001 AD," *Library Journal*, 107 (1 October 1982): 1809-1815.

8. Joseph Becker. "How to Integrate and Manage New Technology in the Library," *Special Libraries*, 74 (January 1983): 1-6.

9. James E. Rush, ed. "Technical Standards for Library and Information Science," *Library Trends*, 31 (Fall 1982): 189-358.

The Technicality of Library Services— and the Service of Library Technology: A Plea for Humanization

Eli M. Oboler

ABSTRACT. Using the 1981 and 1982 annual review issues of *Library Resources & Technical Services* as a basis, the article surveys recent trends in such fields as serials control, collection development, and cataloging/classification/subject analysis, especially considering how the arriving library technology affects long lasting library traditions. Basically, the article is a "plea for humanization," for consideration of the people behind the machinery, and of the people who are served with technical services. It is an endeavor to reconcile the contrasting goals for technical library services of cost-benefits as a primary aim and of human benefits as an underlying justification for all library service.

There is no better place to ascertain what the library profession in America has been doing about technical services, each year, than the annual (July/September) issue of the ALA's official journal on the topic, *Library Resources & Technical Services.* Since 1956 it has been the basic *omnium gatherum* for discussions of the current state of such disparate matters as deacidification, the control of library growth, automatic classification and indexing, and document delivery systems. All these—and more—these days are grist for the mill of technical services.

What looking at the 1981 and 1982 "annual review" issues of LRTS makes very clear is that—to coin a phrase—the technicalities of service in, to, and from libraries are in a transition state. There

Eli M. Oboler is the University Librarian Emeritus of Idaho State University, author of numerous articles and books in the field of librarianship, including the forthcoming *To Free the Mind: Libraries, Technology, and Intellectual Freedom* (Littleton, Colo.: Libraries Unlimited, 1983). Mailing address: Campus Box 8340, Idaho State University, Pocatello, ID 83209.

are a great many references to very complex and abstruse machine-related items—but little indication that these newer ways of doing established necessities are widespread. The key phrases seem to be "first use," "new system," and "testing."

Before attempting to plunge into the depths of crystal-ball-gazing (if the future of technical services *may* reasonably be prognosticated!), come with me on a quick trip through American library technical services as they *are*—not as some machine-fanatics would like them to be.

In her article[1] on the development and preservation of collections in 1980, Rose Mary Magrill stresses that "doing the best possible job with the money available is the underlying theme of much that happened in 1980. . ." On the federal level alone, the rapid decline of funding—from $21.6 million is fiscal 1970 for the Higher Education Act Title II to $12 million in fiscal 1980—is a good indication of how American college and research libraries fared under the political and economic constraints of the 1970s. At a time when there was ". . . declining title output in most categories and a continuing rise in average prices. . ." the research libraries, Magrill says, ". . . were tending to take money from their book budgets in order to maintain serial publications." Putting it another way, "The shrinking dollar value in the face of inflation and the stabilization of library budgets has had a significant impact on collection development."

But surely the newest of the new in computer hardware and software has helped, in this dire situation? Unfortunately, not so. One would think that the development of regional, almost national, bibliographic networks—OCLC, RLIN, WLN, RLG—would mean more cooperation—since clearly cooperation might relieve the pressure of under-budgeting. But competition seems to be the name of the game, even *within* networks. Resource sharing is a lovely phrase—but it is more honored in the breach than in the observance.

In analyzing the current situation in acquisition methods and procedures, Magrill finds that "automated acquisition systems were in the news all during 1980. . ." But AAS's cost money—so-called "seed-money," even, is out of the question for the vast majority of academic libraries in America, in these "austere" 1980s. The ultimate choice, all too often, is to cut down on funds for books—and then use that money for an AAS. Surely, even robbing Peter to pay Paul was not *quite* as sacrilegious!

The abysmal state of most modern library collections—due to the poor quality of book-paper and particularly its high level of destructive acid content gets its share of attention from Magrill. But no machine-operated methods seem very effective in helping preserve library materials. It requires dedicated people working book by book, not mass (which usually turns into "mess"!) operations. Certainly in 1980, as Magrill concludes, there were some ". . .profitable applications of automation to selection and acquisition procedures. . ." But their universal—even common—applicability is decidedly questionable.

In 1980 micrographics, full-size document reproduction, and video technology all contributed their share to library progress. As documented by William Saffrady and Rhoda Garoogian,[2] there was a definite trend, ". . .the integration of technologies. . ." The key word here seems to be "interface"—so that reports of systems which, for example, include ". . .a central computer, a minicomputer, and automated microfiche retrieval equipment" are the highlights of the Saffrady-Garoogian study. There is some indication of "interface" with human beings; two articles are reported on ". . .the problem of library staff development with respect to microforms, and the importance of knowledgeable staff in overcoming user resistance. . ." But the authors admit that such ". . .facets of micrographics. . . rarely receive attention in library literature. . ." And, one must suppose, in libraries, generally!

Video technology, the annual review states, ". . .was in the forefront in 1980." But they admit that "most of the emphasis was. . . on *potential* rather than on actually available products or services." As usual, the prognosticators let their dreams far outstrip realities; for example, one article claimed that ". . .by the end of 1981 the total market for videodiscs will exceed the market for color television," which is, of course, not yet true at the time this is written, the beginning of 1983. There was a feeling—not yet much beyond that today—that ". . .videodisc technology may prove to be an ideal complement to, or may even replace computer-based information storage and retrieval systems." On the anti-humanist, anti-Gutenberg side, one predictor sees the videodisc as something that "in combination with microcomputers. . .has the potential to supplant live instruction and the book itself." We shall see.

On quite a different level of technical processing, the 1981 review[3] of the state of descriptive cataloging was, as one might expect, mainly concerned with the then brand new AACR2 code. But on the technologic level the year's attention was on what form the catalog (not the catalog card) should take—online, microfiche, automated, or variations on these. All had their proponents and opponents, their benefits and disadvantages. The principal human effect, as reported, was that the teachers of cataloging in ALA-accredited graduate library schools felt that the coming of variant catalog forms meant that ". . .emphasis should be on the practical side rather than the theoretical." Whether this means that future library school graduates are all required to be computer analysts or computer programmers was not made clear.

Another phase of information retrieval—subject analysis—almost seems as though it has reached its nadir—in relation to machine-technology—in 1980.[4] One of the established authorities, Hans H. Wellisch, states, unequivocally, that ". . .complete control [that is to say, bibliographic control via the machine—E.M.O.], while achievable (at least in theory). . .can never be fully attained." He claims that ". . .the ideal indexing system or retrieval system. . .is beyond the powers of any system, no matter how large or sophisticated." In other words, the ideal of using the computer to permit universal indexing/retrieval is about as chimeric as the chemist's dreams of the universal solvent.

Wellisch caustically comments on the "progress" of so-called automatic classification and indexing" that "all these quasi-operational 'automatic' projects share a characteristic that might be compared with reports on the manufacture of mechanical birds; after a quarter century of trial and error, some models begin to look bird-like, a few can imitate chirping noises, some can flap their wings, but so far none can really fly or sing. . ." He concludes that this sad fact is ". . .carefully hidden behind some dense verbiage, generally in the last but one paragraph of such reports."

Writing on "The Year's Work in Serials: 1980," Dorothy J. Glasby commented[5] on the high level of interest that year in automated check-in systems. The state of the art is such that ". . .it is clear. . .that individual institutions no longer need to build their own serials control systems from the ground up but can choose instead to participate in more or less (!—*my* comment—E.M.O.) complete systems developed by a utility, by subscription agencies, or by other libraries." Of course, this method of procedure has its problems; using the Procrustean bed system may cause libraries ". . . sometimes (to) have to compromise in terms of their own identified and exact requirements." But *vive la machine!* One interesting result of computerized serials control cited by Glasby is that "serials librarians. . .may be among the first to champion the computer. . . .are now finding themselves about to be given their come-uppance by it."

More significant than all of this is a trend seen by Margaret O. Rohdy in her discussion[6] of technical services management. She sees ". . .technical services is not the back-office, isolated function it once was." She finds that "a growing interest in management science is one response of technical services librarians to the challenge of automation and change in the workplace." And she sees ". . .technical services (as). . .the center of attention in many libraries."

This is a most interesting development. Since the basically humanistic librarian is caught in the whirlpool of swift and pervasive library automation, he/she reacts by wanting to learn to "manage" the new Colossus. Or would "Frankenstein's monster" be the better metaphor? Perhaps the best known critic of what he[7] calls ". . . mechanistic formulas for dealing with complex realities. . . ," Richard De Gennaro, is not alone in his feeling that coincident with the Computer-Video-Networking-Miniaturization Revolution, there is also a decided trend toward "automatizing" library management. This is especially prevalent in library technical services, particularly in large academic and public libraries.

The latest parallel review of the "year's work," which makes up most of the July/September, 1982 issue of *Library Resources & Technical Services* is, in essence, very similar to what appeared in 1981. Rose Mary Magrill says,[8] "Collection development in 1981 departed in no radical way from the trends reported in 1980. . ." Constance Rinehart finds[9] that ". . .some nagging and difficult questions remain," in computerized technical services procedures. Discussing subject analysis, Jennifer A. Younger says,[10] "understanding information-seeking behavior is critical. . ." Benita M. Weber,[11] discussing such topics as "standardization and automation developments in bibliographic control of serials" and "electronic document delivery," concludes, "There is no doubt that developments in all areas related to serials librarianship over the next several years will broaden the scope of our specialization in ways just beginning to be identified and as yet not conceived." *Und so weiter. . .*

Lost in the flood of new and ever newer techniques and gadgets is one of the basic strengths of library technical services. If technical services in libraries become completely the slave/servant of the machine, they will lose their principal tie to library readers' services.

That link is collection development. In a great many small libraries the same individual who selects library material processes them for the shelves. And this is far from being a bad thing.

In the very action of selecting, ordering, handling a book on its arrival, cataloging, classifying, and assigning a subject, the librarian, perforce, deals with a *book,* not a *byte,* a viable addition to both the library's collection and the librarian's knowledge. Of course the giants, with their multi-thousands of additions annually, cannot do too much to humanize the process of book collection—but they can at least try.

I foresee technical services in libraries as an arena where the soul of librarianship is at stake. If we want to sell out to the information gadgeteers, the VDT-fanatics, it only requires setting efficiency and economy as the goals, rather than as the by-products of a properly functioning library. The machine is a tool; service to the individual is a goal. Let's put our priorities where they should be—on the human side of library service, whether technical or otherwise.

REFERENCE NOTES

1. Rose Mary Magrill. "Collection Development and Preservation in 1980," *Library Resources & Technical Services* (July/September 1981), p. 244-266.

2. William Saffrady, & Rhoda Garoogian. "Micrographics, Reprography, and Graphic Communications in 1980," *Library Resources & Technical Services* (July/September 1981), p. 267-276.

3. Constance Rinehart. "Descriptive Cataloging in 1980," *Library Resources & Technical Services* (July/September 1981), p. 277-294.

4. Hans H. Wellisch. "Year's Work in Subject Analysis: 1980," *Library Resources & Technical Services* (July/September 1981), p. 295-309.

5. Dorothy J. Glasby. "The Year's Work in Serials: 1980," *Library Resources & Technical Services* (July/September 1981), p. 310-318.

6. Margaret Rohdy. "The Management of Technical Services: 1980," *Library Resources & Technical Services* (July/September 1981), p. 319-329.

7. Richard DeGennaro. "Library Administration and New Management Systems," *Library Journal* (Dec. 15, 1978), p. 2477-2482.

8. Rose Mary Magrill. "Collection Development in 1981," *Library Resources & Technical Services* (July/September 1982), p. 240.

9. Constance Rinehart. "Descriptive Cataloging in 1981," *Library Resources & Technical Services* (July/September 1982), p. 254.

10. Jennifer A. Younger. "Year's Work in Subject Analysis: 1981," *Library Resources & Technical Services* (July/September 1982), p. 271.

11. Benita M. Weber. "The Year's Work in Serials: 1981," *Library Resources & Technical Services* (July/September 1982), p. 277-293.

Will People Talk to People?:
A Leaping Look at Library Life
in the Coming Generations

Arline Willar, PhB, MS

ABSTRACT. Libraries will remain recognizable as we now know them in the near future. There will be an increased demand and utilization of the library by the public, where the library will function as an information evaluation and referral agency. It will successfully compete economically with vendors offering commercial information products. It will adapt service functions and its organizational structure to meet the demand for a more highly trained professional who possesses a greater arsenal of skills and has more perceived expertise than librarians now do. Specialization in assignments will come through knowledge of subject fields; there will be a sharper division between administrative personnel and the professional group, and there will be a smaller corps of clericals. Most technical service functions will be done in bibliographic processing centers outside the library. Technical service librarians will be absorbed into the public service ranks, become systems analyst consultants, work in bibliographic record centers, or accept administrative tasks. There may be fewer libraries, but the staff that deals with the public will largely be professionally trained. There will always be a library. Could it become an entertainment arena for mental/electronic spectator sports?

People talk to machines. Machines talk to machines. Machines talk to people. Will people talk to people?

The outlook for how automation in the library will affect our daily social and organizational lives has inspired a range of views from the gloomy prediction of extensive displacement of personnel and the disappearance of the worklife we now know, to the euphoric promise that we will be free from all hampering barriers and our service potential will be gloriously fulfilled. My prediction is that

Arline Willar is Assistant Librarian for Public Service, Northeastern University Library, 360 Huntington Avenue, Boston, MA 02115.

while the computer technology revolution in enhancing how information gets disseminated is, and will continue to be, enormous, the library will be recognizable to the observing public pretty much as it is today for the foreseeable future. There will clearly be some internal adjustments of personnel and shifts in how staff are used within the organizational structure. There will be some displacement, as the distinction in how technical service and public service functions are performed will become blurred, and the emphasis will shift to serving the public as the main professional activity in the library. Other changes that will occur in addition to redeployment of professional staff will be an increased ratio of professional to clerical workers, with far fewer clerical positions staffed, an increase in the ratio of professional staff to the community served, and in how library training gets accomplished.

Rather than computer home products displacing the need for library service, I predict there will be an increase in the demand for library service. The number of service components will increase with the library assuming a stronger business stance than that taken at present. This will not mean reducing free information service or traditional programs, but will mean that the library will provide commercial as well as advisory services based on fee products.

The reason that I don't foresee the total demise of the library but instead evolving of increased, although changed, services is that the claim that the computer, robots, and instant information access will change our work lives and social values profoundly is akin to the prediction that scientific capabilities in food technology will result in people satisfying their nutritional needs by popping a food pill. Labor-saving devices, like refrigerators and dishwashers, even though they substantially increased the material comfort of our lives and resulted in a redistribution of labor are not too different from what may result from the computer "takeover." Even though they help us, they didn't turn society on its head. The fears about what coming changes will mean to the profession are exaggerated, as the big breakthrough, the technology revolution has *already* happened, and we have been slowly adapting to it. Costs for hardware will become more affordable, and simplified refinements in applications will gradually evolve, allowing the profession to adapt its service strategies and technical capabilities to fit organizational opportunities well before there is any death knell to heed.

Social needs and needs for one-to-one assistance will still persist. Even though service enhancements via the computer in the public areas will come slowly and incrementally, with much lurching, backtracking and soul-searching within the profession as adaptations are made, the public demand for and dependence upon the library for service will probably increase, for both economic and recreational reasons. With the commercial sector plying the home front with massive (slight hyperbole) overdoses of information, the librarian will give professional advice on what type of information sources a person should use or subscribe to. The library will become an economic middleman, allowing the public to financially participate in subscription to network resources. Some of the economic brokering to use computer generated commercial services will take the form of helping the public determine what electronic information sources and hardware would be useful for home consumption in satisfying a configuration of information needs. The library will also indicate what programs and other products can be leased through a shared subscription relationship, at a reduced cost, through the library and what other alternatives can be provided non-electronically, either in the library or elsewhere. Complex information needs will not be completely satisfied by simple-to-use computer systems. The library's counseling service will assist in data and information reduction for public use and will become the community's major information referral agency.

If in fact the use of computers shifts time spent in the marketplace to time spent at home, the library's role as a social institution could well mitigate against social isolation. The library functions as an unstructured meeting place, a role it can clearly augment as other social changes occur. The computer will not be the only means by which information becomes accessible. People are likely to prefer a printed page to a terminal for many non-work related reasons. Screens will be used to locate information and to access brief pieces of information, but are unlikely to replace the habit and enjoyment of sustained reading from the printed page. Individual ownership of books, even in paperback edition, may diminish because of costs and because other entertainment devices compete heavily with books. For this reason too, libraries are likely to be actively used in reducing information costs.

Over the next twenty years, the interior library landscape will change with the disappearance of extensive paper files, card catalog cabinets and with many self-service terminals appearing throughout the facility. Books will still be seen and documents in the form of printouts will roll off attachments to the terminals. While access to backfiles of many periodicals will be done electronically and while some scholarly, scientific and specialized journals will only be available electronically, and not in print form as we now know them, the publication of general interest periodicals will continue unchanged, and as markets become more segmented, may even grow. It is unlikely that the publication of magazines will be dinosaured into history.

A more subtle change to the observing public will be the staff-to-patron ratio of professionals dealing with the public and the shift from clerical to professional in the proportion of staffing assignments. Most of the professionals in the library will be dealing with the public. There will be fewer clerks, and the work these do will be behind the scenes and not observed by the public. Professionals as information specialists will be highly trained. They will possess and utilize a wider range of skills than they now do and cover a wider range of duties, many of which are now dispersed into discrete and sometimes unnecessarily discontinuous routinized tasks.

Patrons will make scheduled appointments to consult the information specialist for those services that relate to economic choices dealing with systems decisions, but librarians will continue to have the casual, drop-in relationship that has marked their calling.

Functions formerly divided between public service and technical service professionals will merge into skills held and practiced in common by all professionals. Their practice will encompass a knowledge of data bases that allows a searching of client requests at the appropriate level as determined by the complexity of information needed; knowledge of network systems and economies; knowledge of how to access published sources traditionally and electronically as well as a knowledge of only electronically available information. They will have subject search strategy competence (using those skills formerly devoted to discerning and applying cataloging and classification rules, encoding and decoding bibliographic information, etc.) in both general and subject field areas. The differentiation in types of assignments will come from the library's ability to afford specifically trained subject experts, or its dividing up of fields among generalists who train themselves on the job. The trend already appearing in academic libraries to have the collection development technical services people (sometimes call acquisitions or selections or bibliographer librarians) work as reference librarians will become the norm. Librarians as information specialists helping the public evaluate and satisfy information needs intellectually and to make economic choice decisions will be trained in both communication and problem-solving techniques.

Library information specialists will be less concerned with hardware/software problems, as the number, sophistication and simplicity of programs and computers enable them to concentrate upon analysis of the information need at the budget level of funding. They will not be concerned with how to create records and programs, but their expertise will focus on how programs compare as to what they can provide.

Many functions formerly done by technical services professionals (and often by clerks as well) will be done centrally outside the library under contract by commercial agencies. This will include the creation of bibliographic records for owned as well as leased information sources. Supervised clerks will check such records for accuracy to match electronic records. Cataloging and ordering librarians as we now know them will evolve to a type of specialist working in bibliographic record centers. Those whose skills, interests and incentives will enable a shift into the public area will enlarge the scope of their duties, becoming as all professionals in the system, technical generalists.

The library organizational structure will change from a pyramidal hierarchy to a diamond-shaped structure in which a few professional administrators at the top will deal with budget, equipment, contracts and supervision of the technical service clericals. There will be a general eradication of the middle level professional supervisor, as the main bulk of the professional staff will be made up of a large number of generalists, who divide up the work by subject area rather than by complexity of work done. Some supervision will take place, some in-house training to meet individual institutional needs will persist, and responsibility for liaison between the technical areas and those interfacing with the public will be redefined to accommodate the changes taking place.

In the future there may be fewer library units and possibly fewer practicing professionals. Library administration will use on-going consultant help for advice on which networks, which cost structure, which configuration of hardware and software packages it should own or lease, how these might be shared or leased through some kind of rental or fee structure for the library and for its subscribing patrons, and what legal arrangements it would need to make with its clients. The consultant will have a contractual agreement with the library, as regular updating and negotiating will be necessary. Technical systems consulting will almost certainly evolve as a specialty from today's turmoil.

The conclusion is that computer technology with its marvelous potential is not in its flickering guts a beast of prey, ready in descending upon us to destroy the fundamental library mission. That it will enhance the library's effectiveness, upgrade, increase the range, and unify practitioners' skills, strengthen their ability to offer more meaningful and economically competitive sources of information, and create a corps of professionals whose expertise is observed and valued by the general public may sound like Pollyanna crooning in the dunes, as the dinosaur disappears round the corner and another band of experts comes marching in to take over. It would be much more fun to paint a landscape in which the computer offers something totally new, affecting the brain directly, without the needed intervention of the information specialist. If a leap were made into the distant future, where libraries cease to exist in their present form what would be seen as taking their place? Is it possible to imagine the library existing as a social arena, where competitions pitting the strength of one electronic brain against another are held, as an entertainment resource for the community?

REFERENCES

Bachus, Edward J. "I'll drink to that: the Integration of Technical and Reader Services." *The Journal of Academic Librarianship,* September, 1982, p. 227, 260.

Beckman, Margaret M. "Online Catalogs and Library Users." *Library Journal,* November 1, 1982, p. 2043-2047.

Bolgiano, Christina. "Libraries as an Art Form." *The Journal of Academic Librarianship,* November, 1982, p. 289-291.

DeGennaro, Richard. "Libraries, Technology and the Information Marketplace." *Library Journal,* June, 1982, p. 1045-1054.

Koenig, Michael E. D. "The Information Controllability Explosion." *Library Journal,* November 1, 1982, p. 2052-2054.

Marchant, Maurice P., and Smith, Nathan M. "The Research Library Director's View of Library Education." *College and Research Library News,* November, 1982, p. 437-444.

Toffler, Alvin. *The Third Wave.* N.Y., Morrow, 1980.

Zuboff, Shoshana. "New Worlds of Computer-Mediated Work." *Harvard Business Review,* September-October, 1982, p. 142-152.

A View From the Great Pyramid

James C. Thompson

ABSTRACT. The future of technical services will be determined by that of publishing, but change in both is slower than some futurists imagine, and along different lines, for economic reasons. Economics will necessitate a general revision of the underlying assumptions of technical services, and this will have a profound effect on its relationship to the rest of the library and on its staff.

Things are more like they are now than they ever were before.

Dwight D. Eisenhower

Bertrand Russell, in a little-known essay on library management,[1] cautions those who would predict the future, citing "the men who study the Great Pyramid, with a view to deciphering its mystical lore. Many great books have been written on this subject, some of which have been presented to me by their authors. It is a singular fact that the Great Pyramid always predicts the history of the world accurately up to the date of publication of the book in question, but after that date it becomes less reliable." In spite of these wise words, and recognizing that the world has become a dangerous place in any event, I will make a few notes on the future of library technical services, particularly in regard to academic libraries.

By technical services I mean acquisitions (of whatever materials) and cataloging, or, in plain English, purchasing and indexing. The future of technical services will be determined to a considerable extent by that of publishing. I believe that books as we know them will continue to be the basis for scholarly and popular publishing, at least until I am too old to worry about the question. There are important advantages to the printed word for which no automated equivalent is yet on the horizon, including the characteristics of contant reflected

---

James C. Thompson is Associate University Librarian, Fondren Library, Rice University, Houston, TX 77251-1892.

37

light, as opposed to the intermittent radiation of the video screen. More important, a book is comparatively cheap, while electronic publishing must, at least for some time, depend heavily on telecommunication, which is not cheap. So there will still be a need for libraries and library purchasing, though with technical progress will come a shift in the balance in favor of on-line access to mass data banks, some located in libraries, some not. But for now these data bases are limited to mere information, and not the many other things for which people turn to books.

THE OUTLOOK FOR INDEXING

The volume of publication already makes it impossible for libraries to index the majority of new publications through individual examination, even on a cooperative basis. Since most exist in machine-readable form, they can be indexed automatically from their tables of contents and indices, or from the texts themselves. This has not happened yet for two reasons: the cost is still great, and there is little incentive for publishers to participate cooperatively. But manual indexing has shown the commercial possibilities, and sooner or later automatic indexing will be economically feasible, presumably under the control of the interests which produce the documents. How far we have to go is illustrated by the fact that University Microfilms is indexing collections through individual OCLC records which possessors of a collection must call up and edit one at a time.

What assurance will we have that the terms, standards, and so on, used and applied in this automatic indexing will be consistent? What, to use the proper but rather severe library term, of authority control? Alas, the history of agreement on standards is a sorry one, and I have no great confidence that the information industry will have the generosity, or libraries the money, to index new materials in any consistent manner. Even less likely is Phyllis Richmond's prediction that "classification will be mandatory" resulting in "not a great future in the use of keywords."[2] Indeed it appears that online catalogs will be installed in droves before we make any progress toward even a common enquiry language. Granted, ALA has commissioned an Interdivisional Committee on the Catalogue: Form, Function, and Use, but its potential seems limited owing to "the autonomous nature and independent power of ALA's divisions."[3]

Experience and human nature suggest that what a few librarians cannot agree upon is unlikely to find consensus across the vast spectrum of firms and organizations involved in document production and delivery. Two recent papers by Salmon[4] and Lipow[5] offer sobering support for this gloomy outlook.

The proliferation of local automated systems is inevitable. Financial considerations work against the success of a centralized system devoted to the sharing of computer, as opposed to data resources. This is the reason for the current state of the OCLC serials check-in and the RLIN acquisitions systems. RLG doesn't say much these days about financial control, or for that matter about faculty office terminals or centralized catalog conversion; this may be an example of improved performance through a tacit redefinition of goals. But on the question of OCLC and RLIN I make no predictions, except to note that their adherents continue to be equally suspicious of each other's motives. "In this opinion," to quote Russell again, "both parties may be right, but they cannot both be wrong. This reflection should generate a certain caution."[6]

Local systems are capable of imposing some degree of consistency on the data taken from an inconsistent source, but even at its most automated, this process still requires a great deal of human intervention. Conversely, in the absence of authority control, searching must be based on keywords, creating a need for skilled intermediaries. In either case, the market for indexing experts should continue to be a good one; but I fear that authority control even over local data will be beyond the reach of many libraries. In this, as is so often the case, the determining factor will be economic rather than technical.

TECHNOLOGICAL INNOVATION
AND ECONOMIC REALITY

Economics, not potential, is what directs progress in technology and limits its applications. This is a fact of life with which we librarians are loath to come to grips. We need not assume, because the automation of some function is possible, that it is desirable and affordable; yet this assumption underlies much library planning, and causes us not only to rely on what turns out not to transpire, but to ignore at first what does become available.

For many years Athelstan Spilhaus, in his column in the Sunday papers, described the wonderful world of the future, when inventions just conceived would become commonplace. Streets would have moving sidewalks, and every family its own helicopter; automobiles would be piloted by computers while the family played pachisi in the back seat. There are, in fact, electronic sidewalks in some airports, but of course the sidewalks of our cities remain entirely manual, or rather pedal, there not being enough money even to maintain the streets. This fallacy of the possible permeates our planning for library automation. Here are some examples:

The assumption that all libraries should and would automate their card catalogs arose when AACR 2 was looming ominously on the horizon; people hoped and believed that on-line systems with automatic authority control would be invented and installed before the new code was adopted, rendering the change painless. AACR 2 has come (and, according to strict adherents, gone), but we continue to assume that our most important task is to replace the card catalog as soon as possible. Yet for many libraries, the card catalog is still to be preferred as a form of index. Most of the on-line systems now marketed incorporate decisions no longer applicable to today's hardware, and certainly inappropriate to tomorrow's. These include the minimization of storage redundancy, the assumption that circulation transactions predominate, the use of 8-and 16-bit software, and so forth. Unrealistic library demands have contributed to this, whether the vendor has acceded to all the demands, or in frustration ignored them. Hardware and software developments make it likely that the "innovative" systems now being installed in many libraries will rapidly grow obsolete, leaving their owners stuck with white elephants of enormous appetite.

"Integrated systems" look nice in flow charts but are at present chimerical. Transactions in a circulation computer are different, in important ways, from those used to order books, or to catalog them. Even the most advanced systems handle only a few of the major library functions, and divide and reintegrate these according to the requirements of the computer, with no relationship to library organization. A library's users comprise distinct populations whose needs cannot be served equally by any single system; these include staff users, whose commitment to shared systems is occasionally dampened by the same drawbacks which have slowed the acceptance of network acquisitions and serials systems. Masses of existing data cannot reasonably be entered into systems at all, and a large portion of the contents of a typical library is not indexed in any system, manual or automated. Much of what libraries buy arrives on approval, and machine-readable data on these items is not generally available in a transferable form. From the library's point of view, "integrated system" is a meaningless concept. Some integration of data files is possible, but this is limited in extent by the limits of standardization among libraries, the book trade, and commercial data bases.

The end of the office is thought to be at hand, as microcomputers make it possible for people to work at home in "electronic cottages." This is an intriguing prospect, more so perhaps for librarians than for many others, since the advantage may be greatest for mothers of young children. On the other hand, the presence of young children may not be conducive to success at the terminal. Perhaps there are reasons other than necessity for the continued existence of the office, including the fact that centralized work is still cheaper for most employers, and most employers take mundane considerations of that sort into account.

Microcomputers will soon be commonplace in homes, classrooms, and dormitories; their use will eventually be as routine as that of the typewriter or the lightbulb. There is speculation, however, that newly-deregulated IBM and AT&T view them more as terminals for computer utilities than as independent processors. They will make it possible for individuals to have direct access to numerous large bibliographic and text data bases, bypassing the library. On the other hand, these same people currently have the ability to buy their own books and journals, yet they usually depend on the library to do this. One reason is that systems are more "user-friendly" when someone else has to worry about them (see Lipow's article[7] for some unforeseen problems with the concept of user-friendliness). I suspect most computer users will be reluctant to spend much time in the vast costly wilderness of incompatible commercial information systems. Nor do I worry that the library will become an adjunct to the computer center; there will still be a need for large processors run by experts, but local networks of special-purpose machines are already well established and most centers have given up worrying about total control.

After twenty years of library automation, we find that progress is considerably slower than first imagined, and proceeding in somewhat different directions. Economic limitations have changed expectations, and continue to direct the course of development. Resistance to automation can come from strange sources, as when the teachers in California resisted Apple's attempt to give thousands of computers to schools, on the grounds they weren't prepared to train students in their use. Cost savings through automation have been sporadic, unreliable, and in many cases more than offset by costs generated elsewhere in the library. These realities are not apparent in the literature, since most writers on automation projects are also accountable for their success.[8] All in all, automation has not had a profound effect on most library operations. There are exceptions, most notably in circulation, citation retrieval, and the OCLC cataloging and loan systems, and I believe we are reaching the point at which real progress in other areas is within reach. Among the more important determinants are developments in optical storage and in copyright legislation.

THE ECONOMICS OF THE CATALOG

In technical services we sometimes overlook the fact that the catalog is simply one of many reference works, the most expensive, by far, but not always the most important. The catalog is not complete; it omits citations for whatever types of materials the library chooses not to include in it: government publications, maps, parts of microform sets, chapters of books, articles in journals, paragraphs in dissertations. Monographs as units are well represented, because there are comparatively few of them. But only a minority of the library's distinguishable holdings are cited in the catalog, and the proportion is decreasing as serial and on-line publications proliferate. Many items are circulating, missing, or in process; the catalog does not show what we have in the library, only what we think we once decided to have.

In effect, the catalog is a substitute for reference staff—or vice versa, according to the material in question. A library with unlimited funds could provide better bibliographic control with no catalog, provided it employed enough librarians, each of whom would be an expert on a small part of the collection. Conversely, these funds could be spent on a catalog so complete and thoroughly analytic that the user could find what he wanted without assistance; then no reference staff would be needed. But since funds are limited, the library chooses an appropriate treatment for each type of material, according to its resources, and leaves the rest up to human effort. Thus, the catalog serves to pass cost, in the form of work, through to the user, while minimizing the total work required.

Given these limitations, it is foolish to try to make the catalog into a research rather than a reference tool. It can never be a bibliography, for example, or a discography, to the extent of substituting for examination of the works themselves. One eminent bibliographer, for whom I have the highest respect, wants us not only to retain dust jackets but to describe them in the catalog, along with the thickness of the paper. This would, I grant, enable him to ascertain in New York whether it were worth his time to fly to Houston to study a book. But it would be much less expensive for us in the long run to accept a collect call, should such a situation ever arise, and this we will be most happy to do.

Even the best catalog provides no answers a good reference librarian cannot find elsewhere. Yet great expense is devoted to making it as complete as possible, without real regard for the probability of need for the information. An example is the extensive effort put into monographic series treatment. Most series are seldom looked up as series except by library staff. Series work is at once the most difficult and the least productive labor of technical services, and will become increasingly so once catalogs are on-line. It is a fallacy of the exception: a procedure is followed in every case which is of benefit only in a few cases, though the cumulative effort expended is greater than it would be if the exceptions were dealt with as they came up. For most series, a reference source or an occasional call to the publisher will provide all the information needed, at a comparatively small cost.

Library operations have been virtually free from financial accountability in the past, but with increasing interest in automation, a reexamination of these operations is being mandated by the administrators of many libraries. At the same time, economic forces at work both in higher education and in public administration are making inevitable a reduction in personnel devoted to such activities. The effects of these developments will be felt most heavily in technical services, and within that area, in cataloging. Catalogers, in evaluating new methods and standards, will be constrained to pay close regard to cost as well as benefit. Even within the concept of benefit, traditional cataloging has confused its ends with its means.

In the aggregate, books and other library materials lose value over time. There are many exceptions, of course, and research librarians believe that much of what they buy will retain significant value indefinitely. But certainly most works are more useful when new, whether they are critical, creative, scientific, or otherwise. So we cannot justify processing backlogs on the grounds that a better cataloging record may become available on OCLC, or that we can produce a better one ourselves if we spend enough time at it. While we wait for LC copy, the book in question is unavailable to the people who need it most, at the time they most need it. LC cataloging next year is not superior to provincial cataloging today. An assumption is often made that cataloging quality is a function of the average quality of the cataloging done; in fact, from the user's point of view, it is a function of the average quality of the cataloging of everything so far acquired. Works held but not cataloged are useless, and the lack of access to them brings the overall quality of cataloging down to an unacceptable level, however perfect the records actually produced. (Some will argue, in a peculiar contradiction, that the book really is available, since a slip has been filed somewhere. If this were sufficient, however, we wouldn't bother cataloging at all; we'd maintain a slip file and be done with it.)

The work involved in processing a given type of material varies with the effort needed to bring a unit under a specified level of bibliographic control, and with the volume of acquisition. The total workload is a function of the sum of the products of effort and volume for all the types of material acquired. In an operation which is current in its work, the human resources available will be at least equal to the total load. Since neither the resources nor the volume of material added is really under the control of the library, it follows that the effort expended per item is the only variable, and must be adjusted so as to equate the load to the resources. If it is not, then there will be not only a backlog, but a growing one, as in the case of a bathtub in which the tap has a greater capacity than the drain, and also because the unit effort per item will be greater when a backlog exists.

GETTING OUT OF THE BACK ROOM

Economic pressure and greater involvement by top management will make it difficult for technical services departments to devote so much effort to each title at the expense of currency. How does a backlog become chronic, and how can it be eliminated?

At first glance, catalogers seem unconcerned with the continual presence of large numbers of unprocessed items. In practice, however, they are resigned to the existence of the backlog, rather than in favor of it. But cataloging operations are subject to a variety of external forces over which the catalogers have little control. Collection development librarians, automated systems, patrons with priority requests, publishers, and the Library of Congress can all throw monkey wrenches into the best-designed workflow. Technical services people may feel misunderstood and unappreciated, assuming that the backlog can only be dealt with when, and if the administration comes to its senses and increases their numbers.

Unfortunately, the funds available both for people and for materials are determined by the institution's varying wealth, and in terms of the work to be done, there will never be more people than there are today. So as the backlog grows, it is periodically divided into higher- and lower-priority backlogs; the latter is put in storage to be processed as time permits, but since the former continues to grow, this never happens.

Excessive reliance on local tradition inhibits innovative solutions to the problem. Managerial turnover and communication problems among the processing departments promote inconsistencies among and within them (as when the copy catalogers have stricter standards than the Recon team). Staff members lose confidence in their ability to make changes and test assumptions. Under the critical eye of patrons and public services staff, they grow reluctant to make files and records available, and resort to unnecessary cross-checks in a vain attempt to avoid any errors. Eventually the staff becomes more involved with its own processes than their effect on the user, as in the many libraries which keep internal records such as authority files up-to-date while public catalog work falls farther behind. Redundant files eliminate the possibility of the unanswerable enquiry, but at a high cost in effort. (My favorite example, now defunct, was the "departed file" at one university; this consisted of main-entry slips sorted by age and then by call number, filed when the books left the room. Thus it could be proven that a missing book was someone else's problem, since it had "departed" from the catalogers' sphere of responsibility.) Eventually, "Biblish"[9] becomes the predominant tongue, making processing procedures unintelligible and thereby unexaminable. Separate backlogs grow to fill all the available shelves and booktrucks; they are not called backlogs, however, but are given names suggesting that they are about to be processed.

There is a way around this impasse, but it requires that the technical services staff assume a different role within the library and play it with confidence and courage. The essential change is to become accepted as agents rather than servants.

Librarians often treat themselves (and are treated) as public servants in the literal sense, bound to the task of trying to provide unlimited service with limited resources. In fact, libraries and their departments have little control over the resources allocated to them, and librarians should not be apologetic for their inability to satisfy all demands. Just as the library cannot afford to buy all the books everyone wants, its staff cannot provide all possible services; this can be changed only if budget priorities are altered, and while the director must do what can be done in that regard, these are not the best of times for it. Technical services librarians have the right to a reasonable error rate and reasonably streamlined cataloging standards, provided they can demonstrate that they are making the best use of what resources they have. They can only demonstrate this by first effecting it, and then opening their work for examination by all.

The first step is to reach consensus with public services on how to provide bibliographic access to various types of materials. This can be done in conjunction with the writing of a collection development policy. Itemize the distinct types of acquisitions for which different forms of bibliographic control can be provided, and the different types of treatment available (analysis, antiquarian description, MARC title cataloging, personal knowledge, etc.). Assess the volume of acquisition for each type of material, and the effort required in each case to provide each type of access. Agree on decisions that will result in a total load no greater than the available resources. In the absence of consensus, make these decisions yourself.

Before such an exercise is attempted, the outlines of a basic processing workflow should be in place, indicating a realistic procedure for getting most or all items through the pipeline quickly, and including no steps that are more expensive than compensating for their omission. Once this is implemented, the people in charge of it must be prepared to accept a reasonable number of mistakes, to resist pleas for frivolous exceptions, and to decline to provide irregular services which bring routine processing to a standstill. The aim is to get on top of the job and stay there, and to do it before the traditional system breaks down completely.

CHANGES IN ORGANIZATION

If in fact economic change will force technical services department to reorganize so as to better fulfill their public service goals, the relationship between the two areas is bound to be affected. They will not simply be merged, since large units inevitably divide into smaller ones, and this choice of division has a great deal of force behind it. Ultimately, however, technical services exists to support the public service function, and as success in doing so is called to account, overall direction and the setting of policy will be a responsibility increasingly shared with the public services staff.

One issue which never ceases to fascinate me concerns the future of serials departments. Librarians are divided between those who favor the division of technical services on the basis of the type of function performed, and those favoring division according to the type of material handled. Not unexpectedly, most of the latter are serials librarians. This vexing problem, like the arms race or inflation, has no easy solution, though it is treated as equally important by those affected. I rely on Russell's solution in this case: "There is in England a sect which maintains that the English are the lost ten tribes; there is a stricter sect, which maintains that they are only the tribes of Ephraim and Manasseh. Whenever I encounter a member of either of these sects, I profess myself an adherent of the other, and much pleasant argumentation ensues."[10] Serials librarians writing on this issue never fail to suggest that library administrators don't understand what serials people do. I think this is very doubtful, but it is instructive to note that if it is so, then serials librarians are not being promoted to administrative positions. "This reflection should generate a certain caution," to repeat a phrase.

I expect a continued shift of responsibility, and to some extent of power, to nonprofessional units, with professionals serving in a staff relationship and handling only the most difficult functions. There will also be expanded professional opportunity for staff members without library degrees. Library schools simply are not producing enough librarians capable of managing and operating our libraries. Professionalism is a state of mind, which the presence of an MLS does not guarantee, nor its absence deny. Library schools do not teach technical services work in the practical sense, and most network cataloging requires no knowledge of theory or history. On the managerial level, directors will look increasingly for people who can think in economic terms and deal with the business aspects of management in higher education and public administration, and who are willing to make radical changes and take risks. If library schools do not provide these people, libraries will recruit from outside the profession and do the training themselves.

In-house training of staff will become an expensive function in libraries large and small, as the implementation of diverse on-line catalogs and other systems brings to an end a long tradition of bibliographic uniformity. LC's Cataloging Distribution Service, and more recently OCLC, have made the acceptance of standard cataloging cheaper than local variation. On-line catalogs will reverse this, by making it easy to transfer abbreviated or nonstandard records directly from the screen to the system, avoiding the network's checks and edits. (This will force OCLC to change its charging methods, for which they have already prepared by copyrighting the data base.) Libraries already cut corners in cataloging, particularly in retrospective conversion, and they do so for financial reasons. An increase in financial pressure combined with the ability to catalog directly into the local data base will encourage this expediency. The problem is that no two libraries cut quite the same corners, and no two systems display records in quite the same way. In combination with the multitude of command languages and indices in the many systems under development, this means the end of the era in which researchers can go from one library to another without retraining in the use of the public catalog.

Change, even when inevitable, is seldom easy. Libraries with heavy investments in tradition may find the rest of the '80s wrenching and painful. In part this is because the future of libraries is full of conflict. Ideological conflict is not unusual in librarianship, but it has been comparatively restrained in technical services. Recently this has altered, with AACR 2 and RLG providing ample fuel for dispute. As libraries increasingly diverge in their approaches to automation, standards, as priorities, and as numerous systems and operations fail, disagreement and contention will flourish in our profession. At times this will be unpleasant, but not without benefit in the long run, for out of these struggles will come more effective and adaptable libraries for the citizens of future decades.

NOTES

1. Bertrand Russell. "An Outline of Intellectual Rubbish," in *Unpopular Essays* (London: George Allen and Unwin, 1951), p. 144.

2. Phyllis A. Richmond. "Futuristic Aspects of Subject Access," *Library Resources & Technical Services* 27 (January/March 1983), p. 92.

3. Michael Gorman. Letter to Donald Hammer, August 3, 1982.

4. Stephen R. Salmon. "Characteristics of Online Public Catalogs," *Library Resources & Technical Services* 27 (January/March 1983), p. 36-67.

5. Anne Grodzins Lipow. "Practical Considerations of the Current Capabilities of Subject Access in Online Public Catalogs, *Library Resources & Technical Services* 27 (January/March 1983), pp. 81-87.

6. Russell. "An Outline of Intellectual Rubbish," p. 137.

7. Lipow. "Practical Considerations," p. 86.

8. For a rare exception, see F. Wilfrid Lancaster, ed., *Problems and Failures in Library Automation. (Proceedings of the Clinic on Library Applications of Data Processing, 1978.)* (Urbana-Champaign: University of Illinois Graduate School of Library Science, 1979)

9. Biblish is defined by H. H. Neville, "Computers and the Language of Bibliographic Descriptions," *Information Processing & Management* 17 (1981), p. 137. See also Salmon, "Characteristics of Online Public Catalogs", p. 58.

10. Russell. "An Outline of Intellectual Rubbish," p. 144.

Automation of Technical Services: The Challenge of the 1980s

Bernard Dumouchel, MLS

ABSTRACT. The next decade will see the role and functions of technical services within libraries modified. This paper explores the prospect of integrated library management systems, using as example the National Library of Canada's Dobis system. Future developments of technical services are addressed under a topic covering prospects for automated systems. Developments are seen as having a positive impact on services for users.

INTRODUCTION

Futurology has never been used much in technical services to determine the direction to be followed as we have taken an evolutionary approach in changing our functions and goals. The advent of automation/computerization for libraries in the late 60s and early 70s brought with it a need to break our traditional mould and look more brightly at the future. This is especially true of technical services, which were amongst the first to be caught in a revolutionary spin as a result of the automation processes surrounding the bibliographic data file.

The revolution in libraries has grown since the early stage of automation, and is now trying to keep pace with the rapid changes of the computer and microelectronic industries. Will technical services be able to maintain its place and enhance its functions within this changing environment? How will technical services carry on and modify its role of providing documentation and access to this documentation in an environment where information, rather than the document itself, will be playing a larger role?

This paper will attempt to answer these questions through the analysis of changes that are taking place right now and by conjectur-

Bernard Dumouchel is Director, Technical Services Branch, Library of Parliament, Ottawa, Ontario, Canada K1A 0A9.

ing about others likely to occur between now and the end of the decade. The analysis of present changes will be limited to the evolution of technical services in Canadian government libraries as a result of the introduction of the Dobis system. The first part of the paper will explore the prospect of integrated library management systems and the impact on the development of services for users. The prospective element of this paper will be more wide-ranging.

EVOLUTION OF TECHNICAL SERVICES
WITHIN THE DOBIS ENVIRONMENT

Designed as an integrated library management system to support all the main library functions, Dobis (the *D*ortmunder *B*ibliothek-*s*ystem) functions on the concept of a major bibliographic utility in the operational mode of the National Library of Canada. It is operated as a shared system amongst libraries and information centres of federal government departments and agencies. Libraries participate in the development of the system through their involvement with planning and operation of the system, standards and use of records, system functions, products, support services provided to users, and equipment evaluation. Participants sit on a number of user advisory groups whose functions are to help in the developmental process. The Dobis system is run by the National Library of Canada through its Library Systems Centre. Located in the nation's capital region, the Library Systems Centre is fortunate to service libraries found mostly in Ottawa. Thus the problems and costs associated with data transmission over long distances are diminished.

Technical services were and are affected greatly by the introduction of Dobis in their libraries, as the cataloguing module was the first to be implemented. As with other libraries experiencing the automation of bibliographic databases, an impact was felt on the following issues: job security, job enhancement, staff training, review and redistribution of tasks, requirements for new skills, increased efficiency, acceptance of system-based standards, equipment "fright," etc. The automation process dates back only as far as 1979 for libraries of federal government departments and agencies using Dobis through the online pilot projects of the National Library of Canada and the Canada Institute for Scientific and Technical Information (CISTI). Other libraries within the federal government did not wait for the availability of Dobis, and automated certain library functions with the help of other systems before 1979.

Automation of processes at a later stage has been a mixed blessing for libraries of federal government departments and agencies. On the positive side, it has permitted us to benefit from the experience of others and to introduce our automation processes in the least disruptive fashion. The level of consciousness of automated processes and their promised potential was certainly greater in 1979, enabling us to consider and take action on a number of issues still being considered by libraries that had already automated some processes. One of the major actions with a direct impact on user services has been the closing and/or freezing of card catalogues and the introduction of COM (Computer Output Microfiche) and online catalogues as new tools for accessing the collections. In a number of libraries, retrospective conversion projects are underway in order to enhance the collections' access by users and to benefit from available derived products. The online system is also being used effectively to trace a title's critical path from the time it is ordered, received for processing, and finally catalogued for the collection. Dobis products have been developed to provide specialized access tools for staff and users alike in the form of accession lists, serials lists, inventory lists, etc. To us, then, Dobis has opened the door to the new technologies, facilitating and enhancing bibliographical control and access. It has permitted us to survive the introduction of AACR2 with minimal disruption. Most of all, however, it has traced a road and a consciousness of no return: technical services must evolve, use the new technologies effectively and be creative in its approach to providing users with enhanced information retrieval tools.

Expectations amongst librarians in the development of Dobis as a truly integrated library management system had been an incentive to delay automation until 1979 when Dobis was finally available to libraries of federal government departments and agencies. Developmental plans called for the introduction of a number of modules, once the cataloguing module was operational. Such modules as acquisitions, circulation control, management statistics, serials control, and boolean searching are presently at the early planning stage. Developments of software packages in an EDP environment have traditionally lagged behind schedules; Dobis is seemingly no different, to the chagrin of libraries who count on the integration of these functions to meet some of the challenges of the ''information age.'' The ability of the developers of Dobis to provide a fully integrated library management system within the next years is essential for the continual development of the role of libraries as information

centers. The evolution of technical services of governmental libraries will largely be influenced by the rate of development of Dobis
modules. We remain confident in the value of the concept of the
Dobis system and in the possibilities of progress in the development
of new modules to service both technical and user services.

FUTURE PROSPECTS FOR AUTOMATED SYSTEMS

My analysis of the prospect for technical services centers on the
development of new technologies and techniques as these will prove
to be the dynamic force that promote the evolutionary process of the
next decade. In my opinion we will succeed in enhancing the technical services function if we arrive at using the new technologies and
techniques efficiently and effectively to offer better services to
users. Of all the proposed developments for the next decade I foresee that three issues are likely to make their mark. They are: 1) the
question of decentralized versus centralized systems: 2) interconnection; and, 3) the impact of microcomputers.

1. Decentralized versus Centralized Systems

Two camps are presently forming in the library environment as
proponents of decentralized and those of centralized systems are developing new systems and using the newest technologies in identifying their concept as the answer to forthcoming challenges.

Proponents of the decentralized or distributed systems argue tena-
ciously that automating locally certain library functions will serve
their users best because the flexibility offered permits the system to
be moulded in light of specific user requirements. Functions most
likely to be automated locally are acquisitions, serials control, and
online catalogues. Libraries opting for local systems will continue
accessing major bibliographic utilities to create and maintain their
bibliographic databases. Other scenarios are possible but the concept of accessing a major source for bibliographic data derivation in
the cataloguing function will likely remain.

In my view there will be continual development in this field over
the next decade as this option will become accessible to a great number of libraries where computer hardware exists or will be bought.
For technical services this option is certainly a challenge as it will
demand that well-defined links and standards be established in order

that products and services provided to users are compatible with their needs and can be obtained in a user-friendly environment.

Generalized computer services will also grow within the next decade as one of their major disadvantages, telecommunication and computer memory storage costs, is likely to be resolved with the stabilizing of costs. In order to maintain its clientele base, major bibliographic utilities will have to realign their developmental objectives to provide clients with integrated library management systems, as in the Dobis system. Such a reorientation should be taken now to satisfy the needs of libraries that depend largely and/or exclusively on major bibliographic utilities for the automation of their processes.

The benefits of centralized services, within the proposed new environment, reside chiefly in their greater efficiency and their near universal access by libraries. The efficiency factor is tied to a manipulation of bibliographic records that is minimal. Once entered in the system, bibliographic records can be used for different functions without being re-keyed. A record will be entered at the acquisitions stage, modified when going through the receiving and cataloguing functions, used for the online catalogues and the online circulation function, and manipulated for the output of special products for users. The economy in the handling of bibliographic records is certainly apparent but, more importantly, the handling can be done on one system, providing user access to bibliographic records at different stages of processing and within a number of functions. It is, in other words, fully transparent.

Another important plus for centralized services is immediacy of access to such systems by all libraries, large or small. Major investments in computer hardware and EDP staff are not required when one is linked to a central computer system as terminals and printers represent the only important capital costs. I must recognize, however, that telecommunication costs are high, espcially for those libraries located in remote areas. These costs could halt their rapid increase and probably stabilize at an affordable level if we consider the following factors: increased competition amongst communication carriers, inroads of automation within other service sectors such as banks, and developments in the field of satellite communication and dish antenna technologies. A reduction in telecommunication costs and a revised fee structure to reflect the new environment of the integrated library management system should continue to make centralized computer services a viable alternative in the next decade. For technical services such systems provide the incentive for a continued and enhanced bibliographical control function, one in which products/modules developed for user services are themselves constantly expanded and improved.

2. Interconnection

Interconnection, the ability to access multiple databases through a common interface, will probably play a key role in the evolution of technical services within the next decade. Already in Canada a trial of interconnection possibilities has been under way since July 1982, by six major libraries/library systems. The iNET Gateway trial, the name of the common interface system, is being mounted by the Computer Communications Group of the TransCanada Telephone System. Libraries involved have established a Bibliographic Interest Group which is one of seven common interest groups participating in the trial; other groups are found in the fields of banking, petroleum, travel, real estate, broadcasting, and law.

Interconnection permits libraries to access each other's databases through a common interface—the gateway—and thus simplifies greatly the procedures for accessing other computerized systems. The procedure calls for accessing initially the common interface, iNET in this case, through the use of a dial up and password process. Once entered in the gateway system, the user need not go through a dial up and password process to switch from database to database; the process simply calls for ending the communication with the first database, finding the code of the next database in an index, and requesting communication with this database using the appropriate code. The gateway system will automatically connect you to the desired database. "Walking" from database to database becomes then a simple technique. Presently users must follow search procedures that are unique for each database forcing librarians to learn a number of search procedures in order to utilize the system effectively.

It is much too early to evaluate the impact of the iNET Gateway trial on libraries in Canada, but one can conjecture that interconnection will impact on technical services in a number of areas. The acquisition function, be it for monographs or serials, can finally have access to a wide range of databases for the retrieval and use of bibliographic records found in publishers' and vendors' source files. Libraries will have the opportunity to identify and acquire materials more quickly because of the easier access to bibliographic databases and services of vendors and/or publishers. Such a theoretical model will be realized if vendors offering automated acquisition systems review their mode of operation to provide as much flexibility as possible. Pricing policies would need to be redefined in the content of an interconnection environment. The success of these changes could lead to faster turnaround time for ordering and receiving books and other materials. Users are bound to benefit from this proposal.

The most promising element, however, is reserved for the cataloguing function as interconnection will (theoretically) provide access to a number of bibliographic databases and/or bibliographic utilities through a simple and quick procedure. Such access would open the door to a widespread use of the derived cataloguing process to accelerate the cataloguing workflow and increase its efficiency.

There are a number of hurdles that must be overcome before interconnection becomes an asset to the cataloguing function. Firstly, bibliographic utilities and libraries with stand-alone systems will have to agree on protocols and fee structures that facilitate access to their bibliographic databases. Standards, or lack of these, present a major problem also. Libraries accustomed to high standards may find little of use to themselves in bibliographic databases developed according to other practices. This is also true for libraries that have developed bibliographic systems based on local practices. Cost factors should not be disregarded as interconnection automatically brings with it higher telecommunication costs. A library would need to evaluate closely the cost-benefit aspect of derived cataloguing before joining a bibliographic communications network.

Interconnection holds a lot of promise for technical services, given that an environment of cooperation and resource-sharing is created. Interconnection will undoubtedly create greater access to bibliographic databases from which data can be retrieved and/or derived. It will promote on a larger scale the concept and process of bibliographic data derivation, both of which are bound to gain new credentials from now until the end of the century.

3. Impact of Microcomputers

Microcomputers have been available in the marketplace for nearly five years now and have shown a growth potential that is phenomenal. They are very present in libraries, and I foresee an even greater use of such equipment in the future.

For technical services of small and/or special libraries, micro-computers represent an affordable alternative to the automation of processes through local systems based on minicomputers or through medium to large bibliographic utilities. The key elements in the successful application of microcomputers in small and/or special libraries will be affordable costs, flexibility, and local control. With the prospects offered by interconnection, a library with a microcomputer could effectively become part of a macro-distributed system. Users will benefit directly from the automation processes as technical services increase their efficiency and provide information retrieval tools suited to patrons' needs.

Microcomputers offer great possibilities for manipulating information stored in their local memories. Technical services will use this technology to improve their processes and reduce costs. A possible scenario of the late 1980s would call for microcomputers in the acquisition and cataloguing areas to capture bibliographic data via an automatic file transfer system from vendor source files and bibliographic databases in an environment of interconnection possibilities. The captured information would be manipulated to suit the library's need and then dumped either to the local or centralized systems of acquisition and/or cataloguing. Thus a library could benefit directly from its association with vendors and bibliographic utilities by obtaining as much bibliographic data as possible and manipulating it according to local practices without incurring great costs. The microcomputer linked to an automatic file transfer system would cut telecommunications costs because the modifications to records are done locally. Libraries will certainly look at this alternative for their technical services, as I suspect it will enable a greater number of libraries to benefit from automation.

IMPACT OF THE TECHNICAL SERVICES EVOLUTION ON PUBLIC SERVICES

Techology promises to change radically technical services. A greater accent will be placed on increasing its efficiency in order to acquire, catalogue, and make documents accessible in a most timely fashion. Technology promises to help us meet this challenge as automation takes hold in our libraries. The end result of the appropriate introduction and development of automation processes in technical services will have a direct influence on how quickly users can access new materials in the library.

The success of an enhanced efficiency of technical services should be used as an excuse to review, and maybe rethink, the way in which users can access information found in our collections. Commercial databases of periodical and report literature use a number of information retrieval techniques that are quite different from the traditional author-title-subject approach found in most libraries. Should we not aim also to provide users with techniques such as boolean searching, keyword indexing, free-floating thesaurus and abstracting in order to make available enhanced access tools for our local collections? If increased efficiency usually calls for streamlining staff functions and if increased technical services efficiency is achieved through automation, I suggest that we utilize our strengths in document/subject analysis to enhance the information retrieval tools provided to users. For libraries concerned over the usage of their collections, the solution could well come from the provision of better information retrieval tools to display their content.

CONCLUSION

In trying to apply futurology in analyzing the prospects of technical services, my approach has been to fragment the elements of development. I have deliberately avoided painting scenarios involving the factors most likely to change technical services as it would be vain to apply a model for each possible situation found in library configurations. The future will be marked by the flexibility provided to libraries in selecting the appropriate approach and equipment to automate and/or develop already automated processes. Each library will be able to tailor its approach to its environment, its finances, its policies, and its users' needs. I have described some of the elements that could be offered; there will certainly be others.

Technical services will solve the challenges posed by the information age if they succeed in keeping pace with this evolution. An increase in efficiency, more fluidity of processes through automation, provision of enhanced information retrieval tools, and an awareness of changing informational needs of users should be the goals of technical services for the next decade.

REFERENCES

"Canadian Government Installation of Dobis: The First Four Years," *National Library News,* v.14, no.10 (November 1982) : 4-7.

Durance, Cynthia. *Initiatives toward a Bibliographic Communications Network for Canada.* Ottawa, National Library of Canada, 1982. 8 p.

"iNET Trial Conference Held," *National Library News,* v.14. no. 3-4 (March-April 1982) : 9.

Kaske, Neal K., and Nancy P. Sanders. "Networking and the Electronic Library," *Drexel Library Quarterly,* v.17, no.4 (Fall 1981): 65-76.

Kenney, Brigitte L. "Library Information Delivery Systems: Past, Present, and Future," *Drexel Library Quarterly,* v.17, no. 4 (Fall 1981): 36-64.

Newman, William L. et al. "Dobis: The Canadian Government Version," *Canadian Library Journal,* v.36, no. 4 (August 1979): 181-194.

Predictions

Sanford Berman

ABSTRACT. Library automation has some deleterious effects. These are explored.

I truly hope I'm wrong about these three forecasts, but right now they seem likely to happen.

1. AN "AUTOMATION GAP"

Increasingly, library research, funds, and other resources—including book and journal space—go to automated systems. The assumption seems to be that automation is unquestionably "in," represents the total future, and is rapidly supplanting manual systems. The reality, however, may be somewhat different. For largely economic and geographical reasons, *many* libraries—probably a majority—are not now even partially automated and probably won't be—certainly for much longer than the literature and computer-pundits suggest. Some—mainly rural, understaffed, and underfunded—cannot presently afford to maintain more than single-entry catalogs nor perform elementary catalog maintenance (like making cross-references). Closely paralleling the development of a terrific chasm between the "information rich" and "information poor," this library "automation gap" could easily result in the co-existence of two disparate, unequal, and basically unjust modes of library operation: one highly-computerized, presumably more efficient, and providing wonderfully diverse services, from online database searching to instantly-updated catalogs; the other essentially local, labor-intensive, and "traditional" in service-range. In some respects, of course, the "manual" mode may be more *human,* more *personal,* more socially responsible in times of high unemployment,

Sanford Berman is Head Cataloger, Hennepin County Library, 12601 Ridgeway Drive, Minnetonka, MN 55343.

61

better suited to relatively unsophisticated or disabled constituencies, and more satisfying. But doubtless it will be *less* well-financed, *less* integrated into the library "mainstream," and *less* assisted by professional researchers, policy-makers, writers, and publishers.

2. CATALOG RECORD DEGRADATION

Computer considerations have already reduced the intelligibility of catalog records by mandating—via AACR2—"special," arcane punctuation, spacing, and abbreviations. Moreover, long-standing descriptive cataloging policy—especially at the Library of Congress—has minimized the possible utility of catalog entries by failing to supply comprehensible notes that clarify a work's peculiar graphic, language, and other features; specify bibliographic relationships (e.g., among trilogy titles); and further indicate contents and even flavor, approach, or intended audience. In short, the catalog record is *now* defective because of both ISBD conventions and undue parsimony. What appears to be happening, however, is not a trend toward reform—toward spelling-out abbreviations, abandoning foolish hieroglyphics, and furnishing more data about each work so that catalog-users can more easily determine whether a given item is likely to satisfy their needs—but rather a distinct, fast-growing movement toward *limiting* the amount of potentially-useful information available to catalog searchers. This drift is clearly manifest in the favoring of short-entries in online catalogs and the relative difficulty (from a user standpoint) of ever reaching full entries (which, as mentioned, aren't yet as "full" as they should be).

3. IMPEDED SUBJECT ACCESS

Despite the tremendous hoopla over Boolean- and term-searching in online systems, the fact remains that genuinely reliable and comprehensive subject retrieval demands modern, controlled vocabularies, competent subject indexers or catalogers assigning the vocabulary terms on a work-by-work basis and introducing appropriate (and abundant) cross-references to and between primary descriptors. If a work, for example, on the "New Right" hasn't been subject-cataloged under "New Right" and doesn't contain "New Right" in its title, it's not retrievable, even in the most high-tech system. The dreary truth is that in the realm of standard library sub-ject cataloging: a) the predominant "controlled vocabulary"—*LCSH*—is *not* either modern nor sufficiently cross-referenced; and b) online catalog proponents seem basically content with "fancy" searching, often establishing catalogs without *any* authority control whatever and rarely pressing the Library of Congress to, at mini-mum, improve its stock of primary rubrics.

Technical Services,
1984-2001 (and Before)

Michael Gorman

ABSTRACT. A statement is presented concerning the importance of libraries. The use of the computer in centralized cataloging and in access enhancement is discussed, and suggestions put forward concerning the need for an increase in quality and scope of interlibrary cooperation. Finally, ideas are formulated concerning library organization, library education, future forms of cataloging and publication, and the ultimate fate of technical services.

What follows is, to some extent, an exercise in self-indulgence. The editor of this new journal asked me for some thoughts on the future of technical services. Not having the iron self-control of most writers in library journals, I found my thoughts ranging both backward and forward and sometimes sideways. The predictions which this piece contains do not follow some steely thread of logic, but are the thoughts of someone who has been knocking around libraries almost all of his life, usually in a paid capacity, and who has good memories of the past, a passionate interest in the present, and a fundamentally optimistic belief in the future.

When invited to think about the future of technical services, I must admit that my first thoughts are of the past of technical services as I have experienced it. In the twenty-odd years that I have been around libraries in general, and technical processing in particular, I have seen changes in techniques that are quite staggering but no changes in the overall aims. I hope to celebrate my 60th birthday in the Year of Our Lord 2001. 2001 is of private significance, but it and the starting year of my speculations, 1984, are of considerable cultural resonance to us all. Will Winston Smith survive to see the world of Arthur C. Clarke's dreams? Between the arid bleakness of

Michael Gorman is Director, General Services Department, 246A University Library, University of Illinois at Urbana-Champaign, 1408 West Gregory Drive, Urbana, IL 61801.

Big Brother's rule and the cosmic epiphany of 2001 lie all kinds of possible futures for society and for libraries. In looking at those futures I start with a basic premise which can be quite simply put. It is that libraries are of transcendent importance to culture and society, and that the processes that enable libraries to fulfill that role well are of crucial importance to the destiny of libraries and, thus, of civilization.

In the mid-fifties, I had my first encounter with technical services in the basement of a London public library. My job was the filing and retrieval of metal plates upon which were embossed catalogue entries. These plates were endlessly re-usable and covered with a greasy gooey ink. (So much for library work as the "nice clean job" of my mother's dreams.) The plates were handed to my supervisor, a woman who interminably hummed snatches of the Flanders and Swann repertoire while stamping out multiple copies of catalogue cards for the main card catalogue and those in the library's five branches. The catalogue entries were created directly on the plates by way of a weird machine looking like a huge spinning wheel made of cast iron. The woman who spun the great wheel and pecked out the entries letter by letter, was the first, and one of the best of the hundreds of cataloguers I have known. That she has once been Piet Mondriaan's landlady gave her an air of somewhat off-key distinction. That she was widely read, inmmensely knowledgeable, and kind and open enough to discuss cataloguing with a sixteen-year-old library menial meant far more to me. The point of this peer into the distant past is that I have been left with some indelible impressions and ideas which have not changed in their essence over the many years and many miles. These are that cataloguers are, and need to be, informed, dedicated, and open minded; that all technologies should be given a wary welcome; that no solution to a problem is permanent; and, that centralized cataloguing of the bulk of library materials (even in the primitive form which I then saw), is always preferable to distributed cataloguing. I remember asking why, since we made numerous copies of each entry only to type the added entries over the main entry heading; we did not simply omit the main entry heading and supply the same basic entry with different headings. In the mid-1950s that was a simple-minded question verging on the heretical. Nothing that I have seen in the journey from inky metal plates to on-line interactive catalogues has provided a satisfactory answer to my naive and juvenile question.

In thinking about technical processing and its efficacy or otherwise one should always be thinking about the user of the products of technical services—the processed materials and the various keys to their use, catalogues and whatnot. That train of thought takes me back even further in time—to my very young boyhood after the Second World War when Hendon Public Library was the most important thing in my life. Though I was far too young, some of the librarians in that bastion of the northwest London suburb in which I lived would let a small compulsive reader loose on the collections of the "Adult Lending Library." There were some who would not, for them I spun unconvincing tales of a sick mother waiting feverishly for books by Waugh and Wodehouse, Kipling and J. B. Priestley. I usually got in. Once in, I would wander round the shelves looking for interesting reading almost at random. In the course of these explorations I came across, and developed a taste for, the works of a then popular, and now little read travel writer called H. V. Morton. What I could never understand was why his books were scattered around a particular section of the library which I firmly believed was in no order at all. After a life steeped in the work of Melvil Dewey, I now realize that I was adrift in the "910s." I never asked anyone to explain because I was unwilling to draw attention to myself—a juvenile interloper in the adult library world. How many library users are there who, through shyness or an unwillingness to appear stupid or for any other reason, cannot or dare not ask for help in a library when they fail to understand our elaborate systems?

Another feature of Hendon Library was a sheaf catalogue. In this, probably, long-gone type of catalogue, the entries were typed on flimsy pieces of paper which were then gathered into small binders which could be carried to any part of the library. They were a friendly and helpful device, far less cumbersome than the card catalogue, and far cheaper and more flexible than the book catalogue. That catalogue left me with the idea that all catalogues should be useable in a practical way and unintimidating. The lesson is as valuable in the age of the on-line interactive catalogue as it was thirty-odd years ago.

Technical processing is devoted to assisting the (to use a quaint old-fashioned term) reader to locate information and knowledge, to choose and find the right materials for research, leisure reading, entertainment, cultural progress, or for any other of the manifold purposes for which people read or otherwise use library materials. That is, or should be, beyond question. The question which is increasingly posed is "which readers, which library users?" The age which has given us an ever more urgent need to share our resources (because of economic problems and the drift away from public funding of social services) has also given us the technical answer to that need. One does not need to be a starry-eyed technocrat to recognize that the true power of the use of the computer in libraries lies not solely in doing things better, but in increasing the quality of service and the range of service especially by creating new ways of cooperating among libraries.

In Illinois, as in many other parts of the country, there are only two ways to get to or out of most small towns—private automobiles and buses. Under some part of the deregulating procedures sweeping the country, the main bus operator is petitioning to drop services that it deems insufficiently profitable. It will probably be successful. The lines that it will drop are those that serve small towns and rural settlements. In terms of physical mobility, an inhabitant of such a town who does not possess an automobile might just as well be living in the Middle Ages. Paradoxically such persons, once in their houses, will be linked electronically with the Global Village—cable television, the Bell longlines, home computers (which can be used as terminals), and many as yet uncommon electronic devices will remove most limits to communication and the life of the mind. Illinois' state-wide resource sharing system (LCS) will allow the physically isolated person to share in the library resources of the state almost as well as someone who lives in a large town or one rich in library resources. As the darkness closes in, libraries based on the most efficient use of library materials become even more a beacon of hope, a good light in a naughty world. Even when every person has virtually instantaneous access to the fullest bibliographic information, there is still a physical fact to be faced. Books, records, tapes, films, etc., are physical objects which need to be transported before they can be used. Learned persons tell us that we are on the brink of a Paperless (and, presumably, Filmless, Diskless, Ficheless) Society and that this inconvenient necessity will soon not exist. My prediction (fancy word for guess)—which is probably as good or bad as anyone else's—is that in 2001 we will still be transporting significant numbers of books, etc., between libraries. Those involved in technical processing, who have dealt, by and large successfully, with the problems involved in making connections between the users of the library and the materials they need *within* one library will, I believe, be very much involved with performing the same task *between* libraries. One seemingly minor but significant organizational change which this process will demand is the integration of inter-library activities into the mainstream of technical processes. Too long have we regarded inter-library lending and borrowing as fringe activities, have failed to staff them with the right numbers and the right kinds of people, and have isolated them from the developments that have revolutionized mainstream processing.

Given present trends, another significant change in the remainder of this century will be the merging of technical and public services. The division between the two has hurt our libraries and impaired our service to library users. The technological changes which have already occurred and which will soon occur make that distinction as unnecessary as it is harmful. Computer technology enables us to free various levels of library staff from irksome routines and does away with the necessity for centralized groups of professional staff (especially professional cataloguers) by making the information now carried only in centralized files available anywhere there is a terminal. The ramifications of this latter statement are many and lengthy, but principal among them is that the division between technical and public services, though it may seem canonical to many, stands revealed as being born of previous technological limitations. There are numerous psychological and practical problems to be found as the technical services librarians and the public services librarians come together to form professional groups dedicated to all kinds of library service. Those problems will not long endure, and when the process is complete not only will it be to the benefit of the users of the library but also the life of a professional librarian will become more fulfilling.

How are we to prepare librarians for the changes already underway and for the changes to come? I look for major restructuring of library education in three directions. The first is that of continuing education. Though we make efforts in a somewhat uncoordinated manner through professional groups and library schools, there remains a tremendous inequity between the need and the supply. There is a real danger that a generation gap will open between the more established librarian and the younger librarian more informed about the technological realities of the modern world. The second development should be in the library school curriculum. The curriculum, which has had, since Dewey's day, to balance the demands of practicality and theory, is faced with an even more severe challenge—that of becoming more relevant and useful in an always changing library world. I believe that can only be accomplished by the third direction which I foresee—the integration of library schools and working libraries. That (more properly speaking) re-integration is, in my view, the only way in which library education and the practice of librarianship can inform and strengthen each other and can produce librarians who are really equipped to deal with the changes in techniques and philosophy which are bound to come.

What else will happen in technical processing by 2001? I predict that there will never be an AACR3, and that the next general cataloguing code will be a manual on how to create MARC records for the national on-line network. Those MARC records will be different from our present linear records in that they will be multi-dimensional and based on authority file concepts such as those partially elaborated in the WLN system. The national on-line network will be formed by an amalgamation of OCLC and RLIN which will be decreed by a commission set up by CLR, LC, and ARL and formed to deal with the aftermath of RLIN's financial collapse.

I believe that the economics of serials will force a major change in the nature of journal publishing. Librarians will have to deal with a new world in which articles are disseminated from central review institutions on the basis of individual and corporate "profiles." Subject headings, or some new version thereof, will be crucially important in the article dissemination process. There is no doubt that LCSH will prove, to put it mildly, inappropriate and inefficient in this context. For this reason, if for no others, we will see a radical revision of our subject heading apparatus. In the field of subject access, I believe that we will see a move toward the simplification of shelf classification numbers, accompanied by a refinement of the use of classifications in machine systems. For the first time, classification numbers for shelf arrangement will differ from those used for access in catalogues.

The catalogues in our libraries in the near future will not be simply catalogues. They will be the bibliographic component of a complex of interacting systems linked and presented to their users by sophisticated interface programs which will appear to the user of the systems to constitute one system. The systems located in the overall "Grand System" will include (as well as the bibliographic component), circulation, binding, serial control, acquisition, and financial records. They will be a mix of local and national, commercial and private records, and software which are not integrated at the software level but accessible through user-friendly seamless person/system programs. This is all a long way from Hendon's sheaf catalogue but will have the same ends in mind—friendliness and usefulness.

We will see new forms of communication become popular, will have to deal with the implications of cable television, home computers, and the flight inwards which stems from those developments. If the cinema as a place of mass resort seems to have been killed by television, is the public library sacrosanct? Perhaps some as yet unimagined combination of lasers, videotechnology, and holograms may well become the most loved cultural artifact in the next decade—whether it will replace and obliterate the reading and study of *David Copperfield, Psmith in the City, El Cid,* or *The Heart of the Matter* seems rather more problematic. The most confident prediction that I can make is that technical processing librarians will have, in one way or another, to deal with old and new forms of communication, with millions of books, and hundreds of thousands of each of the myriad other forms of communication. The new will add to the old, rather than replace it.

Technical services as we know them now may well not exist by the end of the century. The aims of technical services will exist for as long as there are libraries. The *Technical Services Quarterly* may well have changed its name and its coverage long before then, but its concerns will remain real and the work to which many of us devote our lives will remain worthwhile. There can be few things in life that are as worth doing as enabling libraries to fulfill their unique and uniquely important role in culture and civilization.

Library Automation
in the Year 2000 A.D.

Lois N. Upham

ABSTRACT. An indication is given of some major trends and developments in the area of library and information sciences. Library organization and staffing are discussed, as are production and use of various kinds of non-print media. Some conjectures are made concerning the cost of electronic information.

One is not often invited to predict the future in a scholarly journal, and when one does get the chance (at least this one), the fascination turns to solemnity when the task is actually tackled. It seems at first glance as though the job would be an easy one, but in 1983, attempting to throw the world ahead seventeen years is actually an awesome assignment when you get right down to it. Fortunately, I am not being asked to tackle the whole world, just libraries of the 21st Century. By that time, however, I project that automation will overlap all other aspects of library work, including technical and public service work.

In preparation for writing this piece I have been skimming through a number of books and articles about our technological development and our outlook for the future. Perhaps none of the materials examined was more impressive than the latest issue of a catalog put out by the JS & A Group, Inc., called *Products That Think.* Through it a person can purchase a remote message computer, a computerized thermostat, an electronic pest control system, light bulbs that turn on when you talk to them, electronic "vitamins," a very small but powerful "word cruncher" (word processor)—and a "time cruncher" (a tape recorder that lets you listen at up to three times the normal speed), a personal stock portfolio computer and . . . but I think the point is made. Perhaps more amazing is that each of

Lois N. Upham, Assistant Professor, School of Library Service, University of Southern Mississippi, Southern Station, Box 5146, Hattiesburg, MS 39406-5146.

these items costs under $1000, several of them well under that price. The showcase item of the issue is a commercial flight on the space shuttle—"still in the planning stage"[1] but more than idle fancy. Remember that offer if you feel that anything hypothesized in this article is "too far out."

John Naisbitt in his best seller *Megatrends* discusses ten trends which he feels will reshape the world as we know it. Several of these have important implications for libraries: the move from an industrial to an information society, the move from forced technology to high tech/high touch, the move from centralization to decentralization, the move from institutional help to self-help, the move from hierarchies to networking, the move from either/or to the multiple option, and the move from a national economy to a world economy.[2] Some of these concepts might cause a "traditional" librarian to wince, but then just what are "traditional" librarians anyhow, and why can't they take advantage of the trends?

Christopher Evans gets more specific in his book *The Micro Millennium* among other things, predicting a "decline of the professions." He states that "the vulnerability of the professions is tied up with their special strength—the fact that they act as exclusive repositories and disseminators of specialist knowledge."[3] If, indeed, the specialist aspect of the professions is in danger of being eroded, then what we may be seeking in the future are well-grounded generalists who can adapt rather than highly-trained specialists who cannot.

With all that as a background, it becomes formidable to do anything as "simple" as predict the state of library automation in the year 2000 A.D. Indeed, there is a real question of whether there will be anything quite like libraries as we know them today. It seems we are perhaps pitting the irresistible force (the headlong thrust of high technology of all kinds) against the immovable object (the staid tradition of the institutional library). Optimistically, I do not really think that the one is as irresistible nor the other as immovable as they may seem on the surface. I hope I am correct in this assumption, for in their flexibility and in judicious adoption of the new technologies, I see the revitalization of our libraries—or information centers, or data centers, or resource depositories, or whatever they end up being called. In the following "prophecies," therefore, I am bound to take a more "wishful thinking" approach than a "gloom and doom" one of conjuring up all the terrible things that might happen.

Since one of the big predictions being made is the end of printing/publishing as we now know it, I see the boundaries between technical processing and public services in libraries blurring and perhaps ultimately disappearing. After all, if there are few physical pieces to order, catalog, circulate, and service, why should this not be so?

I come back to the well-grounded generalist; it seems to me that this is the type of person who will be valued in our information centers. These would be people who are able to follow the information process from creation to utilization. Let us proceed from here with a little scenario which *could* be one of the 1000+ factorial outcomes of all the possible pieces available to the information society of the next century.

Picture a teacher sitting at her personal computer. This one is at home, but capable of being hooked into the system at school if necessary. A research project is in mind and some information is needed. She checks through the data files which she has previously created, but does not find what she wants. Having previously completed her application and received her access code to the local information center, she logs into their system to search the subject file.

The subject file maintained by the information center contains not only indexes to a variety of commercially-maintained data bases (both national and international), but also the subject file to their own microform collection, a customized local subject file and the thesaurus to materials maintained in hard copy. Distinction between monographs and articles is made only by a one-character symbol and, indeed, portions of monographs are treated separately where appropriate. Non-print materials are also included and they, too, are identified by special symbols.

The search yields several items of interest. The text of some of them can be requested for review on the terminal screen; two items are on microform in the information center, and the teacher requests that copies of them be mailed to her along with a copy of a chapter from a book which is in the center's collection. One reference baffles her, however, and, changing modes on her terminal, she uses the request function to send a query to the staff terminal at the information center. When a staff member (or an "intelligent" computer) has time to check, a response will be sent to the teacher's terminal. In this case, the material has limited access and is, therefore, not available for public use.

The computer at the information center records the fact that royalty fees are required for access to the commercial files and for copying articles not owned by the information center. This data is, in turn, fed into a worldwide network through which information sources are linked, and applicable charges are calculated (including any currency conversion that may be required). A predetermined portion of the fee will be billed back to the patron at the end of the month, her assigned access code being used as an account number.

An especially difficult inquiry may be referred by the staff to an expert in the field. The expert may not be at the information center. He or she may do all related work from a remote location. As is nicely illustrated in the film based on Anthony Smith's book *Good-bye Gutenberg,*[4] people, through the wonder of high speed/high tech communication arrangements, can locate where they wish and still tie into the mainstream development of their chosen field on a daily basis.

And what of the information center staff? Do they *only* answer queries on their terminals. No, indeed! A certain number will be charged with the task of reviewing and acquiring for their own files electronic, micro, and even hard copies of materials which fill the largest portion of continuing local needs. These will, of course, have to be indexed and entered into their system. Other tasks will include reviewing commercial data base offerings in order to decide which services might warrant setting up a deposit account rather than having to deal with billing on a piece by piece basis.

An interesting phenomenon of the 21st Century will be that, for all intents and purposes, we will only pay for the materials we use. A large portion of library acquisition money is currently spent on "educated guesses." We "guess" what will be used and pay for that use before it actually occurs. This will be changed in the future, charges being made only after usefulness has been established. This should make our information operations much more cost-effective.

Some staff members will be spending time keeping up to date with changes in the composition, entrance vocabulary and protocols of various systems and in turn training not only other staff members, but patrons as well. Staff members will perform a much greater training function in the information center of the future. They will instruct in not only the more traditional avenues of access and retrieval, but will also perform a real technology transfer function. This training can occur in the information center itself, but specialists will also be dispatched to schools, subcenters, businesses, and even homes to assist users.

Individuals who, for one reason or another, cannot personally access the files of the information center, will be able to go directly there for help. Searches will be done and items copied or circulated (controlled through the patron's access code) as required. Especially difficult requests will probably still be best handled by personally visiting the center. Also, there still will be a hard copy collection of books and other materials, for, despite everything, people will continue to enjoy printed volumes—perhaps more than ever since they will be fewer in number. Films, slides, video tapes, etc., will also be available, although home users will actually be able to search for, identify, request, and view such materials at their own terminal, should both the capability and the desire exist.

One other important function that will be performed by information staff members of the future will be that of public relations. This is meant in the broadest sense. If we are to be successful parts of an "information society," information will become a true commodity, and the information center and its staff will become brokers in an important market. In the most altruistic sense, information can help each individual "be all that he or she can be," but this is going to take some encouragement and some salesmanship. . .not to mention persuasion to get the money needed to support the effort. I am inclined, as I mentioned earlier, to feel that these operations will be more cost-effective than the current ones; equipment will undoubtedly continue to get more powerful while its cost decreases, but public money, despite the possibility of, it is to be hoped, modest users fees, will still be needed. It seems, however, a small investment in light of the potentially positive returns to country, world, and society.

I see exciting, if sometimes traumatic, times for libraries cum information centers ahead. I think there still will be a place for persons who are basically task-oriented and I see a greatly increased need for people who want to combine information skills with educational functions and human relations. I think "intelligent" machines will be able to process much routine work and even make decisions about it, but I don't think that machines will replace people. I am, in fact hopeful that machines can free people to use their creativity and imagination, as opposed to using their energy to struggle with day-to-day routines and problems. The "neat" divisions we have today in our libraries will, I feel, blur in the future, but I also think that the intellectual rewards and even the emotional satisfaction can be immeasurably increased. Threatening—perhaps; too bold a projection—I don't think so (recall that Vannevar Bush predicted the Memex[5] in 1949, and although it's been a wait, the realization of something very similar is now finally a possibility). If developments in technology proceed at their current pace, information centers such as the one I have hypothesized could be a reality sooner than 2000 A.D. If developments slow, which I doubt they will, it could be later. I do, however, feel that something *at least* as revolutionary as what I have projected *will* occur. Crazy? The 21st Century will be the judge of that.

REFERENCE NOTES

1. *Products That Think,* 9 (Northbrook, IL: JS&A Group, Inc., 1983), p. 5.
2. John Naisbitt. *Megatrends* (New York: Warner Books, Inc., 1982), p. 1.
3. Christopher Evans. *The Micro Millennium* (New York: Viking Press, 1980), p. 111.
4. Anthony Smith. *Goodbye Gutenberg* (Produced by the BBC, 1980).
5. Vannevar Bush. "As We May Think," *Alantic Monthly* 176 (July 1945):p. 106-107.

The Transformation
of Technical Services

Dan Tonkery

ABSTRACT. Predictions are made about the decentralization of the technical services operation, and about the number and quality of library workers in the library of the next century. Statements are put forward on the electronic library and networking.

By the twenty-first century, the traditional model of technical services organization in most large libraries will be replaced with a decentralized organizational pattern distributed throughout a library system. It will no longer be necessary for the functional activities in cataloging, acquisitions, and serials control to be linked to a manual shelflist, card catalog, or any other type of manual file. Even in 1982, some libraries have begun to experiment with a decentralized arrangement. In twenty years, with the continued development in technology, this approach to the organization of technical services will be commonplace.

In keeping with this decentralized pattern of organization, libraries will find a significant decrease in the number of professional librarians required to operate the traditional technical services functions. Through greater networking capabilities, including linked bibliographic abilities, there will be a much greater sharing of bibliographic information, so that the amount of original cataloging will diminish for the printed material. The sharing of bibliographic information will be facilitated by the establishment of centers of responsibility based on language and format of material, which will have not only the capability to add new records to one or more national databases, but also the capability to update bibliographic records in multiple systems simultaneously.

Dan Tonkery (formerly Associate University Librarian, University of California, Los Angeles), Vice-President and Managing Director for North America, F. W. Faxon Company, 15 Southwest Park, Westwood, MA 02090.

Each library will have significant local computer power and data storage equipment that will enable each individual to have an automated work station to operate as stand alone processor, or an intelligent terminal with as much computing capacity as large IBM systems have in the 1980s. This local work station will not only support the immediate technical services control functions associated with acquisitions, cataloging, and serials processing in a stand alone environment, but also be able to interact with an international bibliographic network utilizing common communication protocols. Each system will be linked to form an international network which will facilitate the routing/sharing of information to member organizations.

Included in this network will be new electronic libraries, which contain large data files which will be "printed out" on demand. The publishing community will undergo a major change. However, one cannot predict that the paperless society will be upon us entirely by the year 2000. Certainly, there will be a reduction in the current volume of printed journals and monographic material. These electronic libraries will contain massive information banks from which libraries can withdraw information, including graphic material. Most of these electronic libraries will offer their services on a subscription or fee basis.

In addition to electronic libraries, one will find that other mediums than the traditional printed work will be available. The most noteworthy example will be the videodisc. By the end of this decade, the videodisc will become a major storage and retrieval device. This device will operate in an erasable, updatable mode, with archival quality output. Libraries with large archival collections will turn to the videodisc as an answer to their storage and retrieval problems.

With the trend towards the electronic library, including the use of videodisc technology, the technical services staff will be required to handle more of what one would consider non-traditional material. Determining what a library owns in order to make a purchasing decision will become much more difficult. Consider that half or more of the "collection" may reside outside of the traditional library. The library will still provide some printed materials, however, the majority of material may reside in one or more computers physically remote from the library. Only on demand will the public service staff activate a procedure to download a copy of the information into a local processor. The library will certainly pay some form of royalty, but only upon use.

The technical services operation of the future is going to be heavily automated with only a small number of staff. Many of the traditional bibliographic problems will be exacerbated by having the end user access the information directly from their own individual terminal. The library may find that it has become an information service that handles print, microform, videodisc, and electronic materials. The next twenty years are going to be an exciting time of transition for everyone in the library profession. The character and structure of the library is changing, and it is our responsibility as librarians to meet the challenges of the future by continuing to learn and advance through education and training.

Our role in the information transfer process by the year 2000 will depend on our ability to change and grow with the technology. Technical services librarians must be innovative, informed, and ready to accept the new challenges coming their way.

The Quik-Trip Syndrome

Karen G. Roughton

ABSTRACT. A statement on the benefits of library automation and how these will grow.

I have a vague recollection of a class in library school during which there was a discussion concerning the proper ambience for an academic library. Most students agreed that the days of the scholarly researcher and the passive librarian were at an end and that the academic library of the future should resemble a supermarket or department store complete with helpful stockboys, cheery produce managers, and electronic cashiers. Reference librarians would function in the role of sales-clerks, aggressively roaming the stacks and public catalog to ask patrons, "Have you been helped today?"

Ten years have passed and the academic library of today has indeed started to offer attractively packaged goods and services. Within the next two decades, technical service divisions, as they exist today, may be obsolete. Differences between public service and technical service librarians have already begun to blur as we share newly automated databases. We will help you write your term paper, search the literature in your field, construct entries for the catalog in the simplest form possible, and we will not worry about precise classification. Who browses anymore anyway? To what extent are these advances? How far are we willing to go with the concept of the academic library as a Quik Trip convenience store rather than a haven for the pursuits of a disciplined mind?

As we approach the close of the twentieth century, it is time to evaluate our image and our place in the University community. We want to make people aware of the multitude of resources available to them, but that should not be an end in itself. We must prove these tools to be a part of lifelong learning; students should not always be

Karen G. Roughton, Cataloger, Iowa State University Library, Ames, IA 58011.

concerned solely with the quickest way to write a term paper. Instilling diligent habits of mind in our patrons should be paramount among all our lists of "goals (and) objectives." Perhaps the years of consumer oriented education are drawing to a close. With automation to free us from much of the time consuming drudgery of bibliographic control we may have an opportunity to witness the second coming of that almost extinct species of educator—the scholar librarian.

The Library Future: Computers

David C. Taylor, BA, MS

ABSTRACT. The factor that will influence American libraries most in the next decade is the computer. Another major influence on libraries is falling budgets relative to the cost of library materials. In the next ten years we should see a tremendous growth in automation, with online catalogs becoming much more numerous and successful. They will become the central databases for integrated library-wide systems used for acquisitions and circulation. Serials may be more difficult to integrate into these automated systems, however. The crying need for research libraries in the next decade—a national information network—is likely to be unfilled. Finally, the author expresses less than profound faith in his predictions.

The most important qualification for a forecaster is not clairvoyance, but a poor memory. For a forecaster to publish, a poor memory must be aided by a poor filing system. A forecaster of the future of technical services should furthermore, not be distracted with too detailed a knowledge of the technical services. Qualifying on all three levels, I accept the assignment to predict some of trends in the future of library technical services. ''Future'' is defined as ten years hence.

COMPUTERS

When the crystal ball clears, what becomes visible in the library's future is computers, computers, and more computers. All increases in productivity in our times are the result of automation. All savings in costs are the result of automation. All the improvements in biblio-

David C. Taylor is Undergraduate Librarian at the University of North Carolina at Chapel Hill, Chapel Hill, NC 27514.

graphic control, in bibliographic access, and speed of processing, are the result of automation, although only some of the recent improvements in public services are due to automation.

Many of the worst problems with library automation ten years ago have disappeared with the new generation of computers. Computers now are less expensive, have increased power, are more convenient, and require less arcane knowledge to use. Likewise we can expect problems we now have, such as lack of uniformity and standardization, poor interface between computer systems, and insufficient software packages to become historical curiosities in another 10 years.

Other problems associated with computers are less likely to go away. I see no easy solution to copyright and bibliographic control problems for electronic publications. We are not likely to find a quick solution to the problem libraries have coming up with the funds to utilize computers. The computer tends to create a class system of haves and have nots because few individuals can afford the equipment to participate in the computer revolution. Don't expect that to change, even though prices are coming down. The nature of database use also encourages the library to charge for its service. Some librarians are contemplating charges for information services on a wide spectrum and find it logical. Others dislike the idea of charging anyone for any service. That debate will probably be exacerbated by events of the next decade.

Some comment should be made here about the backwardness of libraries in making use of the computer. Is there any group of white collar workers in America that have less daily use of word processing than libraries? Isn't that really an indictment of a profession in the business of communication to be so slow to utilize available technology? I don't think so. It is rather, an indication of the undercapitalization of libraries.

Libraries are undercapitalized because they already spend so large a proportion of capital funds. To a university budget officer it appears that the library book fund of $3 million is more than its fair share of the $3 1/2 million the university has budgeted for capital expenditures. Requests from other departments for expensive equipment are likely to be looked on more favorably than the library director's requests.

On the other hand, libraries have been generally slow to take advantage of relatively inexpensive developments like word processing. I have a theory that such innovations travel in pecking order.

Word processing equipment was purchased first by the university President's office and by science departments with a lot of grant money. Then it spread to the Alumni office and other faculty departments. In the library it will appear first in the director's office, followed by technical services, business office, and last of all, by public service departments. Don't ask me to explain this.

The computer will have an indirect effect on libraries through publishers. They have already utilized computers extensively in a word processing and in typesetting, and will seek other cost saving and income producing applications. The creation of data bases and the income they generate is one example. Primary publication in electronic formats will continue to grow in the next decade. However, the electronic form of publication may be in direct competition with the printed publications from the same publisher, so the gains may be illusory. I believe we will see more publications of this kind, and libraries will have to deal with them. I don't believe they will be the general answer to publishers' economic woes, and they will not replace print.

OTHER FACTORS

Briefly, we should recognize other influences on libraries during the next decade or so. Will the U.S. economy continue to struggle? If so, libraries will contine to fall behind in budgets for acquisitions, salaries, and equipment. Even if the economy makes a great rebound in the next few years, which seems unlikely, libraries will probably remain under-budgeted.

The economic squeeze on publishers is also likely to continue, forcing subscription costs and book prices rapidly higher. This will force libraries to acquire fewer materials. Some publishers will prosper because most libraries will continue to want their publications. The publishers who cannot find a large buying public for popular materials or an adequate number of library buyers for scholarly materials will fold.

Commercial information suppliers will increasingly compete with libraries. The online database vendors will serve many users directly in the next decade. The importance of libraries for depth of coverage and service to those without their own computers will not diminish, however.

The bibliographic utilities will continue to survive as competitors.

Pressure on them to cooperate will bear fruit only if all are financially unstable, or, more slowly, if all become financially sound.

Cooperation among libraries in acquiring and making use of publications will have to increase. We desperately need a national information network that will make such cooperation feasible. We can forget the U.S. government as a source of money and leadership for the creation of a periodicals center, a periodicals system, or an information network, which includes libraries, in the next decade, unless the country suddenly becomes very prosperous. It is in the interests of the large research libraries and the smaller libraries that want to borrow their materials to create such a system on their own. Unfortunately I don't believe librarians are likely to come up with the leadership and the collective wisdom to invest the money necessary for such a system to be created in the next 10 years or so. Instead, we will limp along with a scandalously inefficient interlibrary loan non-system, with most of the costs falling on those libraries trying to help others and few costs borne by those who benefit from it. More and more major libraries will drop out of the interlibrary loan free system by adopting fees for their services. When all the major libraries do so, maybe librarians and scholars and university administrators will be forced to think about the problem enough to create a system in the U.S. that is equivalent to the one the British already enjoy.

EFFECTS ON TECHNICAL SERVICES

With the foregoing as prologue, let us forecast some specific effects on the work of those people in libraries who select, acquire, and create the bibliographic control for our library collections. In general these comments will apply directly only to those libraries large enough to have technical services articulated into departments.

Acquisitions of Monographs

Dealers selling to libraries will develop automated systems that connect library, dealer, publisher, and cataloging source. For U.S., Canadian, and European books, these systems will aid in selection and avoid unintended duplication. They will make the ordering process much quicker. Libraries whose orders now take an average of 6 or 8 weeks to be filled, may expect to receive shipment in 2 or 3.

Some more time could be saved if more books were shipped by UPS or other common carriers instead of the U.S. Postal Service. When the special 4th class book rate disappears, more dealers may begin to do that.

More and more library acquisitions departments will be benefitting from in-house automation too. Many libraries are now developing online catalogs. An outgrowth of these catalogs will be integrated systems that include acquisitions operations. Some libraries already have outdated acquisitions or accounting systems operating in the batch mode. Those systems will be discarded and redesigned as part of online systems.

Most university library acquisitions operations now search on the bibliographic utility terminal for confirmation of the identity of a requested book and to make sure the library does not already own it. In an integrated system that search could also include an online BIP and the information found could be preserved in electronic format and ordered by computer printout or online. When the book arrived the record waiting for it could be used for cataloging, for generating payment, and for inventory control while the book was in the cataloging process.

Since we can generally expect most libraries to reduce their acquisitions, we might look for some reductions in acquisitions staff. This would be particularly true for those university libraries that redefine their role and cut back on their acquisition of research material. Many publications in this category require the most extensive and expert searching, and to reduce their number will make the work of preparing orders much easier.

Serials

Serials acquisitions has proven to be a most difficult operation to automate. Much of the reason for that difficulty is the wide dispersal of serial publishers and the lack of standardization in their publications. A library with 20,000 subscriptions is likely to find that they are published by 12 or 15,000 publishers. Of course that is quite different from the experience of book publishing, where most of the 45,000 titles annually produced in the United States originate from no more than 2 or 300 publishers. Keeping track of all those serial publishers undoubtedly creates many problems for libraries.

Of those 12 or 15,000 publishers, many are likely to be undercapitalized, shoestring operations run by amateurs. They undoubtedly cause libraries special problems. For almost a decade I've blamed serial problems on amateurish publishers.[1] Recently I've realized that the nature of a serial magnifies these problems. If a book is published a month late no one is inconvenienced. The late serial causes a problem, because *time* is an added dimension that belongs to a serial, along with the *expectation* of the nature of the next issue, which is based on the appearance, organization, time of publication, and so forth of previous issues. The relation of one issue of a serial to another over time creates more categories of information about serials that don't exist for books.[2] The subscription order requires the library to know when to expect publication and what to expect. Probably twice as many items of information are kept about a subscription order as for a book order. Typically the book will arrive with the copy of the order in it. Except for the first issue the serial almost never will, and may do many of the unexpected things that books do, such as change title, publish late, or early, change format, or change publisher. Somehow the serials acquisitions staff must identify it and find the records that correspond to it. I believe automation of serials acquisitions has not been terribly successful because these factors have not been sufficiently analyzed and because many of the troublesome problems (e.g., identifying the publication) are not presently subject to automation.

Nevertheless, promising serials systems are appearing. The most surprising breakthrough to me has been the success of the serials vendors' systems, particularly Faxon's LINX. I believe its success is due to the wonderful opportunity to generate claims on a timely basis that arises from the ability to compare the experience of several libraries. Still, the most successful system of the future is likely to be a distributed system with functions such as check-in and claiming done locally (with perhaps an automatic query to other libraries through a vendor before a claim is generated). Such a system would be integrated completely with a library's online catalog to produce holdings records and routing instructions upon check-in.

During the next decade many libraries will follow Michael Gorman's advice and break up serials departments.[3] Many of those libraries will wish they hadn't. The special problems associated with serial publishing makes it desirable to maintain specialists on the staff who are familiar with those problems and inventive at problem solving. What we need is automated systems that make it easier to communicate and preserve information about serials. If a reader in the Physics Library notices that the *International Journal of High Pressure Physics* announced in an editorial that the title will change with the next issue, the system should make it easy to pass that information to the people in the library who will check the next issue in.

The next great advance with the acquisitions of printed serials will be industry-wide agreement to put a bar-code identification on each serial cover that is coded for title, volume, number, and date. Once a good number of serials are published with that bar-coded information the greatest error producer and time waster in serials acquisitions will begin to disappear. Don't expect that advance this decade. That's another problem whose solution would cost a lot for the problem solvers to whom it is no problem (publishers), and cost nothing for those who benefit from the solution (libraries).

Cataloging

The OCLC database will continue to get worse until pressure is brought to bear to create a fundamental change in the file, allowing LC verified entries to eliminate all alternative records. Libraries would still be able to access their own records if different from the LC entry, but not be bothered by those of every other library. Luckily, RLIN will survive, so it will be possible to create enough pressure on OCLC for this change to be made.

Many librarians are learning to use their new COM catalogs, and more will soon. Many will soon be using their online catalogs too. The turnkey systems now available from GEAC, VTLS, CLSI, and others are bringing these formerly expensive systems within the reach of many. They are good systems, too, although improvements will continue to be made, particularly in designing effective-user-friendly search strategies.

If acquisitions of library materials drops, it makes sense to expect that cataloging staffs will dwindle too.

Collection Development

Less adequate library budgets will make the choices harder. The collection development staff will have more work to do making those decisions. Much of that work will involve the cancellation of subscriptions. This is a difficult task requiring careful coordination with faculty, the compilation of information about use patterns, consultation of published citation-analyses, and the cooperation with serials staff. It may be necessary for many libraries to tighten the profiles of their gathering plans for books, or to end them altogether and to order all books from reviews, a time-consuming procedure.

I've made reference several times to the possibility that some libraries will decide to change their roles as research libraries. The Pittsburgh study recommended that libraries purchase fewer research materials that may never be used and rely more heavily on interlibrary loans for such material.[4] Several books and articles have been written on this subject.[5] And indeed, it is difficult to argue that each research library should continue to duplicate the holdings of all the other research libraries in rarely used material. In the face of declining budgets, it would make sense for libraries to spend their money on books and serials of immediate use to students and faculty, and not to attempt to anticipate all the future needs of researchers.

That is not so easy, however. Churchill had no desire to preside over the dismantling of the British Empire, and few librarians want to preside over the lowering of ambitions of a library. Nor do they relish the idea of telling their faculty that the library will no longer serve their research needs. This is another reason why libraries desperately need an effective national network that will locate and make available the rarely used research collections at one library for the patrons of another library. Until that network is created, few research libraries will be able to give up the expensive business of collecting research material extensively.

Preservation and restoration of the printed materials in library collections is the most neglected major problem of libraries today. We can expect some progress in this field in the next decade. The most important thing we can do is to persuade paper manufacturers to make more acid free paper and to encourage publishers to use it. This will begin to happen in the next 10 years. We can also expect to achieve a wider awareness of the problem and a better understanding of its extent. Unfortunately, it appears that little can be done to reverse the aging process of brittle paper. It would be impossibly expensive for every library to deacidify the thousands and thousands of deteriorating volumes in its collection. Perhaps technology will come to the rescue in the form of the video disc to preserve in a permanent form the information now in danger of being lost.

FINAL PREDICTIONS

In conclusion, I will revert to my first subject, the uncertain nature of predictions. In addition to the fearless predictions already recorded, I predict that some of these predictions will come true and perhaps even most of them. Some of them will come true, but not in the time anticipated, while others never will. Let us hope that the influences not guessed that will prevent the actualization of some of these predictions will be happy ones, not dire. However they turn out, I predict that in ten years no one will remember or really care what these predictions were.

FOOTNOTES

1. Cf. David C. Taylor. *Title Varies* 1, no. 5 (September 1, 1974), 29.

2. Cf. David C. Taylor. *Managing the Serials Explosion, the Issues for Publishers and Libraries* (White Plains, N.Y.: Knowledge Industry Publications, 1982), 7, 8, 38-41.

3. Michael Gorman. "On Doing Away with Technical Services Department," *American Libraries,* 106 (July/August 1979), 435-37.

4. Allen Kent, ed. *Use of Library Materials, the University of Pittsburgh Study* (New York: Marcel Dekker, 1979).

5. For instance, Cf. Daniel Gore, "Farewell to Alexandria: The Theory of the No-Growth, High-Performance Library," *Farewell to Alexandria, Solutions to Space, Growth, and Performance Problems of Libraries* (Westport, CT: Greenwood Press, 1976), 164-180; and Richard DeGennaro, "Austerity, Technology, and Resource Sharing: Research Libraries in the Future," *Library Journal* 100 (May 15, 1975), 917-23.

File Management
in the Automated Library

Margaret McKinley

ABSTRACT. The acceptability and inevitability of automated technical processing are discussed. How automated record-keeping will change the way in which records are kept and the records themselves is given attention, and the effect of these changes on library organization and productivity is outlined.

Electronic library processing is not a phenomenon that we may expect a future generation of librarians to confront. It is upon us today. While it may well be twenty years before all libraries maintain machine-readable files as a matter of course, the discussion that follows does not concern itself with library technical processing at the end of the century. Some libraries have already entered this world of the future, which relies so heavily on an adequate supply of electrical power and miles of telephone lines. Large and medium-sized research libraries, in particular, are already installing computer-assisted processing systems. Automation has been the impetus for dramatic changes in those libraries. The staffs in those libraries are learning to use new methodologies and new approaches to their work now, and similar changes may be anticipated in the next two decades in even the smallest libraries as automated technical processing invades libraries of all sizes.

Technical services operations have been organized traditionally around paper files. The professional and paraprofessional staff in various departments or work groups is concerned with the management and maintenance of those files. Books, magazines, records, films, and all other communication media pass through these technical processing departments on their way to their final destinations,

Margaret McKinley, Head, Serials Division, Research Library, University of California, Los Angeles, 405 Hilgard Avenue, Los Angeles, CA 90024.

returning only to be repaired, discarded, or compared to other materials. The files in which the existence of these objects is recorded remain permanently, however, and become for many technical services librarians objects worthy of care and preservation for themselves alone. Neat and tidy annotations, accurately filed cards and thorough bibliographic descriptions are as important to some as putting library materials into the hands of users. Some might even suspect that for some librarians, file management is more important than are any user services. On the other hand, the best of the technical services staff can interpret their files as an Indian scout would in looking for twigs out of place in a forest path. They can extract information for the paper records which is all but invisible to the novice or to the uninitiated.

The introduction of automated technical processing in a library will result in the extinction of this way of life. Assuming that a library has had the foresight to develop an integrated system with distributed processing capabilities, the management of the machine-readable files will be shared by staff in many different technical processing and public service departments. (An integrated system is one which provides processing and public access capabilities for all aspects of a library's operations, from selection to circulation. Ideally, work done in each processing phase would build on that done in an earlier phase. Distributed processing capabilities permit similar processing activities to take place in many different geographic locations.)

No longer will there be many small groups of library workers each of whom are custodians of a different set of files. Librarians must adopt a less proprietary attitude towards their files and the Indian scouts among us must learn to interpret a different set of clues.

If a library is utilizing the electronic wonders of automation, there's no longer any good and sufficient reason for catalogers to have their desks situated so that they will have easy access to shelf list and official catalog. Catalogers will no longer need a supply of well-sharpened pencils, typewriters, caches of 3 × 5 cards in various colors, and other impedimenta which clutter so many catalogers' desks. It may, therefore, be possible to seat catalogers at computers and sell their desks to benefit the library in some appropriate way. Automation might, in fact, bring about the rise of a new cottage industry since catalogers should be able to do some of their work at home, communicating with their supervisors by means of messages on CRT screens.

Selectors who formerly maintained lists of items for which they had submitted orders and who complained about long delays in the acquisitions department before orders were placed, will be able to key their requests into a machine-readable file. The acquisitions department will be able to work on the orders more quickly since there's no paper to file or to annotate. Selectors will be able to check the status of their order requests without moving from their offices, without causing distress or consternation in the acquisitions department, and without maintaining separate files of orders requested.

Bibliographic checkers in large libraries have always worn sensible shoes and developed long, loping gaits, or walked in short rapid trots as they moved from card file to card file around their libraries. Automation will end the peregrinations of bibliographic checkers. They'll be able to sit comfortably at terminals, check all the library's files and wear fashionable footgear.

Distributed processing features in an automated system mean that decentralized processing and centralized control of standards and procedures is possible and practical. This is particularly important in serials operations. In large libraries with central serials records files and a number of branch libraries and public service departments, library management has accepted duplicate recordkeeping as a necessary evil. Management has also been resigned to a considerable lack of correspondence between like records in different files. A high error rate in those records has been acceptable. Differing procedures and file maintenance methods in different departments or locations have been permitted.

Automation will bring about radical changes in these long-accepted practices. There will be a single serials receipt file in machine-readable format to which staff in any location in the library will have access. If library management decides that serials mail shall continue to be received centrally, then issues can be checked in only once, either at the point of receipt or at the shelving location. This eliminates one significant opportunity to maintain duplicate files. Staff in all locations updating or altering serials records must adhere to similar standards since records are available to all library staff and perhaps to the library's users. Consistency in formatting information in records is essential if everyone viewing those records is to be able to interpret them. The higher visibility of serials records which is an inevitable consequence of an automated, on-line system, should result in a lower percentage of errors in the serials file since there will be greater opportunities to locate inaccuracies.

The end of the century will surely find technical services departments in libraries still engaged in the business of acquiring library materials and fitting them into collections of all sizes. The paperless files which will be commonplace then will result in startling differences in the appearance of technical services work areas. Vast banks of cabinets holding 3 × 5 cards, acres of desks for staff, and ranges of shelves full of material awaiting processing will have vanished, replaced by CRTs, plenty of empty floor space and lots of empty shelves. The empty shelves must be mentioned since the optimists among us believe that the speed and ease of computer-assisted technical processing will result in the eventual elimination of that *bête noire* of all libraries, the backlog.

Access and Delivery:
Availability of Materials
in a Medium-Sized Academic Library

Joan I. Tracy, MLS

ABSTRACT. An appreciation is presented of the creation of automated library systems. The substituting of data base searches for the use of print bibliographies is commented on, and electronic interlibrary lending and the cooperative acquiring of materials are considered. Other matters touched upon are computer to computer exchanges, traditional and electronic forms of delivery, and automated circulation systems.

> Books are for use; Every reader,
> his book: Every book, its reader;
> Save the time of the reader; and,
> A library is a growing organism.[1]

S. R. Ranganathan's five laws of library science, first promulgated in 1928, are as valid as ever today. In 1983, with more than 9,000,000 titles accessible on-line in OCLC and with many other automated finding aids available, the first four library laws should be more easily obeyed than ever before: Every man (and woman) should be able to get that book (or information in another medium) within a short time. As for the fifth library law, even with reductions in library budgets, libraries keep on growing, but any single library will probably not be able to meet all the needs of its users.

How can a medium-sized academic library continue to provide the materials that faculty and students want and need in a timely manner? Technical services librarians have a responsibility to investigate possible answers to this question.

Joan I. Tracy is Assistant Librarian for Technical Services, The Library, Eastern Washington University, Cheney, WA 99004.

RESOURCES

While the number of titles published in the United States continues to increase, the typical academic library is less able than ever to acquire even a fraction of the new publications available. The subscription prices of serials continue to increase faster than the general consumer inflation rate. Academic libraries must increasingly rely on sources outside their own collections to satisfy user needs.

Automated systems not only help individual libraries carry out their daily routines more efficiently but can also aid technical services librarians develop and preserve collections more rationally and economically. For example, an automated circulation system can produce data to show which parts of a collection are being used most heavily and even which titles are in high demand.

Automated systems that are shared by many libraries can aid all in collection development, even though cooperative efforts are difficult to achieve because, in a funding crunch, each institution must respond to the demands of its own users and the limits of its own budget.

With shared automated acquisitions, circulation and cataloging systems, each library can determine whether a title has been added by another. If the title is expensive or likely to be seldom used, a decision can be made not to purchase it. Equally important, a library can determine that a copy about to be discarded may be the last of that title in the region. Cooperative storage schemes can be developed to preserve last copies.

ACCESS

While I believe that reports of the imminent demise of the book are premature, certainly the future of serial publications, especially scientific and technical titles, is being affected by electronic communication. Increasingly, faculty rely upon computer searches of remote data bases to obtain citations and sometimes copies of articles. Emerging now is the journal which is never published at all, in the conventional sense of the term, but which is displayed on-line or is available through on-demand supply of offprints or telefacsimiles.

Only careful studies, in an individual library, can determine at what point it becomes cost effective to offer data base searches instead of acquiring print bibliographies, or to order articles on demand instead of subscribing to the journals.

In the meantime, and probably for some years to come, academic libraries will rely on traditional interlibrary loan to obtain the vast majority of articles from serials they do not hold. While it may be easy to get the citation, from searching an on-line data base, receiving a copy of the article can take many days or weeks. A widely used data base, OCLC, for example, will show that a library holds a serial but does not give details of holdings. The OCLC serials control and union list modules may eventually provide these details, but, as yet, they are in limited use and accessible only to the libraries using them. Many union lists exist, but often they are incomplete or seriously out of date.

Making detailed serial holdings available on-line in the larger national or regional data bases should be a high priority goal. Although the Eastern Washington University library, for example, is a member of both OCLC and the Washington Library Network, its holdings are shown in detail only in the print or microfiche edition of a union list for the Spokane area, which is described below.

In the United States thousands of libraries search and obtain products from the large data bases: OCLC, RLIN and the Washington Library Network. Hundreds use automated circulation systems. But these data bases are not linked. The situation is like having three long-distance telephone networks and hundreds of local systems. Even if one finds out that a telephone number (title) is available somewhere, one cannot find out whether the person (copy) at that number is home (available for loan).

An electronic link among the bibliographic data bases and circulation systems used by libraries in a region would be a giant step forward in improving the speed and efficiency of interlibrary loan. Furthermore, protocols could be developed to shunt regional interlibrary loan requests through a pre-set hierarchy of lending sources, based on such factors as proximity, size of collection and demand on resources.

Within an individual library, internal routines should be examined to insure that materials which should be available are on hand when needed: locations, loan policies, recall procedures, shelving, repair and replacement, addition of copies for titles in demand.

Locations that restrict access to materials should be examined, too. How many obscure bibliographies languish in reference sections when a location next to the author's works might increase use? Just because a book is called a dictionary or bibliography does not necessarily mean that it must be non-circulating.

During the Falklands campaign, the British Ministry of Defence is reported to have requested a copy of an Argentine dialect dictionary from a university library but was informed that the book could not be borrowed. "If we can get the QE2, we can get your book!" was the reply.[2] Academic library users may not have as much clout, but they should have reasonable access to materials.

DELIVERY

Perhaps before the end of the century, delivery may commonly be in the form of electronic transmission, videodisc or by other means. But at present, and probably for many years to come, books and photocopies will be delivered by more or less traditional methods.

Although the idea of a national periodicals center seems to have been shelved, at least for now, I think that a great deal can be done, on a local and regional level especially, to improve delivery of library materials. The demand for specific books and periodicals can be spread more evenly among libraries of all types and sizes. Large research libraries with holdings of unique titles for a region should be compensated for the demands on their resources.

While teaching in a library school in England some years ago, I visited the British Library Lending Division at Boston Spa and was impressed with its efficiency. Serials were checked in manually, in a traditional manner, but the shelf arrangement was decidedly non-traditional. Libraries in Newcastle-upon-Tyne, where I taught, had joined together to provide a frequent courier service to the Lending Division. With one of the world's largest serial collections readily and quickly accessible within one hundred miles, the libraries in Newcastle could avoid subscribing to expensive or infrequently used titles.

The United States is many times the size of England, but cooperative courier service can, and should be encouraged to share resources among libraries in a geographic area. In the state of Washington, for example, Washington State University and Eastern Washington University, in the eastern part of the state, are investigating the possibility of air delivery of materials from the University of Washington, which is located on the west side and which is by far the largest holder of library resources in the northwestern United States. Another innovation being tested in this part of the country is telefacsimile transmission between the Washington State Library, the

University of Washington, and other libraries in the Pacific North-west and Alaska.

THE SPOKANE EXPERIENCE

The Spokane area is relatively isolated, geographically. For many years, the libraries in and near Spokane have depended on each other, and cooperative arrangements have been worked out. As the largest academic library in the Spokane metropolitan area, the Eastern Washington University library has been an important participant in joint efforts and has gained from them.

In the Spokane Cooperative Library Information System (SCOLIS), for example, five libraries share an automated circulation system based on a minicomputer. The libraries include two large public libraries, two community college libraries, and the Eastern Washington University library. A bar-coded library card from any of the libraries may be used at any other.

If a book is not available in the first library checked by the user, but is available elsewhere in the system, a hold may be placed at the terminal; when available for loan, the book is mailed directly to the home address of the person who requested it.

At the Eastern Washington University library, a title is routinely checked in the SCOLIS data base if it is not held by the library. Only if the title is not held by another library in SCOLIS is the request forwarded to the interlibrary loan technician (if the person requesting the title qualifies for service). Statistics for the first year of operation of SCOLIS indicate that the Eastern library is supplying more books to the other libraries' patrons, by far, than it is borrowing, but this situation might change if Eastern's students and faculty had access to the SCOLIS data base through a public terminal they could use; it is hoped that a public access terminal will be available within a few years.

For each library in the system, each of the others serves as a resource, according to an order established in the computer program. Requests are automatically routed through the list, until an available copy is located. Since the list is in a different order for each member of the SCOLIS system, no one library receives more than its fair share of requests for a title held also by others.

Since November 1977 the five SCOLIS libraries, together with several others which constitute the Council of Spokane Area Libraries (COSAL), have funded the operation of a courier service which delivers material daily at each library. This service makes it possible for patrons of the eight COSAL libraries (including the SCOLIS libraries) to return books at any of the libraries, regardless of where the materials were borrowed. The SCOLIS libraries also collect fines and charges for each other and transmit them via the bonded courier.

A local union list for periodical titles was first published from a computer data base in 1976 and is scheduled for a fourth edition in 1983. Although some of the more than twenty libraries with holdings in the union list use one of the large data bases (Washington Library Network and OCLC) and several have automated circulation systems, only in the regional union list are all their periodical holdings displayed together. The importance of the list to the library community of the region is shown by the willingness of COSAL to fund it, with the expectation of partially recovering the costs through the sale of microfiche and print copies.

CONCLUSION

Perhaps the year 2000 will see people locating sources of information through wristwatch computers and getting delivery via their telephones or home computers. In the meantime, libraries must work together to improve access to each others' collections through electronic communication and devise ways to deliver materials rapidly while sharing the burden fairly.

REFERENCES

1. Shiyali Ramamrita Ranganathan. *The Five Laws of Library Science* (Madras: The Madras Library Association, 1931).

2. *Library Association Record,* 84, no. 7/8 (July/August 1982) : 231.

Musings on the Future of the Catalog

Jerry L. Parsons, PhD

ABSTRACT. Progress in development of on-line catalogs is rapid and impressive. Much of this progress is due to financial pressures: on-line catalogs may be able to provide improved services at diminished costs. Computerized catalogs will enable other, more significant changes in libraries and their operations than are usually perceived, including finally, efficient use of cooperative networks among all types of libraries. This essay reviews some of the pressures leading to the rapid development of on-line catalogs and projects some of the possible changes which will result.

Because I am involved in studying and evaluating potential on-line catalog systems for a large university system, have been writing and speaking to library audiences on that and related topics, and am vain enough to believe that I have a point of view which may be of interest to others, I accepted a challenge from the editor to forecast "concerning the shape, size and use of the on-line catalog." Naturally, as my deadline approaches, I have been thinking more about the topic, reading the many articles about on-line catalogs in the professional literature, and reflecting on the utter foolishness of accepting this assignment. On this note, let me proceed to review some "facts," and see if any conclusions can be drawn.

First, the sudden rush to implement on-line catalog systems needs to be considered. For some years now, card catalogs have been obviously less effective and efficient than librarians and patrons would like. These catalogs are large, cumbersome, labor-intensive monoliths which allow very limited searching. They can be duplicated only with great labor and expense. They allow access only at their location. On the other hand, they are well known to most users and staff, comfortable for most to use and, studies have shown, produce acceptable search results for staff and user alike, especially in those

Jerry L. Parsons, Assistant University Librarian for Administration, California State University, Sacramento, Sacramento, CA 95819.

105

cases where catalog size is kept to a tolerable level (e.g., where branch library catalogs contain only branch holdings). The possibility that the installation of on-line public access catalogs may result in benefits to libraries such as lower maintenance costs, improved search capabilities (e.g., post-coordinate searching), wider access, lower space requirements, etc., obviously has raised the level of interest in development of such systems. In times of economic uncertainty and diminished resources, such as we are now experiencing, the possibility of being able to provide similar or improved services to users at similar or lower costs is too attractive to ignore. Thus, the pressures for and progress in development of on-line services are readily understandable.

One of the basic assumptions here is that users are and will be served adequately by the catalogs, existing and planned. Is this actually the case? Card catalogs have long been criticized as a librarians' tool which hinders patron access to information as much as it aids it. There is some justification for this, especially from the users' point of view. Research reveals that well over half of all library users know, by author or title, what they want when they arrive in the library. Except in research situations, users seldom care what edition of a title they get; most users don't even know what is meant by the edition statement on the catalog card. Few understand classification systems or call numbers at all. Except for librarians' perceived need for "bibliographic control" of collections, libraries might well be organized like bookstores or warehouses: titles could be shelved alphabetically by author or by title. Even shelving by accession number would be simpler for the user to understand. Catalogs, in these simplified systems, might be shelflists, including only cross-reference information and location of the item. For example, visualize a library where all items are shelved alphabetically by title. If the patron knows the title wanted, direct consultation of the shelves is the most rapid access method. If only the author is known, consulting the catalog (which would be alphabetized by author and subject) would provide title and location. This might be the simplest, easiest organization for user access. This system is, of course, insufficient for the efficient, effective bibliographic control of the collection that librarians must maintain so that subject access, subject searching, and other necessary services can be provided.

How, you may wonder, is this relevant to the future of the catalog? The answer lies in the computer's functions. Card catalogs can complicate user access to material when main entry information is known because the catalogs contain information superfluous to those simple inquiries. Such information is included in the card catalog because that tool must perform other functions in addition to serving as a holding and location device, functions such as subject searching or bibliographic checking, which require information unnecessary for simple look-up functions. The computer's ability not only to hold various levels of information but to provide only as much information as is needed allows us to reconfigure our catalogs so that better access to all levels of that information is possible. Several of the vended on-line catalog systems take advantage of this by providing different "screens" for different needs. Thus, the user who needs only to know whether or not a collection includes *The Catcher in the Rye* and its location may use a short record screen. A researcher wishing to ascertain whether or not a certain edition of this work is available, can request screens which include information comparable to that on a catalog card, a MARC record or an OCLC record. I believe that recognition of this flexibility has yet to occur on a broad scale, especially among librarians. More on this later.

Current fiscal constraints, combined with a liberalized interpretation of acceptable levels of service, have produced some innovative library facilities and services. Transportable library branch buildings, which can be trucked from place to place as population shifts occur, are one example. Storefront, "bookstore-type" branches which cater to patrons' demands for popular, mass market literature perhaps most often associated with the Baltimore County Public Library, are another. These trends, and ones of a similar nature, combine the "give-them-what-they-want" philosophy of library service with the reality of tighter budgets. Libraries cannot provide increasing numbers and levels of service when resources are diminishing. As a result, choices must be made concerning which services will be provided, to whom, and when.

Academic libraries, too, have exhibited a variety of responses to similar dilemmas. The extensive weeding of the collections at Macalester College and subsequent emphasis on acquisition of materials based on actual rather than anticipated usage gained much publicity during the 1970s. Debate concerning Macalester's activities centered upon two issues. First, the commonly held assumption that academic library building needs resulting from ever-expanding collections were inevitable and universal was called into question. Second, the effectiveness of academic libraries in satisfying their users' needs for materials, especially with regard to conflicting attitudes about multiple copies, well-rounded collections, core collections, etc., was questioned. Here again, the primary issue may have been a questioning of beliefs traditionally held by librarians: that the library's proper, if paternalistic, role included building "balanced" collections, even if much of the material was never used; and that all libraries, but especially academic libraries, were responsible for preservation of extensive collections, even if that meant widespread duplication of core collections, expensive and on-going building programs, more difficulty for users in finding what they need, inability to fund new library services, etc.

While it may seem easy to scoff at such parochialism in this era of electronic communication, it must be recognized that the attitudes and beliefs discussed above were the product of times when each library was an exclusive resource, when campus users were restricted to using local resources. Under these conditions, academic library collection building and preservation were important and long-term investments. Now, however, rapid methods of communication and transportation, bibliographic databases which are national and international in scope, widespread cooperative networking, and interlibrary lending systems have virtually eliminated the former isolation of discrete library collections. Formal recognition of the changed relationships among libraries can be found in the many cooperative agreements which exist and in the U. S. Department of Education's Strengthening Research Library Resources Program, which funds only those collections judged to be national resources. This program, and the operating principles under which cooperative agreements work, indicate that some, *not all,* libraries are supported in their efforts at maintaining and preserving comprehensive collections.

Academic librarians and faculty have not always adapted readily to changes in the traditional roles and methods of accomplishing their respective tasks. As a result, some programs which are no longer useful have continued because "it has always been done this way." Some aspects of collection building and of bibliographic control may fall into this area. Stress, resulting from economic constraints and growing awareness of alternatives, is changing these traditional practices and perceptions, even in academic libraries. One consequence of such change should be a simplification of standards for local catalogs and a lessening of the complexity in bibliographic record maintenance in local on-line catalogs as they are created, not because they will be better that way, but because they will be cheaper, easier for patrons to use, and because the full MARC records will be available in other locally-held systems.

Sacramento, California, my hometown, is negotiating a long-term cable television and communication system contract. The process is a complex, drawn-out affair that will commit the area to cable development for the next ten years or so. Sacramento, incidentally, is purported to be the last undeveloped major market for cable. One of the so-called public channels on the cable system is to be a dedicated library channel.

The local cooperative library system is planning and developing databases so that an automated circulation system, as a first step, might be obtained. With shrinking budget support, progress is slow. Now that cable is imminent, there is a realization that electronic linking of libraries is feasible, as is direct user access to library information (read catalogs). Further, a primary use of cable may be related to off-campus instructional programs, whether "canned" courses or those broad or narrow cast directly from campuses to extension centers. One of the important corollary uses of cable in these types of instructional programs would be access to library catalog information. In fact, one significant impetus for creation of on-line catalogs may be the requirement to solve information access needs resulting from off-campus instructional programs. Here again, technology enables change (take the curriculum to the student rather than the reverse) and promotes corollary problem-solving (take the library collection index to the user, too).

My fifteen years in libraries have taught me that nothing progresses as rapidly as we think it will. Nevertheless, I conclude that on-line catalogs will become common in and out of libraries very quickly. At first, there will be many variations available, the bulk of them being clones of the card catalog. As experience is gained, however, simple catalogs, many little more than alphabetical lists of holdings, will proliferate. These will be accessible from a variety of locations: libraries, communication cetners, public offices dealing in information, and dial-up locations of all descriptions, especially where home computers are available. Campus libraries, especially, will encourage access from users on and off campus using dial-up capability.

Finally, cable communication will allow access to simple, union catalog databases which will allow inquiries from the home or any other convenient location where a television screen is available. Small keypads, some already in use, will enable users to search these simple library catalogs at all hours and from any location. Locally generated catalogs will become less complex bibliographically and more "user friendly," because the responsibility for bibliographic control will be borne by national databases such as OCLC and RLIN. College and university libraries will collect more to satisfy local demand, will weed materials vigorously without guilt, and will depend on research libraries to collect and preserve the esoteric and special materials which are expensive and seldom used but which need to be available, if not immediately at hand. A "hierarchy" of catalog complexity will evolve, local catalogs being the least complex bibliographically and international catalogs being the most complex. Coincidentally, this is consistent with the tenets of the *Anglo-American Cataloging Rules, Second Edition.*[1] In turn, the development of levels of catalog complexity appropriate to the levels of users' needs will reflect a parallel development among libraries and librarians, that of cooperation rather than duplication.

Thus, the advent of the on-line catalog will enable many changes in libraries and in patterns of library use. While many of these changes will relate to equipment and facilities, I believe that the more significant changes will be ones which involve the interrelationships among libraries themselves. Due to the capabilities of the computer and of rapid electronic communication, the isolation of one library from another can be virtually eliminated, thereby allowing each library to serve its users effectively *and* efficiently.

---

[1]*Anglo-American Cataloging Rules, Second Edition.* Chicago and Ottawa, 1978, pp. 14-15.

Out of the Catalog:
The New Renaissance?

Colleen Power, BA, BS, MLS

ABSTRACT. Large-scale use of the computer is shown to be influencing the look of libraries, library training, and the services libraries are providing. Comment is provided on the online catalog, home information services, and the future role of the library in information dissemination.

INTRODUCTION

In the 8th century, Ireland became the birthplace of western civilization.[1] Her monasteries with their extraordinary libraries provided a refuge for those fleeing the horrors of savage Hun-scourged Europe. Are our libraries once again becoming the birthplace for a new renaissance or a refuge from the gathering technological storm?

Twenty years ago in 1963, library computers were used principally to create the first MEDLARS data base and automate circulation systems. A survey of eighty New York academic, school, and public libraries indicated that only one library had a computer; that was a leased model at a public school.[2] While extraordinary unified computing systems were being tried and found wanting, as at Florida Atlantic,[3] most library discussion centered on the use of electronic data processing equipment to handle the burgeoning workloads being created by rapidly increasing library materials budgets. Acquisitions processes, catalog records, and circulation systems appeared to be the most practical target for the limited, expensive, cumbersome machine storage capacity of that time.[4]

Today the use of online systems in library work has become pervasive, finally reaching the public catalog. Most such systems operate off of in-house separately created software. Major integrated

Colleen Power, Collection Development Coordinator, Science Librarian, California State University, Chico, CA 95926.

systems are present, such as ULYSYS, CLSI, and RLIN, but these have the unfortunate capacity to confound staff and patrons alike.

Why the rush to automated systems? Library budgets, information growth, and technological advances are all contributing factors. Library budgets have grown tremendously over the past several years. Many libraries have doubled their budgets in just ten years,[5] creating the need for improved budget reporting systems. Moreover, the information explosion has brought in enormous increase in library public services demands.[6] Microprocessors with large inexpensive storage capacity are finally within range of most medium-sized libraries, while massive interlocking telecommunications networks make practical shared access at relatively low cost.[7]

Simultaneous with this rise in library technology, a major struggle for adequate budgets is occurring. Many academic librarians find competition exacerbated by demands for high-priced non-print media and machine-readable data files.

Increasing budget pressure and staff reductions brought about in part by selling regents and trustees on salary savings to be gained from the introduction of online systems and in part by the taxpayers' revolutions have major implications for library organizational structures. Reorganization discussions should be centered around three practical considerations: the availability of adequately trained library professionals, what information services the public will demand, and the nature of the technological revolution.

THE LIBRARIAN AS INFORMATION BROKER

Librarians are essentially knowledge brokers. Our services have normally been bought by private companies or public institutions. Several authors estimate that by the year 2010 almost half of library school graduates will be self-employed as independent information professionals.[8]

Already the role of librarians as consultants to libraries themselves has become well-known, with some firms providing technical expertise and trained help for such diverse activities as collection development and reclassification projects. Those librarians who chose to remain within the institutional structure will have to accept profound changes in that structure if the uses to which their knowledge and expertise are put are to be maximized.

Recently new organization structures based upon combined technical and public service functions have been tried at Columbia University[9] and at the University of Washington. Since 1970, a significant increase in technical services participation in library user instruction (over 60% in one survey) has been noted, but appeared unrelated to the advent of automated systems.[10] These trends toward great technical services involvement in user access will however provide a solid framework upon which to meet the increasing technological challenges.

THE PUBLIC DEMANDS

"I have TERM ONE on the screen; what do I do now?" This phone call to the reference desk from a professor at California State University, Chico, highlights the 1983 state-of-the-art in online catalogs. This enterprising professor calling campus information had been given the dial-in port phone number for the new online catalog. Using his office terminal, he was now ready for full access to the university library's catalog system. The questions raised by such incidents have enormous implications for technical and public service. Among these implications are the role of home computers, the methods of library instruction, the security of library records, and the greatly increased interaction of technical and public services in responding to these challenges.

As the approach to the catalog requires an increasing knowledge on the part of library patrons, so does the demand to create simpler and more readily understood systems with keyword approaches and automatic links without unwieldy cross references.

The introduction of the online catalog is a prime example as technical services personnel find themselves in a potentially enviable position. As the new catalogs are being planned and introduced to the public, major dialogs have developed over the various software packages available. Technical services has been drawn into the public area on several fronts and has the opportunity to influence the creation of the online catalog, the tutorial and access points, the training programs for both public and staff, mainstreaming separate manual files and ultimately controlling the collection through statistical management reports.

The online catalog makes possible the ready correction and updating of subject headings, introduces the possibility of more flexible creative authority control and can simplify catalog production. One estimate at CSU, Chico, indicates that error correction time for altering a catalog record had gone from 20 minutes manually to 3 minutes per item on-line.

Although the increased literacy of the post-war baby boom is reaching academic libraries at the same moment as the expanding home computing market, most library patrons are not experienced computer keyboard users. The quantum leap from "look it up in the card catalog" to "look it up in the computer file" is not an easy transition for either staff or patrons.

As library personnel grasp the extent of the coming revolution in use of the catalog and the use of the library in general, the potential implications are enormous. Massive unified networks will allow the smallest branch to establish area information centers. Centers that may be as cheap as a computer terminal.

THE NATURE OF THE REVOLUTION

"You can't curl up with a computer." The printed book will not disappear. Books will continue to exist, especially for pleasure and scholarly collections. The tendency in publishing at present is to publish fewer titles, with very short runs on scholarly materials, and massive runs on casual pleasure reading.[11] Publishers will expand the present successful online news and information services.

Libraries will continue to be used as resources for pleasure reading and for some types of scholarly pursuits. The commercial writer will probably depend upon the home information services using the word processor in combination with other equipment.

As libraries continue efforts to justify their budgets, the building of archival collections will become more important, as such unique local interest collections will become even more valuable resources for scholars unable to obtain materials elsewhere. The presence of pleasure reading materials is also not likely to disappear since American libraries have traditionally geared their collections to the wants of middle-class people, people who cannot afford to purchase massive quantities of materials for casual reading.[12]

What exactly will the future hold? Unbelievable advances in machine storage capacity make practical inexpensive home computers and miniaturized storage modules. Present commercial marketing techniques for home computers are being aimed at children in affluent middle-class homes.[13] These children will be experienced computer network users in less than twenty years. They will demand an excellent level of response to very detailed, refined requests. If libraries are unable to provide this response, private enterprise will respond with alacrity.

Increased machine storage capacity and switching ability will make practical, for those who can afford it, home access to library holdings. In any city in the United States today, private citizens can subscribe to Lockheed's Knowledge Index, to VIDEOTEX, and a variety of other commercially available hybrid encyclopaedic/bibliographic data bases.[14] In any of these same cities, the public library may still have hand-typed catalog and hand-stamped books.

The next step in the home computing industry is online shopping, now practiced on a very small scale.[15] This can extend to delivery of library materials to homes. The systems and materials may be provided by private industry, should libraries fail to meet the challenge.

At that point, our libraries may become refuges for those too poor or too machine resistant to deal with the home computing revolution. It is just possible that the vibrant exciting libraries of the 1980s will become the train stations of 2001.

A grim picture? "Those who cannot remember the past are condemned to fulfill it" (Santayana).

The future is not out of control; it is in our hands. We may be stumbling toward tomorrow, but our imagination and creativity can transcend whatever obstacles are in our way. Now is the real information revolution. We as librarians have the training and ability to make libraries the leaders in this new renaissance. We have the materials, systems, and the organizational structure to provide leadership in training the public for this future. For the poor and those over grade-school age, ours may be the only free resources. Online catalogs and circulation systems may provide us with the key. We have only to open the door.

REFERENCES

1. Toynbee, Arnold. *A study of history.* London, Oxford University Press, 1934, vol. 2, p. 322-340.

2. Weiss, Rudi. The state of automation: A survey of machinery used in technical services departments in New York State Libraries. *Library Resources and Technical Services,* vol. 9, no. 3, p. 289-302, Fall 1965.

3. Florida Atlantic University. *College and Research Libraries,* vol. 24, no. 3, p. 181-199, May 1964.

4. Brown, Margaret C. A look at the future through bifocals. *Library Resources and Technical Services,* vol. 9, no. 3, p. 162-269, Fall 1965.

5. *ARL Statistics.* 1980-81. Washington, D.C., Association of Research Libraries, 1982.

6. Mathews, J. R. Online public access catalogs, assessing the potential. *Library Journal,* vol. 107, p. 1067-71, June 1, 1982.

7. Bradshaw, E. Getting the most from the micro boom. *Management Today,* p. 64-67, August 1982.

8. Neill, S. D. Libraries in the year 2010. *Futurist,* vol. 15, no. 5, p. 47-51, October 1981.

9. Booz, Allen, and Hamilton, Inc. *Organization and Staffing of the Libraries of Columbia University.* Washington, D.C., Association of Research Libraries, 1972, p. 12-13.

10. Pausch, Lois, and Kock, Jean. Technical Services Librarians in Library Instruction. *Libri,* vol. 31, no. 3, p. 198-203, September 1981.

11. Magrill, Rose Mary. Collection Development in 1981. *Library Resources and Technical Services,* vol. 26, no. 3, p. 240-253, July-September 1982.

12. Hald, Alan P. Toward the information rich society. *Futurist,* vol. 15, no. 4, p. 21, August 1981.

13. Rosenbaum, D. Personal computer market barely tapped. *Merchandising,* vol. 7, p. 63, June 1982.

14. Morse, R. C. Videotex in America. *Editor Publisher Fourth Estate,* vol. 115, p. 41-47, June 26, 1982.

15. Maher, T. Shopping by satellite. *National Underwriters,* vol. 86, p. 24-26, July 16, 1982.

NOTE

The University Library at California State University, Chico, has in excess of 450,000 monographs and journals. In Fall 1982, the library installed the CLSI online circulation system and the online public catalog. Forty-two keyboard and touch terminals provide access to the library's holdings, with the card catalog as a back up system for the next two years.

The library is engaged in a massive orientation program for the 14,000 students and faculty. The public catalog system is the pilot project for the nineteen state campuses, with a DEC PDP-11/34 minicomputer, with 256 Kbytes of main memory, four 300 CDC megabyte disk drives, and one 9 track tape drive.

Libraries on the Line

Carol R. Krumm, BA, BS
Beverly I. McDonald, BA, MA

ABSTRACT. The utilization of online systems has necessitated many changes in technical services including the following: 1. Increased cooperation among libraries is obvious; 2. Card catalogs have been closed or frozen; 3. The focus of cataloging has changed from manual to online access with the publication of AACR2; 4. There is a growing realization of the importance of authority control; 5. The automation of serials is in the beginning stages; and, 6. Libraries are exploring implications for user services.

Since the early 1900s librarians have discussed ways of streamlining technical services. However, implementing proposed changes was slow. For example, the first edition of *A.L.A. Catalog Rules* appeared in 1908. Although a committee for the second edition was appointed in 1930, the second edition of *A.L.A. Catalog Rules* and *Rules for Descriptive Cataloging* were not issued until 1949, nineteen years later.

From the advent of automation in the late 1960s to the present, more changes have occurred in technical services than in all the years preceding 1967. Much credit is due the academic librarians of Ohio who conceived the idea of a cooperative automated cataloging system, now the Online Computer Library Center (OCLC).

COOPERATION

Cooperation among libraries is evident today in the widespread use of bibliographic utilities such as OCLC, the Research Libraries Information Network (RLIN), and Washington Library Network

Carol R. Krumm is Cataloger and Assistant Professor of Library Administration and Beverly I. McDonald is Cataloger and Instructor of Library Administration, The Ohio State University Libraries, 1858 Neil Avenue Mall, Columbus, OH 43210.

(WLN) for acquisitions, cataloging, authority work, serial processing, and interlibrary loan. Greater attention to certain areas will make cooperation even more effective. One goal must be the development of better national and international standards of rules and formats. Also imperative is the interface between the Library of Congress (LC) and bibliographic utilities, as well as the interface among the various bibliographic utilities. Additionally, the practice of assigning libraries specific responsibilities in cataloging, name authority work, serials, and interlibrary loan must be expanded.

SELECTED ASPECTS OF TECHNICAL SERVICES

Catalogs

Many libraries are now freezing or closing card catalogs and developing or using catalogs in online or microform format. Some catalogs are new while others have evolved from existing systems. For example, at the Ohio State University Libraries (OSUL) the automated circulation system has been expanded so that it now includes an online public catalog as well as online access to detailed serial holdings.

Before the online catalog can completely replace the card catalog, some problems need to be resolved. In the first place, the online catalog must provide at least as much information and as many access points as the card catalog. Cross references are necessary. Moreover, large academic libraries must decide whether or not such non-Roman scripts as Arabic, Hebrew, and Chinese should be transliterated. Essential, too, are improved search capabilities for national and local online systems. Terminals must be less costly and more efficient to operate and have less down time.

Cataloging Codes

With the publication of AACR2, the focus changed from manual to online access. It has been difficult to keep up with the numerous AACR2 rule interpretations and changes. The inevitability of AACR3 raises the following questions: When will AACR3 be published and implemented? Will there be major changes? Can these changes be carried out without serious upheaval to the system? Will practicing catalogers at the local level have input into future catalog codes?

Authority Files

There is a growing realization that authority files are of primary importance to an online catalog. While some libraries have changed from paper to online or microform authority files, others are establishing authority files for the first time. Links between online catalogs and online authority files enable changes in an online catalog to be made much more quickly and accurately than in a manual catalog. However, decisions concerning authorized forms of headings and links must be made by library personnel.

Especially helpful for technical services processing is online access to the LC name authority index which is available through the bibliographic utilities. Perhaps in the near future there will be access to LC subject, series, and uniform title authority files as well.

Serials

Some libraries are beginning to automate serial processes, such as online bibliographic records, online check-in, and online union lists. An example of online serial activity is the Ohio State University Libraries serial holdings file, which displays detailed holdings statements and permits access by volume and year. These serial holdings are kept up-to-date by online maintenance.

Future online capabilities for individual records should include serial publication patterns, date of next expected issue, check-in, and claiming. Among other areas of interest are online periodical indexes, electronic journals, batch and online searches for journal articles, document delivery, and copyright law problems.

IMPLICATIONS FOR USER SERVICES

Recent cooperative activities have pervaded all areas of the library world from international standardization to bibliographic utilities to individual libraries. Technical services support is essential for public service to patrons. If technical services do not use innovative methods to eliminate backlogs, patrons will not be able to locate needed information.

As patrons become excited about the use of the online catalog, they may prefer to use it to search for information about monographs and serials. Two factors which make the online catalog a viable tool are AACR2 and online authority files. Helpful to patrons are the use of natural language and user-oriented choice and form of entry as indicated by AACR2. Good authority control, including cross references, also assists the reader. User-friendly terminals will permit patrons to find needed information and materials with minimal or no assistance. Recent and projected changes in technical services have enabled library staff and patrons to find what they need, when they need it, in the least amount of time.

Authority Control—Beyond Global Switching of Headings

Kimi Hisatsune, AA, BA

ABSTRACT. This paper is an attempt to stimulate novel approaches to the development of automated authority control. Traditionally, authority control involved modifications to all affected headings when the authority file entries were changed to conform to changes in rules, policies, or new information. In a computer-based system, because of its multi-dimensional capabilities, headings established as valid at the time a work was described by a cataloger need not be updated when rules and policies are changed.

INTRODUCTION

Can authority control in a computer-based catalog be more than a system used to make global changes of headings in bibliographic records? Can it be designed to provide an effective relationship of records without the onerous necessity of changing headings in all of these records each time the catalog code or the local policy changes? If such a design were possible, headings valid at the time they were established would not require modification no matter how many editions of the AACR (Anglo-American Cataloguing Rules) were produced or how many local policy changes regarding the form or choice of headings were made. The record can remain intact as established.

As revealed in Larry Auld's review of authority control in the October/December 1982 issue of *Library Resources and Technical Services,*[1] most leaders in the field of library automation are still looking backward to the traditional, linear concepts of authority control instead of opening their minds to the power and the flexible, multi-dimensional capabilities of the computer. Alvin Toffler's vi-

Kimi Hisatsune, Associate Librarian, Department Chief, Research and Standards Department, E506 Pattee Library, The Pennsylvania State University, University Park, PA 16802.

sion of colliding wave fronts[2] can be seen reflected in the Second Wave thinkers among us who, tightly clinging to old methods appropriate to a former environment, are bewildered by the innovative thoughts being expressed by a few bold Third Wave thinkers who point the way to novel applications of automated power in our vastly changing technological atmosphere.[3]

AUTHORITY CONTROL BASED ON TRADITION

Discussions on authority control invariably return to the concepts expounded by Charles Cutter and to the "Paris Principles" as expressed by Seymour Lubetzky.[4] Helen Schmierer restates these principles concisely by pointing to the two major functions of the catalog: 1) the finding function; and 2) the gathering, or collocating, function.[5] She explains that the finding function does not necessarily require a controlled vocabulary for access, but the gathering function does indeed require a controlled vocabulary which becomes the basis for authority control. Varying forms of names must be worked into a controlled, syndetic structure that pulls them together to provide access, for instance, to all works of a single author.

Malinconico, an articulate spokesman for the tradition-inspired authority control systems, sees control in terms of keeping the headings in records consistent with headings established in the authority records. He describes an automated authority system in which the authority control numbers ensure that "only the latest forms appearing in the authority file are used for all headings in a bibliographic record whenever it is accessed" and "a change made to a single authority record will be automatically reflected throughout the data base regardless of the number of times it is used."[6] Buchinski, another prolific author and an expert on automated authority control systems, describes the National Library of Canada's system as operating in the same way—as so eloquently expounded by Malinconico—and explaines that [authority] "control mechanisms eliminate the possibility of using a heading which is a see-reference as a main or added entry."[7] This is precisely the concept that has traditionally been used in card catalogs with a separately maintained authority file to achieve the collocating function of the catalog.

Because the cards must be filed according to the headings appearing at the top of the cards, whenever a change was made to the forms of headings in the authority file, all corresponding headings in the public catalogs had to be changed so that the old and the new cards would file in proper alphabetical sequence. Obviously, automating this procedure would greatly accelerate the maintenance process. However, should the computer be used merely to develop a one to one transference from the manual to the automated processes as currently proposed by these leaders? Are we not ready to make a quantum leap into a Third Wave mode of operation?

COMPUTER-BASED CONTROL—NOVEL POSSIBILITIES

In 1979, at the Institute on Authority Control sponsored by the Library and Information Technology Association (LITA) in Atlantic City, NJ, two new approaches to bibliographic record control were presented. Neither one seemed to have made any real impact on the tradition-minded librarians, or on library systems development. All subsequent activities or discussions on authority control to date have continued to follow the traditional mode of approach.

At the Atlantic City meeting, Ritvars Bregzis, in his erudite presentation, attempted to explain the difference between an entry syndetic catalog and a record syndetic catalog. He stated that "Our current entry syndetic catalog requires the normalization of the name form itself before the combination of this name with a title can take place." This method, however, causes a "loss of the recorded authentic relationships between the author's name and title as they had been published, occasionally resulting in artificial forms of the author's name not originally associated with the given publication." On the other hand, in a record syndetic catalog, records with alternate entry forms can be integrated and "offers a basis for reconciliation of AACR1 and AACR2 records in the online catalog without changing the entry forms in these records."[8]

Clearly a record syndetic structure would be impossible in a card catalog, because the headings do need to be changed to allow a consistent alphabetical arrangement of entries for the same bibliographic identity. Only in a computer-based system can one hope to develop a record syndetic structure.

At the same Institute, where Bregzis expounded his revolutionary ideas, Michael Gorman stated his conviction "that, if a heading ever had any validity, it should be retained."[9] He suggested establishing an authority record for every bibliographic entity represented in a catalog and described how each would be linked to the related records. His basic concept of retaining the originally valid headings—if not the method he propounds—is highly desirable.[10] It warrants serious consideration for the very simple reason that his ultimate objective is a public-oriented catalog. In fact, Gorman echoed the following opinion expressed by Bregzis at the same Institute:

> . . .the automated method of record-to-record connection holds out the promise for some economy through a simpler management of bibliographic records, for the widening of scope of the catalog by paving the way for a transition from our current cataloger-oriented catalog to a more public oriented catalog. . . "[11]

The design of the user-oriented catalog should not require users to have a knowledge of the choice and form of entries. Furthermore, they should not be required to specify the *type* of access entry, because the name used as an "author" by the users may not have been chosen by a cataloger as the author of a work.

AUTHORITY CONTROL AT PENN STATE

Pennsylvania State University Libraries, working independently and even before ideas expressed by Bregzis and Gorman were known, began with this concern for the general users' lack of understanding of cataloging rules, and developed an information retrieval system that provides access directly from a file of authorized entries to the bibliographic records. Since the file is syndetic in nature, users can use any established form—AACR2, pre-AACR2 or their variants—without specifying the type of entry to search for a record. The authority file, therefore, is the entrance to the bibliographic database. Unlike, other systems, the Penn State system does *not* have two separate databases: one, a file of authorized records, and the other, a file of separately indexed bibliographic records with headings linked to the authorized records. The authorized entries and their variants, or former forms of those entries, are linked together to point to the *records* to which they were assigned—not to the corresponding *headings* in the records. This ensures that regardless of what headings exist in the related records, any valid entry for a specific bibliographic entity used as search terms would retrieve the relevant records.

The authority file, as the main access to the bibliographic record, is composed of what are called "Universal Entries"—which were determined by analysis to be the basic common elements of a set of established entries. For instance, it was decided that the basic elements necessary to identify a personal author (field 100) are the subfields $a (name), $b (number), $c (title) and $d (date). A forename entry (if a saint or a king, for instance) requires subfield $b or a $c, because there are so many duplicate names, such as Mary or John and their variant forms, in the database. For surnames, the database contains numerous cases of common names, including the obvious ones like "Smith, John," which require dates to distinguish one from the other. In these cases of personal names, there may not be sub-sets of entries which link to records that would need to be displayed in some prescribed order, and thus the collocation function is simplified.

These Universal Entries constitute the Grand Gateway to the bibliographic records, including the decision records which contain, in addition to the remainder of the subfield elements not included in the Universal Entry, such data as the source used for establishing an entry, related history notes, etc., normally found in the traditional authority records. The Universal Entry Control drives the total integrated system. It not only provides access to the entire spectrum of bibliographic and processing records in the database but the ability to make global changes to the contents of the access terms when it is desirable to correct a subfield element, but not the earlier choice or form of entry; for instance, when a death date needs to be added to older name entries so as to conform to a current one. Otherwise, the actual headings found in the catalog records need not be changed when rules or policies are modified so long as they were valid at the time they were assigned by the catalogers. Variants of an entry are linked so that all pertinent records for a single bibliographic entity can be gathered and displayed together.

The Penn State system, thus, permits the retention of chronologically proper relationships between the headings and the work described in the records. The type of global changes required in all other authority control systems is not necessary, because the syndetically structured Universal Entries point to the *records* which are pulled together for display and do not simply constitute the authorized forms of headings that *must* be reflected as main or added entries in all records to which the catalogers have assigned them. The system was not designed merely to support the cataloger's need to maintain standardized entry forms. It was designed to retain the internationally agreed upon standard bibliographic description (ISBD) of a work which never needs to be altered. The choice and form of access points to these records, on the other hand, can be changed as desired simply by maintaining the Universal Entry File. Entries can be added, subtracted or modified by authorized personnel to provide a user-friendly approach to the database which should, indeed, be the real objective of an information retrieval system.

PROSPECTS AND IMPLICATIONS

A system design which does not require global changes to valid headings found in records has tremendous implications for future developments in the area of network exchange of information. Since a standard description of a work need not be changed, foreign libraries may freely use their preferred forms of names or subject terms in their own languages as access points. As for libraries within our own country, any preferred variants of established forms in another library's catalog can be used without penalty. If, however, a national standard for entries is required for communication purposes, headings selected and authorized by Library of Congress would probably be the choice of most libraries. Similarly, for standard descriptions of works, LC records following full NLBR (National Level Bibliographic Record) and ISBN specifications would be the desired communication format. However, so long as the full format is readily available in some form, it would not be necessary for local libraries to store the records in full NLBR formats.

In the future, descriptive rules based on a new concept of authority control can disregard previous requirements for choosing the main heading from a possible set of entries to a record. Catalogers wishing to continue assigning main headings, however, can do so without incurring the high cost of having to modify them to conform to changing policies or cataloging codes. Printed lists of titles can be generated using the cataloger's choice of headings or any desired headings appropriate to a specific purpose; and a variety of on-line screen displays are possible in the multi-dimensional computer-based system. Not only can it permit myriad forms of searching techniques, it can provide ready access to a library's database from very remote parts of the world.

The rapid advance in technology is providing opportunities and prospects for libraries that were beyond our wildest dreams in the past, but our profession needs to break away from those traditional modes of thinking that inhibit new concepts from arising and prevent the most effective utilization of the enormous capabilities of the machine. A new approach to authority control is only the first step toward removing the shackles of past practices, so that a truly user-oriented bibliographic system will emerge to help people locate items or information from the vastly increasing mass of publications, and a host of other types of materials continually being added to the library's collection.

REFERENCES

1. Larry Auld. "Authority Control: an Eighty-year Review," *Library Resources & Technical Services* 26 (Oct./Dec. 1982): 319-30.

2. Alvin Toffler. *The Third Wave* (New York: Morrow, 1980).

3. Ritvars Bregzis. "Syndetic Structure of the Catalog," 32-34; Michael Gorman, "Authority Control in the Prospective Catalog." 177-178 in *Authority Control: The Key to Tomorow's Catalog,* ed. Mary W. Ghikas (Phoenix, Ariz.: Oryx Press, 1982).

4. S. Michael Malinconico. "The Library Catalog in a Computerized Environment," *Wilson Library Bulletin* 51 (Sept. 1976): 54-55; Helen F. Schmierer, "The Relationship of Authority Control to the Library Catalog," *Illinois Libraries,* 62 (Sept. 1980): 599-600; Bregzis, "Syndetic Structure," [19]-21.

5. Schmierer. "Relationship of Authority Control," 600.

6. S. Michael Malinconico. "Authority Control in a Bibliographic Network Environment," in *What's in a Name? Control of Catalogue Records through Automated Authority Files,* ed. Natsuko Y. Furuya (Toronto: 1978), 170.

7. Edwin J. Buchinski, William L. Newman, and Mary Joan Dunn. "The Automated Authority Subsystem at the National Library of Canada," *Journal of Library Automation,* 9 (Dec. 1976): 281.

8. Bregzis. "The Syndetic Structure." 25.

9. Gorman. "Authority Control in the Prospective Catalog," 172.

10. Michael Gorman. "Authority Files in a Developed Machine System (with particular reference to AACR II)" in *What's in a Name? Control of Catalogue Records through Automated Authority Files,* ed. Natsuko Y. Furuya (Toronto: 1978).

11. Bregzis. "The Syndetic Structure," 26.

How Will Automation Affect Cataloging Staff?

Gregor A. Preston

ABSTRACT. This article considers the affect of the continuing spread of automation on library technical services in general, and on cataloging staff in particular. Support is given to the view that staff will decline and that the distinction between technical staff and public staff will erode. A mix of technical-public service work is urged for all staff, in addition to a safe and healthy automated workplace. Future cataloging procedures in a fully automated setting are projected, and greater productivity with lower costs are predicted. The automated library should be a better library, but it is vital that change in job content and staffing patterns accompany the new technical environment.

The impact of the automation revolution on library technical services (TS), now in its second decade, continues to spread, both in regard to the number of libraries affected by it, and by the number of library operations which are being automated. In cataloging, serials, acquisitions, circulation, and interlibrary loan (the latter two operations are often called "public service," although I view them as basically providing technical support), more libraries are in the process of shifting towards fully automated systems.

The purpose of this article is to speculate on the implications of this switch from a largely manual, labor-intensive TS operation to a fully automated, technologically-driven one, specifically as it may affect cataloging staff in academic libraries. I would like to explore the potential effects on both professional *and* non-professional staff,

Gregor A. Preston is Head, Catalog Department, Shields Library, University of California, Davis, Davis, CA 95616.

since the latter tend to be ignored in discussions of the future of cataloging.

While this article is intended as an opinion piece, rather than a research paper, relevant citations in *Library Literature,* 1979-1981, were consulted prior to its preparation. Granting this restricted approach, I still was surprised to find no case studies of TS departments which were being completely automated. Perhaps it is premature to expect such studies, but I hope that those TS librarians in the forefront of automating their operations will share their experiences with the library world, since writing on this subject seems to be limited to theory.

CATALOG LIBRARIANS

There is widespread conviction that catalog librarians will dwindle significantly as automation spreads. R. P. Holley asks, "Do catalogers indeed have a future or should they be added to the endangered species list?"[1] He sees their number diminishing with the survivors being employed by the Library of Congress and large research libraries. In other academic libraries, he sees the cataloger restricted to a managing/planning role.[2] M. Gorman, a frequent commentator on the future of TS, believes that "the central processing operation will be staffed almost entirely by non-professional and paraprofessional staff. Professional involvement will be restricted to policy-making and a limited amount of supervision."[3] In today's libraries, bibliographic utilities have made it "impossible to justify maintaining the large staffs or professional catalogers which have been necessary in the past."[4]

While I am in general agreement with the accuracy of the above predictions, I do question whether the withering away of catalogers will be as total or take place as soon as some observers posit. F. W. Lancaster et al., blithely projected that "beginning in the early 1980s. . .technical services have been practically eliminated. . . [in] academic and many special libraries."[5] In their futuristic scenario, "descriptive cataloging. . .is now entirely centralized, through cooperation between the Library of Congress and the publishing industry."[6] Catalogers exist only at LC and library networks, since "catalog departments have disappeared in all but the larger academic and public libraries."[7] Such sweeping assertions are premature, to say the least.

Cataloging is definitely not a growth stock. Yet, have catalogers in academia really declined in recent years and, if so, has the decrease been significant? My impression is that the process has been gradual and is likely to remain so through the 1980s.

TECHNICAL SERVICES DEPARTMENTS

What will TS departments look like, assuming they still exist, a decade hence? Again, there is general consensus that TS will be centralized, eliminating the traditional TS departmental divisions, and that eventually the distinction between technical and public services will be abolished. In this view, there will be movement away from specialization towards the librarian as generalist, with librarian subject specialists performing cataloging, reference, collection development, etc.[8]

Gorman presents the most persuasive case for the erosion of the technical-public services dichotomy. "That distinction has undoubtedly wasted money and human resources because the specialization implied by two types of librarians within one library has not allowed either category to reach full efficiency." Examples include catalogers with subject expertise who have no public contact or collection development duties, reference librarians whose ignorance of cataloging results in poor public service, and the problems of implementing library-wide plans due to lack of understanding, lack of communication, and often the mistrust which exists between the two "factions."[10]

It seems clear that centralization of TS is being driven by automation and bibliographic utilities. Libraries in which the bibliographic record exists in online form from time of order through final cataloging will profit from the efficiency of having staff who can create and track the record through the entire process. However, the concept of the "compleat librarian," while encouraged to some extent by advances in automation, will occur only through conscious acceptance by library administrators of the utility of switching from a specialist staff to a generalist staff. Otherwise, it seems more likely that, at least in the near term, TS staff will simply decrease as a consequence of higher productivity and less original cataloging which result from automation and networks. It is, after all, much simpler to merely reduce staff than it is to revolutionize long-entrenched library divisions and job responsibilities.

NON-PROFESSIONAL STAFF

Assuming that a gradual decrease of professional catalogers does occur, what will happen to non-professional staff in the fully automated library? It seems safe to predict that their numbers will decrease significantly as well, due to a sizeable increase in productivity. Each remaining staffer will be supplied with a VDT since very few, if any, paper forms will survive. Within this automated setting, various workflows and procedures are possible, of course, depending on size, type, and philosophy of the library in question.

Hopefully, the TS workplace will be ergonomically sound. At present, there is growing awareness that attention and research must focus on the potentially harmful effects of VDT use. While the Food and Drug Administration recently offered the opinion that VDTs are safe, saying the "video screens do not produce levels of radiation *known* to be hazardous and the low-frequency waves they do produce have never been *shown* in clinical or epidemiological studies to have any biological effect"[11] (emphasis mine), such a statement is neither unqualified nor the last word. In addition to radiation fears, some VDT operators have complained of eyestrain, headaches, and dizziness. More studies, such as one being conducted by the National Institute for Occupational Safety and Health, are essential.[12]

The enthusiasts of automation proclaim that it will eliminate the drudgery of manual tasks, and it is true that with an online catalog, such work as catalog card filing will become obsolete. However, the automated environment may give rise to a new problem: staff do not enjoy spending a full working day interacting with a VDT. According to A. Lipow, at the University of California, Berkeley, "the introduction of technology and online cataloging is evoking a lot of complaints from catalogers who say, 'I'm now tied to the keyboard. I used to get up and walk around a lot and now I'm an extension of this terminal.'"[13] In my experience, cataloging staff efficiency and concentration begin to flag considerably after a one to two hour stint at the terminal, even among those staff who are enthusiastic about online cataloging. For this reason, retrospective conversion staff at the University of California, Davis, whose work consists largely of VDT use, are all half-time employees.

In the ideal automated library of the future, then, all TS non-professionals will spend a large percentage of time each day in public service work: at the circulation and information desks, reshelving material, and so on. Staff fulfillment and morale can be considerably improved by a combination of technical and public assignments. Thus, on both the professional and non-professional levels, the division between technical and public service will disappear. The result will be a more knowledgeable, satisfied, and productive work force.

AUTOMATED CATALOGING PROCEDURES

What might a typical cataloging operation consist of in the automated academic library of the not-so-distant future? Staff, during the portion of time they spend in TS, will be responsible for each bibliographic record from time of order through final cataloging and processing. When an order is generated, it will be sent to the vendor (online, of course) and at the same time it will be added to the library's online catalog, either in full bibliographic format, if it has been cataloged, or in a brief, "on-order" format, if it has not. When the physical item is received, the bibliographic record is updated and the process continues until the item is housed at its final destination. At all times, library users will be aware of the current status and location of all material via the online catalog.

The manager of cataloging activities will be a professional, responsible for three functional operations: original cataloging, cataloging with copy, and catalog maintenance. These operations will not be performed within distinct, separate units as they commonly are now, since all staff will work in other areas of TS operations and the library. Depending on library size, the cataloging manager may do all original cataloging or may supervise a few professionals who contribute original records in specific subject areas to the national database. The latter will consist of cataloged items from the Library of Congress and selected academic, public, and special libraries.

The cataloging with copy function will be the largest cataloging operation on an FTE basis and will process *all* material with copy— no distinction will be made between LC copy and other contributed copy. There will be a much higher degree of standardization and acceptance of shared cataloging than exists today. The overall skills needed in the cataloging with copy operation thus will be lower than is necessary now, since less local variation and critical judgment will be required. There will still probably be a need for an experienced non-professional to supervise this operation. Typically, when copy is found in the online system, the copy cataloger will check it for errors, and add location and local information. The record will then be transferred online from the national database to the local catalog. Some "local" catalogs may exist as statewide or regional cooperative catalogs and thus contain so many records that staff will search them first, and only if the record is not found will they search the national database. Ultimately, the "local" catalog and the national or international database may be one and the same.

At the same time the "add to local catalog" button is pushed, an attached printer will spew out a call number label which can be immediately affixed to the item, along with a date-due slip (unless this is done by Circulation at time of check-out), and the item can be whisked to the stacks. Thus, in addition to the filing unit, the material processing unit, as such, will be abandoned.

Authority work for items with copy is not done locally, since all cataloged records will have "built-in" authority control, including cross-references, created at the time of cataloging. Some maintenance work to catalog records will still be performed, i.e., transfers, withdrawals, and other internal housekeeping, as well as error-correction and the reporting of same to the national database. Special staff will not be required for this function.

All of the non-professional cataloging functions will experience a great leap in productivity as a result of full automation and the creation of a cooperative, national database. However, original cataloging will become a more time-consuming activity than ever before. The machine-readable record will contain even more "fixed fields," "tags," and "indicators" than at present; furthermore, great care will be taken by the professional cataloger to create a first-rate record with full authority control, since each original record will be cataloged only once for the whole nation.

SUMMARY

Like all prognostications, predictions about cataloging in a fully automated library may bear little resemblance to the ultimate reality. While the future cataloging scenario discussed here may seem reasonable now, it could prove embarrassing to read 10-20 years hence. Still, I would be unpleasantly surprised if, by the year 2000, TS operations are not fully integrated, TS staff has not been greatly reduced, there has not been a large-scale jump in TS productivity accompanied by a dramatic decline in TS costs, and if most of us are not cooperating through a national database.

In the meantime, we need to know how best to reach this future TS world. We need to share information on how the most automated of libraries are "doing it good" in TS. We are really only halfway, if that far, along the road to full automation, and to avoid detours and flat tires, we need surveys and studies, both practical and theoretical, to enable us to reach our "final" destination as painlessly as possible.

I am convinced that the automated library will be a better library for users and staff. It promises to eliminate the drudgery of narrow, repetitive, manual tasks and lead to the emergence of the complete library worker, professional and non-professional alike. It should allow us to channel precious resources into library materials and services and to provide users with a higher level of sophisticated benefits than ever before.

At the same time, I believe we must be aware of the need to change with the times, to reorganize staffing patterns, and to change job content in order to intelligently utilize full-scale automation. We need to investigate the problems which inevitably accompany new technology and to respond to these problems in timely, creative, humanistic ways. If libraries fail to adapt to our changing work environment, they run the risk of creating a tyranny of technology, by focusing on the machine and not on the interaction of human with machine. We need to develop automated equipment, work stations, and job mixtures which are safe, healthy, and satisfying. We must avoid simply overlaying automated systems on procedures and workflows designed for the typewriter-photocopier 3 × 5 library world. Those libraries which are able to successfully design new synergies in technical services will reap the many benefits which can be realized in the transition from labor-intensive to machine-dependent library operations.

REFERENCES

1. Holley, Robert P. "The Future of Catalogers and Cataloging," *Journal of Academic Librarianship*, May 1981, p. 90.

2. Ibid., p. 93.

3. Gorman, Michael. "Technical Services in an Automated Library," in *Proceedings of the Clinic on Library Applications of Data Processing, University of Illinois, 1979*, University of Illinois Graduate School of Library Science, 1980, p. 57.

4. Ibid., p. 51.

5. Lancaster, F. Wilfrid, Laura S. Drasgow, & Ellen B. Marks. "The Role of the Library in an Electronic Society," in *Proceedings of the Clinic on Library Applications of Data*

Processing, University of Illinois, 1979, University of Illinois Graduate School of Library Science, 1980, p. 182.

6. Ibid., p. 180.

7. Ibid.

8. Funk, Carla et al., eds. "Into the '80s: the Future of Technical Services," *Illinois Libraries,* September 1980, p. 584-598.

9. Gorman, "Technical Services," p. 54.

10. Ibid., p. 55.

11. "FDA Finds No Radiation Risk in Video Terminal Screens," *Library Journal,* October 15, 1981, p. 1976.

12. Ibid., p. 1977.

13. Freedman, Maurice J., & S. Michael Malinconico, ed. *Nature and Future of the Catalog: Proceedings of the ALA's Information Science and Automation Division's 1975 and 1977 Institutes on the Catalog,* Oryx Press, 1979, p. 140.

The Past, Present and Future of a Cataloguer

Ruth B. McBride

ABSTRACT. Libraries are coping with technology and tight budgets, present and future pressures, in a variety of ways. Through the use of automation, libraries are able to reorganize technical services departments more efficiently and reassign professional cataloguers to other positions in the library. Benefits of such reorganization are more productive use of resources, wider professional experience for cataloguers, and better service for patrons.

Considerable concern is being expressed by librarians about the future, concern precipitated largely by technological advances and tight budgets. Much has been written about how libraries, and technical services departments in particular, are adjusting to the present and planning for the future. Card catalogues are being closed, online systems are being developed, bibliographic utilities are being joined, cataloguing records are being standardized, networks are being formed, resources are being shared, and staff is being reassigned. Laudable efforts are being made to utilize technology and cut costs without jeopardizing book budgets and patron services. How does this affect the individual librarian, the cataloguer? It may be necessary for many individual librarians to accept these changes and prepare for new assignments, using their knowledge and expertise in different ways. The Technical Services Department at the University of Illinois at Urbana-Champaign is continually analyzing its operation and making changes. My assignment at UIUC has changed from original serials cataloguing, to supervising a "copy" cataloguing operation, to circulation services.

Ruth B. McBride is Central Circulation Librarian, and Assistant Professor of Library Administration at the University of Illinois at Urbana-Champaign, 1408 West Gregory Drive, Urbana, IL 61801.

When I was first exposed to automation in the Library, in the form of OCLC and LCS (Library Computer System), the circulation system of the University of Illinois, my limited vision went only so far as eliminating the need to consult routinely a myriad of printed bibliographies to catalogue materials, including NUC (National Union Catalog), NST (New Serial Titles), the local shelf list, etc. I saw myself with a larger desk, an LCS terminal on one side and an OCLC terminal on the other, busily churning out cataloguing copy without taking a step. In my naivete, I did not realize that when such terminals did appear in the Library, most of the LCS terminals would be clustered in the Circulation Area for public use, and the OCLC terminals would be tightly scheduled and supervised from 7:00 a.m. to 9:00 p.m. for use by the support staff. I was correct, however, about their lessening my need to consult the many printed bibliographies. The end result, initially, was that my cataloguing copy was no longer sitting in boxes waiting to be typed, but was sitting in boxes (in the form of OCLC catalogue cards) waiting to be filed. The basic information, however, was being added weekly, via an OCLC-LCS interface, to the LCS database for immediate access by patrons and staff.

As a serials cataloguer at UIUC, my primary responsibility was to provide cataloguing records for serials and analytics, the "component parts" of monographic series. We had always used LC catalogue cards and proof slips to catalogue those titles for which such information was available. In fact, there was little or no original cataloguing of analytics, and we depended almost entirely on "standing orders" for LC cards for those series which we and the Library of Congress analyzed. With the availability of OCLC, we immediately cancelled our standing orders for cards, and began producing cards for both serials and analytics on OCLC. We were using automation, as most others were, to do the same things we had always done, only faster, and presumably more economically. Beginning in 1978, certain administrative decisions were made which did not change what we were doing as much as how we were doing them. The Serials Department, which was responsible for the acquisition, cataloging, and processing of the estimated 3,000 new serial titles received each year, as well as the maintenance of the 90,000 title serial collection, was decentralized and integrated according to function with other units in the Library. Largely because of my responsibility for analytics, which was primarily a copy cataloguing process, my new assignment was in the Automated Records Department, comprised mostly of support staff and devoted to the rapid cataloguing of monographs and serials with OCLC copy. Later decisions involved "closing" the card catalogue in late 1979, and developing an "on-line" catalogue containing full bibliographic records with WLN (Washington Library Network) software.

I suspect that what is the recent "past" in technical services at UIUC is still the future for some institutions, though reading the literature and talking to colleagues indicate that many are on the same "fast track." When discussing the immediate future of technical services and, hence, cataloguers, there are certain recurrent themes in the literature. Holley notes that "reduced budgets, less emphasis on perfection, greater use of assistants, standardization and automation have had a profound effect upon the professional responsibilities of catalogers."[1] Kennedy identifies four phenomena to which she attributes the changes which are occurring: networking, MARC format, AACR2, and economics.[2] Gorman points out the need to take advantage of cataloguers' skills by eliminating the technical versus public services concept.[3] Automation makes such reorganization possible; economics makes it necessary. Atkinson suggests that automation, by eliminating paper files, will enable decentralization of departments and reorganization of personnel into smaller, more human, service oriented groups of "holistic" librarians.[4] (A "holistic" librarian is defined as one who is responsible for a whole range of services in a special area, from acquisitions to cataloguing to reference, and everything in between.) According to Atkinson, such changes will be more cost-effective, an aspect not to be overlooked by administrators.

It is generally agreed that there are certain identifiable forces at work which are creating changes in the cataloguer's professional life daily. However, it may be Lancaster who provides a glimpse of the world of the future for cataloguers and all other librarians as well.[5] "In general, computers first change how things are done and later changes what is done," says Lancaster. For the most part, we are in the era of the former. Such things as computer conferences, electronic journals, machine indexing and translating, etc., have yet to affect most of us. We are likely to continue to deal with printed paper materials and patrons for some time, though possibly providing information in new forms as part of our expanding services. Nevertheless, Lancaster agrees that there is a future for librarianship, involving an increase in information services and decentralization of professional activities.

Simply adjusting to the technology and the changes it is creating may take all of our energy and resourcefulness. It is important to assess technological advances continually and apply them to the basic goal of improving services to our patrons. Automation enables us to become a part of large networks to share cataloguing information. AACR2 and MARC have helped to standardize that information, enabling us to assign more cataloguing tasks to support staff. On-line catalogues enable us to decentralize our organization to utilize the skills of professionals more fully. Machine-readable authority and subject files with on-line conversion capabilities will further relieve us of labor-intensive tasks. At least until the future as described by Lancaster is reached, there will be a need for cataloguers. In fact, the Library of Congress may be considering the expansion of the CONSER project, to give responsibility to institutions other than LC for certain areas of original cataloguing and authority control. Still, the duties of cataloguers are changing and will continue to change. Routines which were efficient last year may no longer be efficient, and organizational charts may become out-of-date quickly.

The Serials/Analytics Unit of the Automated Records Department at UIUC catalogues all of the analytical titles received by UIUC and approximately 80% of the new serial titles. Support staff have been trained to search, revise, classify, and process most of the serial titles using OCLC, and, at the same time have eliminated a sizeable backlog which developed prior to establishing the unit.[6] In fact, professional tasks in the unit now involve little more than training, advising and some problem-solving. This is a clear-cut example of the use of technology to assign tasks to support staff and free professional librarians for other responsibilities. The result of that organization, plus a reorganization which included the Central Circulation Department in General/Technical Services, was a new assignment for me (half-time for a while, then full time in early 1982), that of Central Circulation Librarian. I am the only professional librarian in a department which maintains a Central Bookstacks Collection of over three million items, circulating them via LCS to faculty, students and staff, and patrons throughout the state of Illinois. A nonprofessional Circulation Manager is responsible for the daily operation of the Department, staffing, training, scheduling, etc. A number of former serials cataloguers have been similarly reassigned broader responsibilities in the Library, ranging from Head of Original Cataloguing Department to Head of the Library and Information Science Library, and from Chief Classifier in the Rapid Cataloguing Unit to

Sociology and Social Work Subject Specialist in the Education and Social Sciences Library.

Plans are underway at UIUC for other cataloguers, who are now doing original cataloguing, to move into departmental libraries, sharing their cataloguing responsibilities with other subject specialists, and working more directly with patrons to provide "readers services." In my opinion, such reorganization enables cataloguers to use their considerable expertise to serve users, to develop their own base of knowledge and activity, and become involved in new areas of librarianship, an opportunity heretofore rarely offered to cataloguing staff. (After all, catalogers are frequently viewed as the "deprived" members of the profession, per Holley, Gorman, Atkinson, and others.) It is difficult for me to peer very far into the future but, whatever it may bring, I am convinced that it will not only improve our professional lives, but, at the same time, increase our ability to fulfill our ultimate goal, that of serving our patrons.

REFERENCES

1. Holley, Robert P. "The Future of Catalogers and Cataloging." *The Journal of Academic Librarianship* 7 (2) (May 1981): p. 90-93.

2. Kennedy, Gail. "Technical Processing Librarians in the 1980s: Current Trends and Future Forecasts." *University of Kentucky Library Occasional Papers* 1 (1) (August 1980): p. 1-11.

3. Gorman, Michael. "Doing Away With Technical Services Departments." *American Libraries* 10 (7) (July/August 1979): p. 435-37.

4. Atkinson, Hugh. "The Impact of Closing the Catalog on Library Organization." In *Closing the Catalog: Proceedings of the 1978 and 1979 Library and Information Technology Association Institutes,* D. Kaye Gapen, Bonnie Juergens, eds. (Phoenix, AZ: Oryx Press, 1980): p. 123-33.

5. Lancaster, F. W. *Libraries and Librarians in an Age of Electronics.* (Arlington, VA: Information Resources Press, 1982)

6. McBride, Ruth B. "Copy Cataloguing of Serials According to AACR2 using OCLC: The University of Illinois Experience." In *The Management of Serials Automation,* Peter Gellatly, ed. (New York, NY: The Haworth Press, 1982): p. 135-49.

Serials Cataloging
and the MARC Format:
Time for Reassessment

David E. Griffin

ABSTRACT. Although few would question the benefits brought to bibliographic control by the MARC format, it may be time to reexamine the format in light of today's cataloging needs and make adjustments where necessary. Fields that at one time seemed promising in the serials format may have since lost their rationale and contribute little today. The question of subject headings for serials is raised and the tendency toward briefer cataloging records noted; the "r" level record of the Washington Library Network is described as one example of brief cataloging records.

In the cataloging of serials (if not quite yet in other aspects of serials control), the Luddites have been routed. Few today would doubt the advantages of machine-readable bibliographic records, for serials or for just about any other type of material a library might collect; and the question "Can we automate our cataloging?" has been answered with a resounding "yes" over the past dozen years or so. But with answers sometimes come only more difficult questions, such as "What are the limits of automation?" or, "In our eagerness to escape the limitations and inefficiencies of our old ways, what new inefficiencies have we inadvertently introduced?" It is this type of question—hardly the dramatic fare of the first heroic days of automation—that we will likely be grappling with during the next few years.

The MARC format for serials itself is a good example of the mixed blessings of the application of the computer to cataloging. Leaving aside the benefits of on-line search and retrieval, the advances made

David E. Griffin is Serials Librarian and WLN Serials Reviewer at the Washington State Library, Olympia, WA 98504.

143

in even traditional technical services functions since the appearance of the MARC format would hardly be questioned today. Efficient production of catalog cards, union lists, or directories from a central data base is alone enough to justify machine-readable cataloging—and this is just one of the more obvious benefits.

But there is evidence to suggest that the continued development of the MARC serials format is out of touch with the needs of most libraries, whether large or small. New fields have been developed with feverish regularity and little demonstrated need, while the rationale for some existing fields remains untapped in every data base in the nation. There is little evidence that any library really wants or needs more information about any serial than what is contained in the body of the description plus certain categories of notes (linking entries, variant titles, issuing body and numbering peculiarity notes, perhaps a few others) plus name and subject entries. In other words, the basic information that is pulled from the MARC record by agencies' programs to appear on catalog cards or perhaps as entries in microfiche catalogs. Or another way of saying it, and one often neglected: the information of interest to public service librarians and the patrons they serve.

The basic cataloging information is just the tip of the iceberg in most MARC serial records, a fact that is not necessarily bad in itself. Many fields exist to provide some benefit apart from creating the record, such as on-line access, possible search combinations, or enhancement of a related product, such as a serials directory. But some of these fields have remained undeveloped by every agency in the nation. At the time of their introduction the fields may have had a promising rationale, but over the years they have been made redundant or obsolete by other developments—or have just become too expensive to develop—or (can it be said?) no one is really interested. For whatever reason, development of some of the fields has always been low priority everywhere and is probably becoming lower. The time has come to reexamine the MARC serials format, not only in terms of its logical structure, organization, and consistency but even from the point-of-view of the continued usefulness of particular fields;[1] if it can be shown conclusively that a field is no longer serving a useful purpose, LC and CONSER should no longer include it routinely in the serial records they create and authenticate. (The rest of us would gladly fall in line.) The creation, inputting, and eventual updating of data that no one really wants costs us all.

In what ways, for example, do libraries use the abbreviated title field, and what developments for the field does anyone have in mind? What is the future of the venerable key title, now that AACR2 has introduced the concept of uniform titles to distinguish non-unique titles? What plans are underway to develop the "main series" linking entry, or is it just a redundant field everywhere, adding that much more time and expense to the creation of a cataloging record? Is there really any need for the vast majority of variant access titles routinely input in the format, or should the 212 field be reexamined? Which of the fixed fields are of use, and which remain meaningless? Does anyone attempt to accurately encode the "title page" and "index" fixed fields, or could we all agree to set the fields to the default value, "unknown"? And even some of the standardized fields, developed with the advent of AACR2 and applicable to all formats, seem to some a case of overkill: the 007 field, for example (physical description fixed field for microforms), and even the 039 (level of bibliographic control and coding detail). There may be good answers to questions such as these, but the questions still need to be asked.

Much of the unwieldiness of MARC serial records need not be blamed on the MARC format, at least directly, but on existing cataloging requirements and how they are interpreted by the Library of Congress and others. How useful, for example, is it to include the price of a serial on a cataloging record? Isn't it already out-of-date by the time the record is created and unlikely to be updated, even when the record is changed for other purposes? Would an acquisitions department ever use a price on the cataloging record for ordering purposes? And if some notes might be useful, would it automatically follow that more are even better? Suppose a journal is indexed by twelve different indexing or abstracting services. Should all twelve be included in the record in separate "indexed by" notes? If that sounds unwieldy, which ones should be included, if any, and what likelihood is there of such information being updated?[2] (The same questions can be asked for "distinctive title" notes and corresponding added entries.) Rather than routinely including "Available on microfilm from University Microfilms" on a periodical record, perhaps it would be more economical to indicate only when a periodical is *not* available from UMI, as a colleague once joked. And aren't the 242 and 776 fields (translation of title by cataloging agency and additional physical forms available) really pretty silly?

Another aspect of the problem can be seen on the MARC tapes themselves. As new fields are added and appear routinely in records, the records become longer and longer, and the quality of inputting steadily deteriorates. Mis-taggings, typographical errors, and even the garbling of the text of entire fields have steadily increased in the MARC serials records to the point of being more than a minor problem.[3] The steadily-lengthening records are, of course, usually unencumbered by the addition of any subject headings in the majority of serial records distributed on the MARC tapes. There are many reasons for this, from the philosophical to the political to the logistical, and it is true that LC's own level 5 records are eventually replaced by full-level records in most cases. But the fact remains that it is a tenet of faith among some who pronounce on "national" serials cataloging policy that subject access for periodicals (some would say for all serials) is of no great benefit. One wonders how rigorously the tenet has been tested in the front-lines of libraries—the reference desks—and how many public service librarians would share it.

The question of subject headings aside, there is much evidence to suggest that there is already a reaction away from cataloging overkill, even at the highest levels. The "minimal level cataloging records" developed at the Library of Congress (level 7 for serials, which include records created by NSDP but not authenticated by LC and LC serial discards), and separately under discussion by the Government Documents Round Table (GODORT) of the American Library Association are one reaction to the lengthy cataloging that has developed along with the MARC format.[4] Another is the increasing willingness of many libraries to *use* brief records and the gradual acceptance of the notion that brief is not necessarily synonymous with "bad" (nor "lengthy" with "good"). The "r" level record allowed in the Washington Library Network, for example, in which participants can input a brief cataloging record for older material from a shelf list or other source document rather than from the item itself or LC copy has gradually won acceptance even by some participants that have traditionally been viewed as "purist" in their cataloging standards. The "r" level record adequately (if briefly) identifies the item; all headings must be in current form; records for monographs must include subject headings, and although subjects are not required in the serial "r" level record, they are also usually included. A signal of their acceptance is that several libraries that do not input "r" level records themselves are willing to attach their holdings to them. The brief records can also be easily upgraded to full-level through the WLN "Change" protocols by any participant who has the item in hand or LC copy and desires a more complete record.

There are, perhaps, different levels of cataloging appropriate to different formats and materials, and the alternatives being developed by various agencies around the country are encouraging. The MARC format remains one of the great achievements of information sciences, but the time has come to assess the subtle effect its continued development has had on serials cataloging, and to reexamine what we really need in the MARC record. To be mesmerized by the computer to input fields because a space exists for them on the screen is the worst sort of folly. What's wrong with cataloging that describes a serial economically (in more than one sense), is transcribed accurately, and provides all useful access points?

REFERENCES

1. For an overview of recent developments in reassessing the MARC format, see James E. Rush, "The MARC Formats: Their Use, Standardization and Evolution," *Journal of Library Automation* 13, 3 (Sept. 1980):197-199; and, D. Kaye Gapen, "MARC Format Simplification," *Journal of Library Automation* 14, 4 (Dec. 1981):286-292.

2. Another perspective on the limitations of the "indexed by" note is found in Joe Morehead, "A Status Report on the Monthly Catalog and Serials Supplement," *The Serials Librarian* 4, no. 2 (Winter 1979):137-139.

3. I have observed this gradual deterioration during the 3 1/2 years that I have reviewed the MARC serials tapes for the Washington Library Network. (Each incoming record that matches against an existing record by record identifier or title match must be reviewed and decisions made on replacement, rejection, or retention.)

4. The LC level 7 records would contain the main entry, full title, key title, imprint, and some fixed fields. The focus of the GODORT proposal is on elimination of personal name authority work. "Memorandum to Bibliographic Standards Committee from WLN Staff," Washington Library Network, June 3, 1982.

'Til the End of *Time*

Martin Gordon, MLS

ABSTRACT. Stabilized or decreased staff levels, alternative means of article receipt, and automated record processing will be the three major distinguishing features of college periodicals units at the close of this century. These changes will be more evolutionary, less abrupt than they are apt to be in larger university serials sections in which the new "high tech" methods will be tested against today's time proven ones. Both technical and user services staff will welcome these adjustments as will the public they serve.

At this very moment, the United States and other developed nations are undergoing a metamorphosis from industrial to information societies. Even as I pen these words, power, social and economic wellbeing and political stability are being transferred to those who are able to access, absorb, and utilize increasing amounts of information. Every time we read about economic affairs, this point is brought home again and again.[1] All signs indicate that this evolutionary watershed will be as significant to our culture as was the industrial revolution in the 19th century. Since the roots of this transformation have already taken hold and cannot be reversed, although the rapidity of their growth is somewhat in question, what then will be their fruit for those of us who expect to drive to work, hang up our coats, and wrestle with title changes and shrinking budgets in the year 2000 much as we do today?

Unless the world puts itself through a cessation procedure by dint of its nuclear prowess, the college periodicals unit will function in a manner very similar to today. There will be, however, three major areas of change even at the college level which will be the result of embryonic efforts being made in the early 1980s.

First, the college periodicals librarian will find along with his colleagues, that there are fewer student assistants and fewer, or at best

Martin Gordon is the Periodicals Librarian at Franklin and Marshall College, Lancaster, PA 17604.

149

the same number of support staff as there are today. Declining birth rates and economic retrenching within higher education as a whole, presently obvious to all, will continue to be felt in the 1990s. One cannot escape drawing this conclusion from the evidence at hand.[2] In fact, the position of periodicals librarian is apt to be markedly different from that defined today, with most occupants holding second masters degrees (whether these degrees will be of assistance in capturing and retaining the "knack" needed in successful serialism is food for an article in itself!)[3] The periodicals librarian will be called upon for an increasingly diverse ranges of duties that will be challenging and rewarding in themselves but that will remove that position to a certain degree from the operations of the department. To be successful in dealing with this situation, the periodicals librarian must closely examine existing policy and procedures with an eye towards:

a. breaking multi-task procedures down into their component parts, eliminating the "niceties but unnecessaries";
b. defining these parts in terms permitting ready understanding by a wide range of staff so that the responsibility for their fulfillment can be easily transferred as need be;
c. creating wherever possible self-service user access areas as opposed to more costly staff-assisted ones;
d. resisting (when appropriate) additional departmental responsibilities by clearly defining department goals and having staff job descriptions available for review as well as explanations in terms of hours per week of student assistant support; and
e. cultivating the good graces of the financial aid office so that student assistants the department receives are more apt to be of use.

The successful handling of decreased staff levels and duty diversification will yield increased staff satisfaction with the daily routine, and should therefore increase productivity per hour of labor available for departmental activities.

The second area of marked change which will occur has already been heralded (in paper copy) almost to the extent of the amount of material it aims to replace. The electronic receipt (at first through adaptations of present day inter-library loan units) of periodical articles is in place today in the prototype mode. The ADONIS (Article Delivery Online Information System) program developed by four

European publishers as a reaction to, and an effort to control photo-copy of their titles, is currently operational with the British Lending Library as the "electronic" recipient.[4] Other single publisher ven-tures in digitalized storage and electronic transmission of text are being launched on this side of the Atlantic. For example, the prestig-ious *Harvard Business Review* will be offered to its readership in this stark, cathode-ray medium.[5]

At the college level, this alternative form of receipt will be wel-comed as a blessing because it will relieve the pressure felt by many of us in having to continually fence with faculty over the "failed university" concept of collection development wherein *all* worth-while titles are considered for subscription without the important criteria of audience being addressed. Research titles justifiably re-quired by faculty in their research and for use by senior majors in highly developed collegiate programs may, at this near future point in time, be utilized through the direct purchase of "separates" via the library's inter-library loan system or (eventually) by retrieving on coin operated CRT/printer modules short abstracts of articles. If their budget permits, full text will also be able to be printed with per screen charges, providing publishers not only with the lost cost of subscriptions but also lost advertising revenue (if any) as well.

Will, then, the periodicals staff become the lamplighters of the in-formation industry?

No, they will not. Despite oracles in our midst today who already have tape measure in hand to measure the paper journal for its cof-fin,[6] I cannot help but draw an analogy to the *beneficial* relationship established in the college library environment between online biblio-graphic search tools such as DIALOG and BRS, and paper product services from the Wilson group on up. Just as not all searches justify electronic communication with a distant data base, so too will we see that the 65,000+ periodicals currently indexed in *Ulrich's Inter-national Periodical Directory* supplemented, but not replaced, by online text retrieval. In fact, the very economies which electronic and other technological advances have made so far will be felt equal-ly in paper production as well as in alternative products.[7]

We must also consider when assessing the impact of online text retrieval on the college's journal collection, a latent function dear to many of us "old guard" librarians as well as the clientele we serve. As one of my professors once admonished me at the outset of my first acquisitions course, the McLuhan adage "the medium is the mes-sage" holds true in reader selection of information as much as it does in leisure entertainment decisions. It is inconceivable to me that liberal arts institutions such as mine that do so much to advance the union of all three major disciplines in a total learning experience, will espouse the retention of humanistic knowledge by solely relying on electronic communication. The various aspects, as I have indicated above, have been discussed in detail elsewhere; and since it is not my intent to decry the advent of this new tool we will all utilize to some degree, let me close this second part of my discussion by remarking that as I review my own subscription list of approximately 1700 titles I see 200 or so titles that would be expendable in paper form, given access capability online. For each of those I could name another which I desperately would like to be able to afford at this time (and which perhaps I will when the former group are not housed in their entirety in the library). I therefore see the periodicals librarian as well as public services staff rejoicing because dollars freed by paper subscription cancellation of relatively short article dependent, mixed frequency titles such as *Life Sciences* or *Journal of Organometallic Chemistry* will be available in part to fulfill long desired goals, such as increased levels of subscription to basic, indexed titles that are apt to be less expensive for the college library to house in their entirety in paper format (or microform) than to retrieve repeatedly online. The resulting mix of paper/microform collections and increased access to titles not subscribed to in the traditional sense will further strengthen the college library as the information center of the college community.

Finally, I can see the time coming well before the end of this century during which there will be widespread reliance on automated record and retrieval systems. Then the microcomputer will be as affordable for libraries as are the electric typewriters of today. The entire college library technical services division will not only be able to realistically budget for these systems, but also purchase software to accomplish the myriad functions of in-process order and standing order files, visible card file units and bindery files, to name but just a few. The periodicals unit will be unable to defend (as it can today)[8] the retention of manual systems. The automated systems will be able to be searched immediately from user service desks so that the up-to-the-minute holdings, claims and bindery information can be employed in solving user request difficulties without public service staff having to take the infamous "walk to the Kardex." These systems will be far more flexible and "user friendly" than the larger, vendor maintained data bases predominantly available for use today. This will simply be a facet of increased memory capability brought on by the prevalence of microchip storage, and also because the software used by these systems will be written by front line serialists themselves. The college periodicals unit will benefit from the success (and failures) of systems first installed in larger university serials departments. Adopted systems will have nearly all the flexibility of today's manual systems, or they will not be used!

Thus we can see a future that is not dissimilar in purpose or scope from that of the college periodicals unit today. This future will, however, be a less frustrating, and more productive one for users and public services staff as they deal with serials, because access to collection holdings will be less mysterious and far more efficient. The collection itself will be more basic and interdisciplinary than today's college subscription lists in which the discerning eye can readily pick out a core of "opening day" titles directly supporting student research surrounded by a group of scholarly, faculty oriented titles, which can only be of penumbral value to the primary intent of the college journal collection. The staff that is responsible for the administration and maintenance of the collection will be less task specific, and as a result more aware of and empathetic toward user services needs.

REFERENCES

1. "Jobs, Putting America Back to Work," *Newsweek* 100:81 (Oct. 18, 1982).

2. James J. Unland. "An Investment Banker's Advice to Colleges," *The Chronicle of Higher Education* 25:64 (Nov. 3, 1982).

3. Betsy McIlvaine. "Librarians and Advanced Degrees," *College and Research Libraries* 42:47-48 (Feb. 1981).

4. "The ADONIS Document Delivery System: Scientific and Technical Publishers to Control Photocopy?" *Serials Review* 8:55 (Summer 1982).

5. "Electronic Publishing:Steps Forward—and Back," *Publishers' Weekly* 221:27 (June 4, 1982).

6. Thomas Hickey. "The Journal in the Year 2000," *Wilson Library Bulletin* 56:256-60 (Dec. 1981).

7. The Future of the Scientific and Technical Journal System. In P. Hills (ed.) *The Future of the Printed Word.* Westport, Conn. : Greenwood Press, 1980.

8. Huibert Paul, "Automation of Serials Check-In: Like Growing Bananas in Greenland? Part II," *The Serials Librarian* 6:39-63 (Summer 1982).

The Fallacy of the Plugged-In Periodical

Bill Katz

ABSTRACT. The online phenomenon is widely touted, but even the most up-to-date information retrieval system lacks some of the advantages the print-on-paper journal provides. These are listed, and a plea is made for the use of common sense in the adopting of computer librarianship.

According to an old Saint Bernard I know, there are many treacherous accidents on the mountain of prophesy. Even the most agile soothsayer slips on some inept guess and is lost on the slope that diminished Marshall McLuhan's performance. As it is easier to separate the morning's batch of periodicals than it is to evaluate descriptions of future events, I'd like to point out not the future, but the small pebble that may trip the princes of projection, and send them rolling down the prophesy mountain.

It is the prophesy about how electronics will replace my dog-eared issue of the *Atomic Data and Nuclear Tables.* A computer terminal, television set, overhead projector, microform reader or videodisk is going to adopt the *Reader's Digest* and yesterday's run of the *Anglican Theological Review.* Instead of pacing my flat as I await delivery of the *Home Economics Research Journal* from the tardy postman, I shall charge to an electrical outlet, plug in the machine, and after an earnest study of start-up procedures shall with wide, rapt eyes gaze upon the open pages of *The Atlantic Community Quarterly.* No matter that the little green letters look like a procession of drunks in a heady wedding ceremony, at least the *Quarterly* is on time and available.

The excuse for this performance of speed over the less than punctual postal employee is that I am a busy, not to mention fascinating, man who requires instant access to the latest in everything from the

Dr. W. A. Katz, School of Library and Information Science, State University of New York at Albany, 113 Draper Hall, 135 Western Avenue, Albany, NY 12222.

columns of the *Banking Law Journal* to the best male bottled scents. I'm a scientist, you see; or, a visibly disturbed social scientist or businessperson; or, possibly a blatant library scientist. My urgent and serious demand for information is matched only by my addiction to passionate engagements at conferences where I deliver papers and offer up proceedings which, in turn, are part of the terrestrial material of more journal articles and obsessively compulsive citations by equally busy cohorts.

How much speed, though, really is necessary in rushing periodical content to reader? Actually, not much. The reason is inherent in the way we all gather information. Articles are major sources of background data, yet it is romantic dramatization or error to suppose any scientist won a Nobel prize or the factory prize turkey shoot by stumbling across Eureka in a journal. So what's the real rush?

Moderately dependent magazine people find, too, that a silicon chip in itself does not produce useful information. No matter in what form, a magazine does require a writer, an editor, even someone to make the data available via a controlled or free text search. All of this takes time, and while one may eliminate the printer and postman in favor of the computer, the actual amount of real time saved is negligible.

Americans and too many western Europeans seem fascinated with the 100 yard intellectual dash, failing to understand the necessity for sleep, patience, and watching television, or reading for something more than the giggles of mining useful information. Taking advantage of this natural failing, undissembling salespersons suggest the computer will save time. Time for what? No one, other than philosophers of leisure—and they are about—address this aspect of the closely watched periodical in a machine.

Fortunately, few of us seem impressed with the computer tied journal or, for that matter, newspaper. Media experts are puzzled, for instance, by the reluctance of Americans to take the local newspapers via the television set. The teletext and videotex experiments of the past decade are given much publicity, but have been limited to "fewer than 1500 households."[1]

So study follows users, and hardware salesmen (an apt term, that) follow up the slopes of the mountain of prophesy, unaware they will soon slip and fall over a buried learning machine or a rusting Edsel. The slightly self-deprecating charm of the latter day pitchmen is his studied earnestness as he lures otherwise visibly sane periodical people to disaster.

More bluntly, the show biz of consigning periodicals to a post-Gutenberg TV screen or clattering printer is a dramatization of folly. It is a play written by con men whose idea of tragedy is the loss of the *Playboy* centerfold and who consider a winning performance the attenuated voice of jargon. Few, if any, read. Few, if any, really appreciate the difference between chipping away at an article in the bathroom or in bed and doing it before a disorderly microform reader.

This is not to vote Luddite, for the dragging up of index and abstract information at a terminal beats rushing about the library looking for the index normally used to support the dying fern. It is to vote for common sense and to recognize five distinctive needs found only in printed journals: (1) They are easy to read, an odd notion, perhaps. (2) They are inexpensive, at least in comparison with the cost of even a rapid printout or straining one's eyes at a reader. (3) They require only attention to themselves, not to a mass of machinery which is often more pleased to backfire than to function. (4) They are neatly packaged and sometimes pleasing to study at bus stops or between television commercials. (5) Finally, they are charming tactile experiences, or as one executive recently put it: "You can begin anywhere in a periodical, front or back, fold over corners for reference, tear out pages, underline passages, blow away blow-in cards, cut out coupons, save the whole magazine. . .for future use."[2]

For the quality of life, for the sake of sanity, for—at a more mundane level—the sake of the periodicals budget, let's spend more time charting the foothills of reality than the mountain peaks of prophesy. The gap between the yet to be realized periodical online[3] and the 65,000 or so periodicals pumping out joy and turmoil in print form, is wide enough to insure that we have plenty of time to think about the appalling possibilities of the plugged-in periodical.

REFERENCES

1. "New Video Systems. . ." *The New York Times,* October 14, 1982, p. D4.

2. Kobak, James. "New Consumer Magazines." *Folio,* September, 1982, p. 97. This issue of *Folio* is devoted to the next 10 years in periodicals and offers an excellent overview, at least of the consumer-commercial type magazine.

3. I am aware, of course, that BRS now offers the full text of the *Harvard Business Review* online, and there are several scientific and technical magazines available only in microform, as well as full text legal services, newspapers and business services. Still, if I am correct, I think this trend is unlikely to develop for other than highly esoteric journals. Here one might argue that if they are online they probably should be in this form only and, as such, are they really periodicals?

Union Lists of Serials' Futures:
Buy? Sell? or Keep What You've Got?

Marjorie E. Bloss, MLS

ABSTRACT. There are a number of internal and external variables that influence the compilation of a union list of serials: ascertaining if there is a need for a union list initially, and if there is, establishing administrative and fiscal responsibilities, determining cataloging rules and the standards for holdings statements and input standards that are to be followed, and selecting production methods. In this article, many of these components are examined with regard to the anticipated technological changes of the next 17 years.

Crystal balls always seem to cloud over at the crucial moment. Ouija Boards can be dismissed as pressure-sensitive. Tarot cards need an intermediary for interpretations, and oracles have lost favor in recent years. Predicting the future of any event or any one subject is best done after the fact. This hasn't stopped us from trying, however. Of course, when prophecies are viewed from the future vantage point of which they spoke, more often than not they are quickly dismissed with a knowing smile and an air of superiority. Just as it was impossible to anticipate the impact of the silicon chip on library technology 17 years ago, something equally revolutionary will undoubtedly nullify today's pronouncements for the year 2000.

A union list of serials is a political animal with a multi-faceted personality. Fundamental to its existence is the cooperation of its participants. This cooperation takes many forms, from administrative and financial commitments to inter-library loan agreements, to agreements to adhere to the rules that govern the representation of bibliographic and holdings data and input standards for those data, to production of the list, and finally to on-going maintenance. Be-

Marjorie E. Bloss, is the Union List of Serials Project Director for the Rochester (New York) Regional Research Library Council, 339 East Avenue, Room 300, Rochester, NY 14604. She chairs the American Library Association's Committee on Union Lists of Serials, and is a member of the IFLA Working Group on Union Catalogues of Serials.

159

cause a union list of serials is such a conglomeration of variables, it is close to impossible to discuss only one aspect of the union list process without including the others. As a result, a number of factors that touch on union list compilation will be considered in this article.

In order to attempt to paint the background for any potential union list of serials picture in the year 2000, a few demographic and fiscal assumptions need to be made. Basic to this entire library scenario is an inference that there will be no major growth in population in the United States. If current trends persist, fewer dollars will be available for the support of libraries. This in turn will force libraries of all types to make organizational and structural adjustments. Even so, libraries will be expected to provide higher levels of service at greater speed and at less cost. There is one even more fundamental assumption in all of this, and that is the assumption that we haven't annihilated ourselves with the latest weaponry. If we have, it is a foregone conclusion that a union list of serials won't be uppermost in anyone's thoughts. For the purpose of this article, however, an optimistic view will prevail.

How will libraries in general and union lists of serials in particular, fare in the year 2000? Will a union list of serials have any place in the library world at that time or will it become extinct due to technological developments and perhaps even due to changes in philosophical and economic outlooks? If they do continue to have a place in the libraries of the future, how will union lists of serials function? How will they be accessed and the titles included in them be located? In this article, two primary aspects of the future of union lists will be examined: the first, determining whether or not there will be a need for union lists of serials at all in the year 2000; the second, if union lists do exist seventeen years from now, how they will compare to the lists of today. Before even attempting to guess at what the future holds in store, it is necessary to view the union list of serials within its environment of 1983.

CENTRALIZED OR DECENTRALIZED BANKS OF SERIALS

Today, there seem to be two differing points of view concerning the necessity for union lists of serials. Prevalent in the United States is the belief that because no one library subscribes to, or owns retrospective runs of all serials, a union list of serials is a basic tool for resource sharing. In the creation of such a list, a group of (usually) independent libraries either regionally based or with common subject interests agrees to cooperate by lending or photocopying materials requested by the other libraries. The purpose of a union list of serials in this case is to combine titles and holdings data of each participating library. Against this backdrop, a union list of serials is instrumental to a member library's knowledge of what is or is not retained for interlending purposes, as well as potentially being used for coordinated collection development or for determining who retains the last subscription of a title in a region.

The second point of view attempts to diminish the dependence of one library on a number of others for materials not in its collection and therefore, the need for a union list of serials to access them. This is done by means of a central collection of serials that has a wide coverage of titles. The British Library Lending Division (BLLD) is organized in just such a fashion. Established in 1961 as the National Lending Library for Science and Technology, it became the Lending Division of the British Library in 1973. Some 150,000 titles, both current and ceased, are retained at the BLLD in one central collection for national interlibrary loan in the United Kingdom.[1] Maurice B. Line, in his article "The National Supply of Serials—Centralization versus Decentralization"[2] contends that a central collection such as that at the BLLD can offer better service for several reasons. First of all, there is a much greater commitment by the centralized agency to maintain its collection because this is its *raison d'être*. Second, supplying the appropriate materials to the requestor will occur in a shorter time period because this is the primary activity of the staff. As a result, user satisfaction will be at a higher level with a centralized interlending system. Finally, there will be economic advantages for the other libraries in the country because it won't be necessary for them to subscribe to as many serials, or to retain as many backfiles. Potentially, this could free up their budgets for the purchase of additional materials or services.

IS THERE A CENTRALIZED PERIODICALS COLLECTION IN OUR FUTURE?

Could it be that the United States has missed the boat these many years by not creating a national periodicals agency? Or, as suggested by Line in the previously cited article, do the chromosomes of librarians contain an innate genetic impulse that causes them to compile multitudes of meaningless union lists of serials?[3] If there are such strong arguments for the establishment of a national serials collection, why in this country are we balking at what appears to be common sense?

The concept of a national periodicals center has not gone unnoticed in the United States. Considerable discussion and controversy have raged over even the possibility of the establishment of such a center. Yet another feasibility study was initiated in 1980 during Jimmy Carter's presidency[4] in time to be snuffed out altogether with a change in administration. The fact that the Reagan presidency has given no support whatsoever to any federal funding for libraries points out a basic impediment to the creation of a national periodicals center. Its existence would balance precariously on the political philosophy of the party in power. This is clearly no way to run a program.

Even if there were some mild entertainment of the idea of creating a national periodicals center in the United States, the initial financial outlay for its establishment would deter even the staunchest supporter. The collection itself would have to be housed somewhere, for one thing. For another, an outlay of many millions of dollars would be needed for current subscriptions and serial backfiles. And of course, staffing such an operation would be a costly must. While the arguments for a centralized collection of serials for the purpose of interlibrary loan can be persuasive, at this time the creation of such a system is simply not feasible financially in this country. Unless economic conditions change, unless there is a realignment of national values, chances are slim that this situation is going to change in the future.

If this weren't enough, there is more than just a financial deterrent to creating a national periodicals center. Fundamental to any interlending program is the delivery of the requested material to the appropriate place with the utmost expediency. (This is due in large part to the "I needed it yesterday" syndrome of the majority of users.) At this time, there is no system of document delivery that fills the bill. This can't totally be attributed to the fact that the United States is a large country. While modern air service does speed up delivery from airport to airport, the multiple handlings involved negate any gains. Before a centralized periodicals collection is established, there will have to be a streamlining of the process that is to be used for document delivery. While future technological innovations like facsimile transmission and the electronic journal may someday partially solve this problem, older serials retained in the more conventional forms of hard copy and microform will still have to be delivered by traditional methods.

The creation of a centralized collection of serials for the purposes of national interlending appears to be remote in this country. A more realistic possibility might be a national union list of serials. In the vast majority of cases, union lists in the United States have been compiled regionally. *New Serial Titles (NST)* is the publication that comes closest to the concept of a national union list of serials. Recently, however, the production of *NST* has been generated from the CONSER database. While as full a cataloging record as resides in the CONSER database is included in *NST*, the only indication of holdings is a code for the reporting library. The lack of enumeration and chronology data has resulted in *NST*'s scope changing from primarily that of a union list of serials to that of a cataloging tool. No change in this policy is anticipated.

Does this matter? Which would be the larger problem: To have to wade through thousands of holdings statements for the same title, or to have to consult several regional union lists in order to locate the needed volume? In the 21st century as is the case today, attempts to supply interlibrary loan requests will come first from libraries close to home. Regional union lists and not national ones, therefore, will remain the major hub of union list activities in the year 2000. In turn, resource sharing will continue to be handled mostly on a state-wide or regional basis rather than on a national one. If there is even a slight possibility in the future of a centralized serials collection, its foundation will be built on these already established boundaries rather than on untested national ones.

Now that the extenuating circumstances have been examined, it seems reasonable to conclude that in the United States at any rate, regional union lists of serials will fulfill as important a need in the year 2000 as they do today. Their compilation and the way in which they and the materials in them are accessed will now be considered.

COMPILING A UNION LIST OF SERIALS IN THE YEAR 2000

Today's national bibliographic databases will continue to grow and their capabilities will strengthen by the year 2000. The framework for these activities is mostly in place right now; it's a matter of refining and fine-tuning some of the components. Creating a large database of serials from which a union list can be derived is an expensive venture. This will be as true in the 21st century as it is today. Most libraries and regional networks will find themselves using pre-existing databases for their union listing activities. Also, as is the case today, the standardization of a number of procedures will be at the core of any union list originating from a file created by many individuals. The fundamentals of compiling a union list in the 21st century will be identical to those of today, namely, the CONSER Project, cataloging rules, standards for holdings statements and data entry, and the methods used in accessing union lists.

The CONSER file will continue to be the main source of bibliographic records used by compilers of union lists of serials. When this project began in 1973, it was viewed as a cooperative venture initiated by librarians who wished to build an authoritative machine-readable database of serials records. Adherence to current cataloging practices and the establishment of data input procedures have been agreed upon by the twenty project participants. These conventions, including *Anglo-American Cataloguing Rules,* 2nd edition (*AACR2*) and the MARC-S format, standardize content, choice and form of entry of the bibliographic record itself plus the way in which the data are entered into a computer. As time goes on, the procedures that govern content and data input of cataloging records will be improved and simplified but in no way diminished or eliminated. Any conjecture as to what edition of *AACR* we'll be using in the year 2000 will be left for others to determine. Whatever the number the code, we will most emphatically be following standardized cataloging for years to come. So that a modicum of sanity can prevail, the glaring differences between ISBD(S) and the *Guidelines for ISDS* and the Library of Congress' guidelines for the creation of uniform titles for serials will be resolved. A single set of rules is quite sufficient. Three different methods for the representation of a title are unmanageable for the cataloger and impossible for the user.

When the CONSER Project began, it was funded and administered by the Council on Library Resources. Although the original plans called for the project to be taken over by the Library of Congress, this never occurred, and it remained a part of the OCLC database. The housing of the CONSER file in the OCLC online database has made a political issue out of a project where none was intended. Because some of the original CONSER participants are now members of RLG, their contributions to the CON-

SER file are limited. The technological developments for the linking of databases is not the issue here. The stumbling blocks are those of a political and managerial nature on the part of OCLC. Hopefully, there will be a break in the stalemate long before the year 2000 so that the building of the CONSER file can again be fully realized. Now that OCLC is breaking into the European market, serial projects similar to that of CONSER will easily take hold on a more international scale. When projects based on mutual cooperation occur, contributed cataloging should be encouraged and shared with as few restrictions as possible.

COMPONENTS OF A UNION LIST OF SERIALS

Traditionally, the bibliographic description of titles contained in a union list of serials has been extremely brief. No standards or criteria have ever really been established for defining the appropriate data elements for a union list record. If the database used for a union list contains the full MARC-S bibliographic record, decisions concerning the content of the union list record become less and less important. If the database forms the basis of an integrated, online system that uses the same bibliographic record for a variety of functions (i.e., acquisitions, cataloging, serials control, union listing, etc.), each one will require a certain degree of data manipulation contingent upon the function, as each activity has specific and unique requirements. With improvements in hardware and software in the next seventeen years, individualized display formats customized for distinct functions will be accommodated with ease. An online display for a union list of serials' record could look very different from the one used, say, for checking in the same serial. A similar flexibility in the manipulation of bibliographic data will exist for the offline products that are generated from the same machine-readable file. Of course by the year 2000, accessing union lists of serials will, for the most part, be done strictly online. By that time, there is an excellent chance that even the smallest libraries will own a microcomputer that can access the major bibliographic utilities. Paper or COM union list products will be used only in the most remote locations or for public distribution.

Equally important as the bibliographic data in a union list of serials are the holdings statements. A considerable amount of work has been accomplished in recent years on the standardization of serial holdings statements. As of this writing, compilers of union lists in the United States have one established standard and two potential ones with which to concern themselves. The American National Standard Institute's *Standard for Serial Holdings Statements at the Summary Level* (ANSI Z39.42-1980) and the draft *Standard for Serial Holdings Statements at the Detailed Level* describe the order of holdings as they should be displayed, and the punctuation recorded therein. The *MARC Format for Holdings Statements,* on the other hand, forms a framework for the machine transmission of holdings data.

Such great strides have been made in the area of holdings statements recently that it seems a foregone conclusion that the *MARC Format for Holdings Statements* will be approved within the next few years. By the year 2000, however, rather than our having separate standards for the display of detailed and summary holdings, only one standard will exist. This standard will combine components of the Summary Standard and the draft Detailed Standard. In the same way that the participants of a union list will be able to select the desired bibliographic data elements, they will also be able to decide which elements of the holdings standard are relevant to their needs.

THE IMPACT OF TELEFACSIMILE AND THE ELECTRONIC JOURNAL

The previous paragraphs examined the content of the bibliographic and holdings data used for a union list of serials. Will there be changes in the ways serials are transmitted and published in the year 2000 that will affect union list compilation? Although *AACR2*'s definition of a serial includes much more than periodicals, this category is often what first comes to mind when the term is used. Periodicals form the cornerstone of any union list of serials and for a union list of periodicals, they comprise the entire building. What will be the result if the format of this cornerstone begins to change dramatically due to telefacsimile and electronic publishing?

The facsimile transmission of journal articles for interlibrary loan purposes had its origins in the 1960s. Since then, a number of libraries have experimented with this method of document delivery. Facsimile is used primarily for the copying and transmitting of articles and documents already in a collection. To date, however, user need and demand remain uncertain.[5] This, in turn, makes library administrators hesitant in appropriating large sums for the necessary equipment. In addition to reluctance in the purchase of equipment, other difficulties have had a part to play in the slow acceptance of this process. For one, bound journal articles do not copy especially well with facsimile equipment. For another, the equipment manufactured by one company is seldom compatible with that manufactured by another. These problems are not insurmountable, and experimentation to perfect telefacsimile continues. By the turn of the century, telefacsimile will be in general use for the resource sharing of older serials both in hardcopy and in microform.

With regard to future trends in the publication of journals, Thomas B. Hickey, in his presentation at the first annual Serials Conference, described the journal in the year 2000. What he foresees is not a facsimile transmission document, but one where the actual text of an article is compactly and digitally stored as ASCII characters.[6] Articles "published" in this manner will be made available over a particular network, either to be read online or, if the user desires, to be printed out for use at a later date. Hickey anticipates that scientific societies will take the lead in building online databases of their journals and making them available through networks. The larger commercial publishers will follow shortly thereafter. Hickey goes on to say:

> Individual publishers will in some cases retain complete control over their databases—maintaining them online themselves. Others will form consortia or lease their databases to central services.[7]

In 1983, computer software is, for the most part, only at the developmental stages for accommodating full text databases. Even so, it seems reasonable to anticipate that these capabilities will be a reality in seventeen years. Whether or not a large number of journal articles will in fact be written and stored online at that time is a point of conjecture. Due to financial constraints, it appears that an actual conversion to electronic publishing will lag behind the technological developments in this area. In 1980, a Delphi study on the future of electronic publishing polled librarians, publishers, and technologists as to the extent of that method of publishing in the year 2000. With regard to the electronic publication of journals in particular, it was felt that fewer than 25% of the titles in the fields of science and technology, social sciences and humanities would be converted at that time.[8] While the study points to the feasibility of a paperless journal eventually, realistically it appears that even in the year 2000 we will have a long way to go before this becomes commonplace.

Even so, we can begin to speculate and anticipate developing trends for union lists of serials based on the advances made in electronic publishing. While the implications are large for the compilers of, and participants in a union list of serials, they will be especially major for the user of the list. Some mechanism within the union list itself will be needed to indicate that a particular library has access to, or holds a title (or more likely, part of a title) only in machine form. Indication of this will probably be handled in a similar fashion to today's designations of microformats in a union list of serials. There will be a further ramification for the user, however. In the same way that today's libraries subscribe to certain databases for literature searches, so will they subscribe to a commercial database for the online journals of the 21st century. It is difficult to believe that accessing these databases will be a free service to the user. Again, parallels can be drawn to today's literature searches where costs are passed on to the user.

The cost factors simply of viewing or obtaining an electronically stored article may have an undermining effect on the journal database itself. On the other hand, an article published in such a manner certainly eliminates the guesswork of interpreting a call number and determining the location of the title in a library, only to learn that the desired article is at the bindery or has been razorbladed out of the volume altogether. Whether one or the other of these trends will predominate remains to be seen. It is very likely, however, that electronic publishing will produce some new patterns in the traditional concept of "net borrowers" and "net lenders" of serials. If cost is a factor, users may turn to the smaller libraries that don't subscribe to the journal online but retain it in their libraries in hard copy or in microform. The implications of electronic publishing will also be felt within the structure of regional networks themselves. In the same way that some United States networks serve as brokers for the services of the national bibliographic utilities and databases for literature searches, similar procedures will be extended to include data bases of journals. Once this is the case, there is a real possibility that a literature search could be initiated, a union list of serials searched, and the actual article requested and printed out all at one sitting and at the same terminal. Granted, it is doubtful that this vision will be realized by the year 2000, but it should be a reality sometime in the 21st century.

As more journals are initially stored and retrieved online, fewer subscriptions will be placed for the hardcopy or microform versions. Both individual libraries and any centralized collections of serials will discover that their remaining physical volumes (hard copy and microforms) are becoming more retrospective in nature, with the popular titles the major exceptions. Perhaps this factor more than any other could point the way to centralized periodical centers in the United States. These centers will consist only of retrospective holdings that are infrequently used rather than containing collections of retrospective and current titles. If they are to be created at all, these centers will be built on a statewide or regional basis as was previously described. Union lists of serials will continue to hold the key to any group of regional serials holdings, be it centralized or decentralized, retrospective, current or inclusive, hardcopy or electronic.

SO DO WE BUY, SELL, OR KEEP WHAT WE'VE GOT?

As was established earlier in this article, union lists of serials will be a thing of the future as they have been a thing of the past. Without a doubt, buy! Do so, however, with the knowledge of the existing and relevant standards, and who is or is not following them. This should also be the basis for "selling" or "keeping what you've got." As library systems become more and more integrated both internally and externally, international and national standards will continue to grow in importance. Adherence to these standards will form the bridge not only to a number of library functions including union listing, but to the 21st century as well.

REFERENCES

1. Line, Maurice B. "The National Supply of Serials—Centralization versus Decentralization," *Serials Review* 8, no. 1 (Spring 1982):63-65.

2. Ibid.

3. Ibid., p. 65.

4. Huff, William H. "Serials" in *The ALA Yearbook 1981* (Chicago: American Library Association, 1981), p. 269.

5. McKean, Joan Maier. "Facsimile and Libraries," in *Telecommunications and Libraries* (White Plains, N.Y.: Knowledge Industry Publications, 1981), p. 118.

6. Hickey, Thomas B. "The Journal in the Year 2000," in *Serials Management in an Automated Age,"* (Westport, CT: Meckler Publishing, 1982), pp. 3-10.

7. Ibid., p. 7.

8. Lancaster, F. W. "The Future of the Library in the Age of Telecommunications," in *Telecommunications and Libraries* (White Plains, N.Y.: Knowledge Industry Publications, 1981), p. 141.

Union Cataloging—The Future

Ruth C. Carter MA, MS

ABSTRACT. Most cataloging today takes place in a union cataloging environment in that it is intended for one or more catalogs which receive cataloging from two or more sources. Union cataloging has implications for cataloging at an individual institution in at least two ways. First, original cataloging contributed to a union data base must meet the standards of that union catalog. Secondly, use of cataloging done at another institution is one important return from participation in a union catalog. This statement reviews features of union catalogs and cataloging. It projects likely developments in the next three to five years and suggests ways in which union cataloging can be expected to evolve.

Opinions on the future of union cataloging show a great dichotomy. The divergence in viewpoints exists at least in part because union cataloging implies agreed upon standards, and adherence to elaborate standards can be costly. One school of thought holds that there must be a return to consideration of the needs of the individual institution first and foremost. On the opposite side are those who believe that because libraries will continue to be interdependent, there will continue to be cooperative programs including both resource sharing and collection development. Therefore, in order to make known resources and facilitate their use by others for possible loan or for consideration of them in cooperative collection development decisions, they must be described and the description communicated and exchanged.

Normally the description of resources held takes place through cataloging, and in many cases the exchange of cataloging takes place through the contribution of records to a shared or union catalog. Consequently, cataloging must take into consideration not just the catalog of the individual institution but that of one or more shared

Ruth C. Carter is Head, Catalog Department, G-49 Hillman Library, University of Pittsburgh Libraries, Pittsburgh, PA 15260.

union catalogs. Most cataloging done in libraries today is union cataloging, i.e., it is intended to be shared in whole or in part with other institutions, and as a result the cataloger must take into account what is necessary to make the catalog record accessible in the union catalog. Ordinarily this will involve some adherence by all participants in a union catalog to a particular set of standards. Union cataloging often also implies utilization of cataloging done at other institutions.

At the present time there are some questions about the cost effectiveness and benefits of union cataloging. This may lead to some rethinking of what is best for an individual institution. Nevertheless, it seems clear that in the immediately forseeable future of 3-5 years, there will be more not less union cataloging. The union environment considered by an individual cataloger or the planners of the entire processing and cataloging work flow may exist on many different levels and in many different facets. In order to project the future, it is helpful to review what these may be.

The sharing of cataloging can take place in at least two directions. On the one hand, it may involve the use of a record created at another institution. Alternatively, it implies contribution of original cataloging to a union catalog. In both instances the union catalog will carry an indication of which participating institutions hold which titles.

The scope of any particular union catalog may vary considerably. A union catalog may cover a single format or type of material or it may contain cataloging for many types of materials in several different formats. A union catalog may be limited to one large institution with many separate cataloging units or it may be groups of independent libraries cooperating to form a union catalog within a local area, a state or a region, or it may have a national base. It always implies that cataloging will be received from two or more sources and incorporated into one unified catalog.

A union catalog may contain cataloging from libraries of similar type on a local, regional or national basis—for example, law or medical, or library science libraries. A library may participate in more than one union catalog. The major bibliographic utilities represent union catalogs on a very large scale. Cataloging participants in these utilities (OCLC, RLIN, WLN, and UTLAS) are all engaged in union cataloging. Participants in these utilities use existing cataloging already in the union data base and contribute their original cataloging to it.

Union catalogs exist in different forms. The bibliographic utilities are examples of online union catalogs. Union lists of serials are, in effect, union catalogs for one type of library material. Many union lists of serials have been, or are in book format. Union catalogs may also be in COM fiche or film or, in many cases, they are in the form of a card catalog. Although new union catalogs are unlikely to be card catalogs, there are many existing union card catalogs, some of which are still actively being maintained and expanded. Many difficulties in union cataloging occur when the new cataloging must meet current standards for online union cataloging and yet somehow integrate intelligibly into an existing card catalog that was constructed over a period of time, and in accordance with various sets of rules and standards. For example, a university library may participate in a bibliographic utility and also maintain an active union card catalog. In many universities there is not a single cataloging unit. Therefore, the card catalog is a union catalog if it receives cards from all the various cataloging units within the university.

There are problems inherent in union cataloging. Because the cataloging is distributed, there is a need for standards for the format and content of the data entered. This is necessary in order that all data relevant to a particular search can be retrieved if the user desires a comprehensive search. In other words, there must be some rules for doing union cataloging. At the same time, it must be recognized that union catalogs often are built over a long period of time with concomitant changes in rules and policies and that total consistency is unlikely, if not impossible.

To maximize the possibility of retrieval of items relevant to a particular search, a union catalog normally provides some method for authority control. As machine readable authority files grow and system designers become increasingly sophisticated in their application, more of the burden of collocation or bringing like items together can be placed on the machine. In the past, however, most of the responsibility was placed on the cataloger to do the necessary authority work and create records meeting the necessary standards. This is still a necessity in the case of card catalogs.

In theorizing on the future of union cataloging, the most obvious point is that libraries in general, large and small, widely-based and special, are moving to machine-readable, mostly online systems. Nonetheless, the shorter term of three to five years, can still be seen as a transition period for the majority of libraries. It seems probable that there will be continued emphasis on cataloging each item once to full national standards. Thus, whichever library handles an item first must be very conscientious about providing full cataloging in accordance with current national standards. That library and the other libraries that will be subsequent users of the record will be able to tailor the record to their own needs either at the time of cataloging or through specifications used to introduce a new catalog record into a local machine readable system. Fortunately, the computer provides many opportunities for adapting standard records to local needs and requirements. In general, the next few years should see the trend continue in which an individual cataloger may catalog fewer items. However, those items originally cataloged will be more complex because they will need to meet not only local needs but those of a union cataloging environment.

A corollary to the demands of original cataloging is the clear trend that professional catalogers will be limited more and more to original cataloging or at least to the cataloging of items that require in addition to everything else the assignment of classification numbers. Many institutions are shifting to the use of well-trained paraprofessionals to handle almost all member or shared-copy cataloging. In the past most non-professionals were restricted to working with Library of Congress cataloging copy or a very controlled list of acceptable member or shared-copy cataloging records. Now, however, there is definite recognition that in order to achieve necessary production levels and cost effectiveness in terms of where an individual's effort is applied, balance is required between ultimate perfection and practical application. It is increasingly understood that the most effective use of the time and effort of skilled professional catalogers is in cataloging items another highly trained, and presumably conscientious cataloger, has not already cataloged at another institution. Original catalogers, whether they are cataloging serials, monographs or media, can be expected to be involved increasingly in the maintenance of online catalogs, whether union or at an individual institution. When those online catalogs receive data from multiple cataloging sources, the complexities increase dramatically. In the short term of the next few years, but not indefinitely, there also must be allowances made to fit what is projected for long-term future machine-readable data bases into current manual catalogs. This too increases the complexities of cataloging in a union cataloging environment.

A few generalities on the future of union cataloging seem possible. These include: 1) the complications that arise from trying to fit current cataloging into both present and future machine-readable catalogs and existing card catalogs, will decrease as more card catalogs are closed, frozen or completely replaced; 2) because of the flexibility of retrieving data from a machine-readable, probably online catalog, there will be less concern regarding the order of data elements in a catalog record and less concern about extra data elements—in general, more will be better than less; 3) there will continue to be a greater willingness to accept cataloging done at another institution—both because of increased confidence in the standards employed at individual cataloging agencies, and because original cataloging is so complex that in order to have the time to meet the standards for original work, it is simply not cost effective or productive to have original catalogers redoing what some other professional cataloger has already done; 4) large scale union cataloging such as through the major bibliographic utilities can be expected to increase in the near future of 3-5 years. Looking beyond that period to the end of the twentieth century, the potential clearly exists for increased reliance on regional, state, or local union catalogs and cataloging rather than emphasis on nationwide data bases; 5) there will continue to be a need in a union catalog environment to monitor input to a union catalog through mechanisms such as edit programs at the time data is input; and 6) provision of authority control mechanisms to permit full retrieval, will remain essential.

In terms of authority control it is probable that machine-based authority systems will eventually be so sophisticated that the problem of satisfying user searches regardless of the particular terms or form of names used, will be a non-issue. In the future any individual cataloger in any individual union cataloging situation may not be burdened with elaborate authority control routines. However, it is certain that somewhere there will have to be individuals instructing the computers in terms of necessary and appropriate links whether they are for forms of names or subjects. In general, access points will be a primary focus of concern in making either copy or original cataloging machine-readable for either union or individual catalogs.

In conclusion, it seems that a high percentage of cataloging will continue to be union cataloging on one level or another. It also seems reasonably certain that more existing cataloging copy will be processed by highly trained paraprofessionals. At the same time the original cataloger, because of external or union catalog demands, will become even more skilled. Possibly the most skilled of all will be the persons responsible for catalog maintenance now often called catalog management. To manage online union catalogs they must know not only the intricacies of cataloging but have a firm grasp on both the capabilities and limitations of the machine. Even more importantly, they will have the skill to relate the two in order that the users of the catalog of the future, union or otherwise, can benefit from our cataloging, most of which will to one extent or another continue to be union cataloging.

Technical Processing of U.S. Government Printing Office Publications: Issues and Prospects

Charles R. McClure
Coy L. Harmon

ABSTRACT. A review of library literature indicates a continuing concern for the lack of access to government publications. Among the many reasons suggested for the limited use of documents is the limited technical processing applied to documents in various libraries. This article examines the historical development of the technical processing of documents and briefly reviews the potential application of computer-assisted techniques in processing and accessing government publications. Following a discussion of the Guelph Document System and CODOC as working models of documents control systems, the paper considers additional automation strategies and examines such issues as the need to catalog or otherwise process documents, the training of documents librarians for online processing, the increasing use of microforms in documents publications, and the role of equipment and materials vendors in the processing of documents. The article concludes by discussing prospects for future technical processing of documents.

U.S. government publications comprise a basic source of information in areas such as technology, public policy, national security and defense, health sciences, and energy. They provide, for example, statistical information and the results of research. Currently, some 1,365 libraries are depositories for U.S. government publications distributed by the Government Printing Office (GPO) and re-

Charles R. McClure is affiliated with the School of Library Science, University of Oklahoma, and Coy L. Harmon is with the University of Oklahoma Libraries, University of Oklahoma, Norman, OK 73019.

177

ceive these publications on the condition that they be made available for public use. These depositories mainly comprise academic libraries (66%) with the remaining percentage among large public, state, and federal libraries. Further, a larger number of additional libraries purchase government publications on a regular basis, either directly from the GPO or through a jobber. Yet, despite the high quality of many government publications presently issued, the effectiveness of their dissemination through the depository library program, and an emerging broad awareness in the library community about their importance as a means to meet the information needs of clientele, government publications housed in libraries are frequently unaccessible and underutilized.

Such a pronouncement may at first seem harsh, but a review of major research studies shows a need to increase access and use of government publications (Hernon, 1979; McClure, 1981; McClure & Hernon, 1983). Although a number of reasons might explain the limited exploitation of U.S. government publications in many libraries today, the area of technical processing has a considerable impact on the access and usage by diverse client groups. Further, technical processing procedures will have significant influence on the overall utility of government publications collections in the future.

For purposes of clarification, technical processing will be defined as those activities conducted by a library to make a specific information resource ready for public and staff use. Typically, these activities include acquisition, cataloging and classification, and labeling/marking. Indeed, technical processing is a *support* activity, i.e., a process that assists in making information resources bibliographically identifiable, logically organized, physically available and ultimately, accessible by the patron. In short, technical services is not an end unto itself—especially in terms of accessing and using government publications. For a thorough discussion of the technical processes, including networks and automated systems, the reader may consult *Introduction to Technical Services for Library Technicians* (Bloomberg & Evans, 1981), and *Introduction to Library Technical Services* (Bernhardt, 1979).

This paper examines technical processing of GPO publications largely in the context of libraries with depository collections and, thus, in many instances, separate collections. For non-depository libraries, technical processing of government publication is (1) typically accomplished in the same manner in which other materials are processed, (2) minimized by use of check-in files only, not cataloged, or placed in a vertical file-type organizational structure, or (3) unnecessary since the library does not actively collect and make available government publications. By and large, primary responsibility for making U.S. government publications accessible and available for use falls on the designated depository libraries.

After a brief review of the historical development of technical processing vis-à-vis government publications, a number of selected issues having significant impact on effective technical processing of government publications will be discussed. The paper concludes with a discussion of prospects and recommendations to improve technical processing. But, underlying these discussions is the belief that greater attention must be given to developing effective technical processing procedures for government documents and integrating such processing with overall library technical services.

AN HISTORICAL PERSPECTIVE

With the exception of a few local technical programs developed by innovative libraries, usually to satisfy a need peculiar to a given library, most technical services operations, through the early decades of this century, centered on the basic functions of acquiring and cataloging monographs. Some libraries fully processed serials, but few attempted original cataloging of government documents. Working with major bibliographic tools such as the *National Union Catalog, New Serial Titles,* and the *Monthly Catalog,* processing departments acquired and cataloged materials in the same manner for several years. Typically, the products of the traditional technical processes were the card catalog, serials list, and a few other printed holdings lists developed out of local needs. The dependency on printed bibliographic sources and manual processing techniques forced a 3 " x 5 " mentality upon libraries and left technical services librarians reluctant to assume new processes, especially the formidable process of bringing bibliographic control to a growing body of government publications.

In the 1950s and 1960s, a combination of evolving technology and highly favorable library budgets resulted in a proliferation of in-house automated programs, the most ambitious of which were automated circulation systems. As libraries rushed to develop their own customized systems, the standardization and quality control that had been hallmarks of libraries for so long often suffered due to the lack of knowledge and experience with automation. That many of these early automation attempts of the '50s and '60s did not live up to expectations is well known, but a few survived to serve as models for later attempts at automation by libraries which had reevaluated their automation needs and priorities. Among the higher priorities for subsequent automation attempts was the need to have programmers and analysts who had a thorough understanding of libraries and their many functions and processes. Such knowledge would enable the analysts to design systems to automate existing functions rather than attempt to change functions to conform to preconceived notions of library automation.

One of the more positive effects of earlier automation attempts was the application of microforms in libraries not only as a bibliographic tool but as the format for bibliographic products. Expanded holdings, old and worn out materials, and specialized holdings lists (union catalogs and serials lists), were all candidates for fiche or film (Saffady, 1978). The use of microforms was not only a departure from the traditional 3 x 5 cards and other printed formats, but also made it possible for libraries to broadly distribute their holdings at a reasonable cost to other libraries. However, one of the major drawbacks to microformatted holdings was a library's reluctance or inability to maintain currency. Microfilming was innovative and space saving, but it was also time consuming and, at times, costly.

In the 1970s, libraries once again considered automated systems; many libraries had adequate financial resources to develop their own systems or to contract for an outside system developed especially for libraries. From previous experience librarians had learned what to look for in automation and sought systems that would enhance necessary operations rather than change them. They also wanted systems that required little software maintenance locally. Concurrent with this new surge toward library automation was a growing number of commercial organizations dedicated to automated library systems. Companies such as CLSI were advising librarians on hardware capabilities and developing software packages for complete automated circulation systems. The more innovative libraries with qualified programmer/analysts were developing their own systems which covered a wide range of functions and provided numerous computer assisted outputs.

Generally absent from these local programs, however, were efforts to bring better bibliographic control to government documents. This absence of effort was due in large part to a long-standing low priority placed on the bibliographic control of documents and to the changing nature of the technical processes themselves. A notable exception to this situation, however, was the Guelph Document System which was implemented in 1965 by the University of Guelph. This in-house batch system, based on simplified *coding* procedures (not classification), provided both a catalog and catalog-type access to the local documents collection. It was later adapted online and used by other libraries. A batch consortium among libraries in Toronto was eventually formed and took the name CODOC. The union file from this consortium is produced on microfiche for the contributors and made available to other libraries on a fee basis (Gillham, 1982).

Until the late 1970s, the general approaches to technical processing of government publications were limited indeed. By and large, the vast majority of libraries with significant documents collections continued much as they had in the past: select item numbers from the GPO, receive the daily shipments of government publications, check the shipment against the "Daily Shipping list," put the Superintendent of Documents Classification (SuDocs) number on the received document, perhaps mark the document with an ownership and date received stamp, and place the document on the shelves in SuDoc arrangement for public use (Harleston & Stoffle, 1974).

Cataloging and production of card sets typically would not be done, and the SuDocs classification number (although based on issuing agency) was seen as adequate "subject" description. In-house bibliographic control techniques were minimal with perhaps possible use of a KARDEX Serials check-in system or, in some rare instances, a short-title shelf list. In general, however, the typical documents collection does no cataloging, relies on SuDocs classification, has minimal in-house control procedures, and processes materials only to the point of transferring the SuDocs number onto the publication prior to shelving (Richardson et al., 1980).

AUTOMATION AND GOVERNMENT PUBLICATIONS

In a typical library attempting automation, librarians were caught between continuing traditional methods and processes, and adapting to the evolving technology of online systems. A consuming interest of libraries developing automated systems was the hiring of librarians trained in the nature and use of automation, and the retraining of librarians as the transition from manual processing to automated operations progressed. The most difficult aspect of retraining librarians was instilling in them the confidence that after decades of doing things one way, the new, computer-assisted ways could be mastered.

But, because government publications departments often had responsibilities for their own processes—training of documents librarians in automation did not occur. Further, document librarians appeared to show only minimal interest in the possible applications of automating various technical services. The combination of (1) not being integrated into overall library technical processing, (2) demonstrating minimal interest in possible applications, and (3) failure to obtain retraining in automation skills allowed many documents librarians to continue as if automation of library technical services was neither happening nor impacting on their area of library operation.

ONLINE BIBLIOGRAPHIC SERVICES

The technical processing of library materials, especially the cataloging of books, took a quantum leap forward with the appearance of OCLC, Research Libraries Information Network (RLIN), and the Washington Library Network (WLN). OCLC was established in 1967 to provide online services for colleges and universities in Ohio, but the system rapidly expanded to include other libraries and was soon available nationally. OCLC remains the largest network in the United States, but the data base of RLIN has grown considerably and now contains over 7.5 million records.

RLIN is an online processing service offered by the Research Libraries Group (RLG), an organization owned and governed by the member libraries which are representative of some of the major research institutions in the United States. In addition to online cataloging functions, RLIN also offers an acquisitions subsystem, authority files and research options not available from OCLC. Subject searches of the entire data base or of a specific library's holdings are possible. Online access to government documents, however, is limited. Beyond the traditional online services, RLIN is actively pursuing and promoting shared cataloging and distributed processing as partial solutions to the ever increasing body of library materials.

Like OCLC and RLIN, WLN offers online cataloging services with output in the form of tapes and catalog cards as well as computer output microform (COM). The data base is the smallest of the three major noncommercial bibliographic networks and does not emphasize U.S. government publications; however, the Bibliographic Subsystem features both name and subject authority control. An acquisitions subsystem that features the major acquisition functions from ordering to payment of accounts is available for both books and non-book items. The WLN circulation control system is being made available to members outside the state of Washington (Bloomberg & Evans, 1981).

OCLC: An Untapped Resource

Through the 1960s and the early years of the 1970s, major library automation was still a remote possibility in many libraries. For those who could afford it, automation was often locally produced for local access only. There was little effort among libraries to produce systems compatible with others already in operation, and the turnkey systems on the market were not readily available for multi-library installation. With the development of OCLC and the decision to offer it nationally as a shared data base, many librarians began to realize the potential of online services. Although it has been used primarily as a cataloging tool, OCLC expanded over the years to include an effective, time-saving interlibrary loan function, an acquisition program, and a serials control system.

As librarians have gained familiarity with OCLC, the utility of the data base has increased. Not only does OCLC store the monograph and serial records input by member libraries, it also receives the cataloging output of the Library of Congress via dumps of MARC tapes. Since 1976 OCLC has also loaded the government publications listed in the *Monthly Catalog*. With the Government Printing Office currently issuing well over 45,000 titles per year (not all of which are included in OCLC), many libraries may soon consider OCLC as the primary bibliographic source for the processing of documents. Further, the GPO is also a CONSER participant, inputting a large number of serial records into OCLC; however, the series entry must be known in order to access the record. Individual author/title entries can be identified once the series record is found.

One of the most significant enhancements to OCLC in terms of accessing government publications was the 1980 implementation of the "086" Government Document search key (see OCLC Books Format C80-1, 086 Government Document Number). When a document is searched on OCLC, the SuDoc number appears in the 086 field; the call number, if any, will appear in the appropriate call number fields. Although the hit rate through the 086 search key is high, the loading of the MARC tapes is slow, thereby taking away part of the advantage of the online processing of government documents. Access is further limited by the lack of the 086 field for many documents already in the OCLC data base. Where the 086 search key is available, however, the experienced searcher can quickly generate a list of records as specific or as general as needed. The 086 search key can be shortened to retrieve more than a specific record or lengthened to narrow the scope of a search.

In addition to search capability by personal author, title, and the SuDoc number in the 086 field, monographic government documents may also be searched by item number in the 074 field (see OCLC Books Format C80-1, 074 United States Government Printing Office Item Number). The item number key has acquired added significance with the distribution by GPO of the *GPO Depository Union List of Item Selections,* a microfiche listing of government document item numbers and all the depository libraries which receive those numbers. Unfortunately, this reference tool does not indicate the year the library began selecting a specific item number. Nonetheless, each depository receives the *Union List of Item Selections,* making it relatively easy during a search to determine which libraries hold currently selected item numbers. This new listing, begun in September, 1982, and cumulated quarterly, could benefit technical processing as well as aiding in interlibrary loan activities for government documents.

Still under consideration by OCLC is a 1980 proposal by GPO to implement an automated holdings system for GPO-cataloged items. Under the proposed system, all depositories would automatically be listed for each document loaded into the OCLC data base. The system would indicate holdings even for those depositories not cataloged in the OCLC system. The utility of having holding depositories immediately listed for each document is apparent; however, maintenance of accurate holdings records would be a local responsibility and may place added pressure on documents librarians to process claims, enter changes, and update records.

The possible applications of OCLC for government documents technical processing, which have been nicely summarized by Walbridge (1982), include the following:

— *cataloging subsystem:* produce complete sets of catalog cards for government publications included in the data base.
— *serials control:* identify and produce bibliographic records of serials included in the data base with potential applications for local "check-in" and recording of serials holdings.
— *public access:* availability of public access OCLC terminals can directly support bibliographic access and identification of government publications.
— *online access:* with use of the 086 search key, document librarians can immediately obtain bibliographic information regarding any document classified under the SUDOCS classification scheme and included in the data base.
— *acquisitions:* ordering and accounting of materials (not government publications) that may be used in support of a government publications collection.

Despite these possible applications, the actual number of depositories exploiting such services specifically for government publications is unclear.

First, it should be pointed out that simply because the host library has an OCLC terminal, use of the terminal for government publications technical processing does not necessarily follow. A recent study of use of OCLC by depository librarians indicated that fewer than 5% had an OCLC terminal in the documents area (if a separate collection), only 1% had any training on OCLC applications, and that the most frequently mentioned applications used by the librarians were to obtain the SuDoc number or bibliographic information about a publication and *not* to input records (McClure, 1982).

Limiting the utility of the cataloging component of the system are the following concerns: multiple records in the OCLC data base with conflicting bibliographic information, incomplete coverage of the various non-depository publications, ongoing disagreement about the use of AACR II for main entries and the limited use of subject added entries for GPO publications. Nonetheless, the availability of those records within the data base marks a considerable step toward effective processing of GPO government publications. Unfortunately, there is virtually no research regarding actual use of OCLC by depository collections, analysis of government publication records within the data base itself, or the degree to which local libraries use any of the various subsystems for government publications in an *integrated approach* with other library technical processing.

Additional Automated Processing Strategies

The principal contender as a bibliographic utility for government publications is the Guelph Document System, developed in the mid 1960s at the University of Guelph and available today through participation in the CODOC consortia. CODOC does not follow prescribed rules of AACR and thus has considerable flexibility. It can generate government publication bibliographic records, holdings lists, and various union lists. Further, it is appropriate for "any government information source," and its developers suggest that the coding system can be easily adapted for use in a broad range of libraries (Gillham, 1980, 1981, & 1982).

Although a few libraries in the United States have used the CODOC system, it is largely unknown, and its appropriateness for depository library collections has not been carefully evaluated. In addition, specific costs and benefits of the system have not been compared to OCLC or other internally developed systems. Probably due to its origin in Canada, the apparent reluctance of documents librarians to experiment with automated systems, and a steep initial lease fee of $10,000, the system has yet to be exploited in the United States. But use of such a system forces a non-integrated approach to technical processing of government publications. Depending on the local library situation, such an approach may or may not increase access to government publications.

An example of an excellent in-house system that produces a simplified shelf list and other bibliographic products has been developed by Morton at Carleton College. Specific objectives of the system (Morton, 1982) include:

— the ability to retrieve a record by keying on a single record component, e.g., SuDoc class, title, or even key word in title,
— the ability to retrieve any record by keying on any combination of record characteristics, e.g., combinations of keywords in a title, the item with year published, or date received with author, etc.

This approach to processing has a number of advantages over OCLC and CODOC because it provides for collection management analyses to be produced as well as the standard bibliographic records, holdings lists, and shelf lists.

Further, this approach is built upon DATARIEVE software and allows numerous other applications with this particular software. As Morton suggests, another advantage lies in the system's capability to review titles in light of a depository's statutory obligation to retain depository materials for a period of five years, allowing collection analysis of holdings, and producing an updated shelflist as often as needed. Perhaps best of all, data entry is simplified, does not require adherence to AACR, and typically can be accomplished by paraprofessionals.

Although online data base searching is only infrequently seen as a tool for assisting in the processing of government publications, it can be of value. The acquisition process for government publications can be significantly simplified by identifying and ordering government publications directly from the terminal. For instance, bibliographic records from the GPO can be identified and verified from the *Monthly Catalog* and the *Publications Reference File* (PRF). After the correct item has been identified, it can be done for either hard copy or microfiche publications and is likely to be of special usefulness for non-depository collections.

A similar process can be used for a number of non-GPO publications as well as government publications made available through private firms. For instance, all publications listed in *Congressional Information Service* and *American Statistics Index* can be ordered directly online; government publications in a number of the federal data bases such as NTIS and ERIC can also be ordered online. For libraries wishing to simplify their acquisition of government publications, use of online bibliographic data bases to assist in acquisitions has a number of advantages:

— reduces in-house record keeping and invoicing,
— exploits the use of deposit accounts if so desired by the library,
— reduces the ordering to receipt-of-materials time lag,
— combines the process of bibliographic verification with the process of ordering, and
— allows ordering to be done from any physical location at which a terminal is located.

Unfortunately, this strategy is largely ignored by most librarians, apparently because of inadequate training related to online data base searching, minimal access to terminals, and concern about significantly increasing the number of microforms being purchased (Mc-Clure, 1981).

Finally, note should be made of the potential applications of microcomputers for processing of government publications. While there is minimal reporting in the professional literature of microcomputer applications for government publications, the possibilities, are limited only by the imagination. Indeed, current costs (1983 dollars) are approximately $2,500 for a 64K microcomputer system with a disk drive. Given the likelihood that microcomputer equipment and software costs will continue to decrease, additional use by libraries seems to be likely.

The appropriateness of microcomputers for a "self-contained" and separate depository collection encourages microcomputer applications. Following the lead from CODOC and the system developed by Morton at Carleton College, simplified bibliographic information can be input into a data file or a number of data files for such activities as:

— serials control list (which could include more than 50% of all government publications received),
— labels production,
— microforms title, SuDoc, or Series control file, and
— specialized holdings lists.

The major limitation with the micro, obviously, is storage space; however, the current price for a ten megabyte hard disk for a micro is approximately $3,000—likely to provide more than adequate storage for many in-house processing chores in a government publications collection.

A new and vigorous phase of library automation is clearly upon us. Not only are there numerous local systems, many of which support multiple locations and distributed processing, but there are also national systems and regional vendors that provide a broad range of services to a number of libraries. There is also a growing number of systems that combine aspects of local systems, turnkey systems, networks, and network vendors to provide the total range of automated services needed by a library (Hoover, 1980). Libraries are now exploring the potential of national data bases such as OCLC and RLIN, and access for both public technical purposes is becoming more efficient and affordable.

With the growing number of publicly available data bases of government documents, more librarians may wish to catalog documents online, especially with OCLC. The cataloging of documents still lags far behind the processing of other materials, however, and the disparity may no longer be due to the lack of cataloging resources or the degree of difficulty traditionally attributed to government documents. With online access through multiple access points, libraries can no longer justify the relegation of documents to the bottom of the processing list. Nor can we continue to assert that documents require an expertise beyond that of the typical processing department.

ISSUES AND PROSPECTS

The preceding sections have provided a selective overview of the background and current status and technical processing for GPO publications in the context of the depository library. They have suggested that, in general, government publications technical processing has continued much as it has in the past and has been relatively untouched by new technologies and innovative processing procedures. As noted in the first section of the paper, the "3 × 5 catalog card mentality" appears to dominate government publications technical processing—if technical processing is seriously considered for documents in the first place! This current state of affairs can be understood only in the context of a number of issues which still remain unresolved and must be addressed if a library is to develop an effective plan for technical processing of government publications.

To Catalog or not to Catalog

Perhaps the critical issue to address related to processing government publications is whether the library wants to catalog such materials, and if that answer is yes, to then determine *the degree* of cataloging that will be required. Currently, most depository libraries do not catalog the majority of government publications, preferring to accession those received and typically put them on the shelves in SuDoc or agency and year order. The reasons offered for not cataloging government publications include:

— too costly and requires additional staff,

— cataloging rules for government publications are inappropriate and numerous changes for each government publication are necessary, regardless of the bibliographic record available in a given data base,

— the emphasis of the GPO on micropublishing (expected to be 50% of all titles by 1984) complicates the cataloging process,

— adequate bibliographic access to government publications is obtained through standard hardcopy indexes and online bibliographic data bases, and

— much of the cataloging detail for government publications is non-informative.

These reasons may or may not be valid for a particular depository setting. General card catalog use studies suggest a wide disparity of usefulness, effectiveness, and access due to cataloging (Lancaster, 1977, pp. 19-68). Reasons for cataloging government publications usually revolve around the assumption that having complete cards in the main card catalog or integrated into the library cataloging system will improve access and availability to government publications. Unfortunately, there is no evidence or empirical research that strongly supports one case or the other (Waldo, 1977).

But, recently advances in technology have minimized the importance of the cataloging issue. Since bibliographic records are available in OCLC for publications listed in the *Monthly Catalog* since 1976, and with the increased availability of hard copy government publication indexes such as *CIS* and *ASI* in recent years, bibliographic access to GPO publications has improved; further, with the availability of numerous government publications data bases online, the importance of cataloging government publications is being replaced by the importance of having a logical means to classify and arrange the documents (such as SuDocs) on the shelves. Indeed, one might argue effectively that access and availability of government publications are severely impaired when classified in a non-SuDocs classification scheme.

GPO Administrative Decisions and Activities

Although the GPO has taken a greater interest in processing issues related to government publications since the mid-1970s, much is still required if the local librarian is to be supported for the cataloging of depository publications. Records produced by the GPO between 1976 and 1980 were done independently of the Library of Congress and may have been changed by LC—thus the "correct" version of a government publication for this time needs to be determined. Beginning in 1981 the GPO was established as the center of authority for cataloging federal documents—taking over that responsibility from the Library of Congress. Also since 1981, the GPO has participated with the LC in the name authority cooperative project. This cooperation between the GPO and the Library of Congress must be extended to meet a number of current problems affecting GPO cataloging.

Four primary problems are yet to be resolved. First, in the area of subject cataloging there is no GPO/LC agreement. The GPO subject headings which appear in the *Monthly Catalog* may be different than those assigned by LC and thus, different headings may appear in OCLC. Second, the GPO does not provide documentation for the computer tapes it produces of bibliographic records. When the GPO sends the tape to the LC Cataloging Distribution Service, it simply duplicates and sells the tape. With no documentation for the tapes (since 1976) libraries will find it very difficult to load and manipulate the tapes for any number of possible applications.

The third problem relates to error correction. Currently the GPO does not distribute a tape correcting previous errors such as is done by the Library of Congress. Although GPO provides corrections for its book catalog, the records in OCLC and other utilities are not corrected. Finally, it should be pointed out that the GPO provides a bibliographic description of the printed copy of a publication and *not* the microfiche. Typically, standard bibliographic information about the microfiche—such as reduction ratio, number of fiche, positive/negative are not provided. Thus, when all 1365 depository libraries receive a microfiche of the publication, the GPO provides bibliographic information based on the hardcopy. These four problems, as well as other difficulties, are discussed in much greater detail by an excellent article by Myers (in press).

The GPO must take an aggressive stance toward improving the cataloging processes and provision of bibliographic records. The need to rely on the GPO for these activities is apparent. Yet, unless adequate attention is given to these and other issues (such as adding item number designations to records loaded in OCLC and eliminating a significant cataloging backlog as of late 1982 at the GPO), government document librarians and any other librarian attempting to exploit automated access to government publications records, increased networking and resource sharing, and construction of in-house *integrated* catalogs, will be stymied.

Training and Retraining Documents Librarians

Another issue that must be raised is the limited degree to which documents librarians have embraced the new technologies related to government publications technical processing. Clearly, other librarians can share equally such an assessment, but currently most document librarians are unfamiliar with the workings of OCLC, have limited knowledge of online bibliographic data base searching, are unable to design and develop in-house automated processing systems such as that developed by Morton at Carleton College, and have not been supported by their libraries to obtain such training and increased competencies (McClure, 1982).

Because of this inability to understand, design, and implement automated technical processing innovations, as well as myopic views on documents processing by library administrators, documents librarians have been largely excluded from the planning process for processing applications that are being developed in other areas of the library. Thus, the ability to *integrate* library technical processing of government publications with other processing procedures is minimized, and in a number of cases government publications are left to the traditional "3 × 5 catalog card mentality." Once documents librarians become more conversant with technology applications by continuing education or other methods, they will then have to educate other librarians as to the importance and possible applications of government publications processing in that particular library. In short, training related to government publications processing is likely to be needed throughout the library.

Microforms

The use of microforms by the GPO as a means to distribute government information has grown significantly in recent years, and new microfiche is the primary format for GPO distribution. this change has a number of implications for the technical processing of government publications, including:

— providing adequate storage facilities under proper climate conditions,

— reducing ability to check for quality control of received microfiche, and make certain that all microfiche on the Daily Shipping List are, in fact, received,
— obtaining adequate bibliographic information on microfiche
headers that is eye-readable,
— reducing document mobility within the library—both for processing as well as for use,
— ensuring that microfiche relates to the functional needs of the
clientele and collections in the rest of the library,
— forcing separation of microfiche from other government publications, and perhaps from other materials in the library, and
— producing greater difficulty in maintaining correct shelf order
of microfiche.

In short, unless depository librarians carefully consider new forms
of management techniques and collection development for processing microforms, "they will be fated to recurring diazo and silver-
halide nightmares in which they are pursued through never-ending
rows of microfiche cabinets. . . ." (Morton, 1982b, pp. 257-258).

The other side of the microforms question is the ability of the
documents librarian to exploit microform technology for increased
effectiveness of processing and better access to information. The
best example is the use of COM catalogs such as that discussed by
Brown and Schlipf (1982). They have reported on a process by
which micrographic and computer indexing reduces file bulk, produces security copies, easily updates a COM catalog, and allows for
rapid retrieval and distribution of a local documents collection. Such
a perspective clearly shows that microform technology, and in this
case COM technology, can be effectively exploited for the benefit of
technical processing and user access. Additional attention to such
strategies by document librarians is needed and will be necessary in
the future.

Vendor Applications

While automated technical processing systems have been developed and are currently being expanded for "regular library materials," attention given to government publications systems is limited.
If government publications are cataloged similarly to other materials
in the library, if complete records are available, and if the bibliographic information fits the available formats supplied by the vendor, then processing of documents may be included in a vendor sup-

plied turnkey package. However, the more likely situation is that only minimal bibliographic records are available for U.S. government publications (and virtually none for international, state, and local documents), and the vendor simply is unable to assist the library when it comes to processing government publications.

Recently, one of the authors of this paper asked seven different vendors of automated processing systems (including serials, acquisitions, and cataloging) for specifications on the application of their systems to government publications. Only one of the vendors provided a clear and logical explanation of what their system could do for processing of government publications (after asking three different salespersons), and then the vendor finally concluded that the system really was not "geared up" for processing government publications. As long as government publications technical processing is inadequately considered in the major turnkey processing systems, librarians will be forced to develop in-house systems or attempt to "piggy-back" processing of documents on other systems as best they can.

Shared Processing and Retrospective Conversion

Assuming the availability of terminals, sufficient staff, adequate training, and the financial resources to process government documents online, a library must next determine if processing will be inclusive or selective. It is a major undertaking to catalog all government publications received in a depository library. Even if it were possible to catalog all currently received documents, very few libraries could seriously consider the retrospective cataloging of all previously received documents. At this point it becomes obvious that sheer numbers and not necessarily the complexity of the material may constitute the major obstacle to the online processing of government materials. Technology holds the answer to the problem, and that technology is currently available.

For many years the Association of Research Libraries (ARL) has advocated shared cataloging as an equitable solution for the vast quantities of uncataloged microforms in libraries, and this position is supported by different studies (Information Systems Consultants, 1980). Consortia of various sizes have also been formed to reap the benefits of shared cataloging. The CODOC system itself is a prime example of cooperative effort in the processing of documents. Among the major bibliographic utilities, shared cataloging has evolved as the only realistic approach to the processing of materials which, due to quantities, format or some other factor, do not get priority cataloging in many libraries. Several members of the Research Libraries Group (RLG) recently implemented a shared cataloging program aimed at the timely cataloging of selected sound recordings. Each participant has responsibility for specific labels, and the priority processing of assigned labels makes cataloging for a large number of sound recordings immediately available to the rest of the participants, and to the whole of the RLG membership.

Another shared cataloging program soon to be implemented by RLG involves priority cataloging of all volumes of selected monographic series. Emphasis will be on foreign language series and those English language series which are not readily cataloged by the Library of Congress. The goal is to identify important series and give priority cataloging to all volumes in those series so that other members will have prompt access to member or LC cataloging. By sharing the cataloging responsibilities, the burden on any one library is not great while the benefits are substantial. These examples illustrate possible strategies that can be applied for the cataloging and processing of government publications.

For both the participants in a bibliographic utility and other network members, online access to a growing number of documents records would greatly facilitate the retrospective conversion of government documents collections. Through receipt of archival tapes, a library could then easily generate paper, fiche or film copies of a documents catalog or produce an integrated catalog, depending on the classification systems used and the access points desired. For libraries with online catalogs and circulation systems, the simultaneous input of documents' records or the loading of archival tapes into the system could result in online access to the local documents collection with a variety of access points.

Even with the technology of today, which is rapidly evolving at both the local and network level to allow online management of virtually all library functions, the body of government documents yet to be cataloged poses a formidable long-term project for one library to undertake. Shared cataloging or shared processing of some degree would seem to be a logical approach to the problem. Members of large networks such as OCLC and RLG could share the responsibility of documents cataloging based on a division of materials by item number, or in some other fashion suitable to the needs and capabilities of the participants.

PROSPECTS

Traditionally, government publications have been relegated to a low priority in many library settings. Low priority of the documents collection is an historical condition that is not easily changed. In fact, it is best described as an attitude in the library that presumes limited importance of government publications. Removal of this constraint requires time and careful planning, political involvement on the part of the documents librarian, and the development of a strategy of integrating or "piggy-backing" government publications into other areas of library operations and services. Until government publications are better integrated, in terms of administration, services, and attitude, increased technical processing will be dependent primarily on the personal interest and commitment of the documents librarian.

Prospects for carefully reviewing the importance, need, and strategies for government publications technical processing are continuing to improve as more librarians, and especially library administrators, come to realize the value of government publications received under the depository library program. Further, OCLC has provided enhancements that address the unique needs of government publications, but much is still to be done—such as the inclusion of the holdings symbols automatically on the items received by the various depository libraries. Despite these positive factors, reduced budgets, priorities at the GPO, and the need to encourage documents librarians to become more active and knowledgeable about automated technical services can still limit advances in this area.

The decision to process documents must be made locally, and the documents librarian should have a major role in influencing that decision. Whether processing is done centrally or in the documents collection also must be a local decision, but with online access to a data base such as OCLC, processing should not be a task beyond the capability of a typical processing unit or documents staff trained in online techniques.

It remains to be seen if libraries will take advantage of existing technology and cooperative efforts to improve bibliographic control for government publications or if there will be a continuation of a wait-and-see philosophy. For some libraries the Superintendent of Documents Classification System may be adequate for their needs, and online processing of documents may not be necessary or advisable. For other libraries, the lack of processing and bibliographic control may result in continued underutilization and physical chaos. For libraries which want or need online capabilities to better serve their patrons, the framework for cooperative efforts exist. Participation in shared cataloging programs may offer the greatest potential for success in achieving efficient and cost effective results.

SOURCES

Bernhardt, Frances Simonsen. *Introduction to Library Technical Services*. New York: H. W. Wilson Company, 1979.

Bloomberg, Marty, and Evans, G. Edward. *Introduction to Technical Services for Library Technicians*. Littleton, CO: Libraries Unlimited, Inc., 1981.

Brown, Jeanne Owen, & Schlipf, Fred A. "The Use of Microfiche and COM Indexes to Improve Municipal Document Control," *Government Publications Review,* 9 (1982): 289-310.

Gillham, Virginia. "CODOC as a Consortia Tool," *Government Publications Review* 9 (1982): 45-53.

Gillham, Virginia. "The Guelph Document System," *Government Publications Review* 7 (1980): 211-216.

Gillham, virginia. "In-House Procedures in a Library Using CODOC," *Government Publications Review* 8 (1981): 411-416.

Harleston, Rebekah M., & Stoffle, Carla J. *Administration of Government Documents Collections*. Littleton, CO: Libraries Unlimited, 1974.

Hernon, Peter. *Use of Government Publications by Social Scientists*. Norwood, NJ: Ablex Publishing Corp. 1979.

Hoover, Ryan E. *The Library and Information Manager's Guide to Online Services*. White Plains, NY: Knowledge Industries, 1980.

Information Systems Consultants, Inc. "Bibliographic Control of Microforms," Richard W. Boss, principal investigator. Unpublished report prepared for the Association of Research Libraries, 1980. (NEH Grant RC-00093-791243).

Lancaster, F. W. *The Measurement and Evaluation of Library Services*. Washington, D. C.: Information Resources Press, 1977.

McClure, Charles R. "Online Government Documents Data Base Searching and Use of Microfiche Documents Online by Academic and Public Depository Librarians," *Microform Review* 10 (Fall, 1981): 245-259.

McClure, Charles R. "Technology in Government Document Collections: Current Status, Impacts, and Prospects," *Government Publications Review* 9 (1982): 255-276.

McClure, Charles R., & Hernon, Peter. *Improving the Quality of Reference Service for Government Publications*. Chicago: American Library Association, 1983.

Meyers, Judy. "The Effects of Technology on Access to Federal Government Information," in *Documents Librarianship: A New Technology,* edited by Peter Hernon. Westport, CT: Meckler Publishing, in press.

Morton, Bruce. "Implementing an Automated Shelflist for a Selective Depository Collection: Implications for Collection Management and Public Access," *Government Publication Review* 9 (1982a): 323-344.

Morton, Bruce. "New Management Problems For the Documents Librarian: Government Microfiche Publications," *Microform Review* 11 (Fall, 1982): 254-258.

Richardson, John V. Jr., Frisch, Dennis C. W., & Hall, Catherine M. "Bibliographic Organization of U.S. Federal Depository Collections," *Government Publications Review* 7A (1980): 463-480.

Saffady, William. *Computer-Output Microfilm: Its Library Applications*. Chicago: American Library Association, 1978.

Walbridge, Sharon. "OCLC and Government Documents Collections," *Government Publications Review* 9 (1982): 277-288.

Waldo, Michael. "An Historical Look at the Debate over How to Organize Federal Government Documents in Depository Libraries," *Government Publications Review* 4 (1977): 319-329.

Indexing into the 21st Century

Marietta Chicorel

ABSTRACT. Some suggestions are made as to what comprises a good index and as to how indexes can be used more effectively in serving the library user.

"An educated consumer is our best customer" goes a slogan of a local retail store. The store owners are referring to a consumer who is educated in the uses and applications of their sales product, and who would presumably recognize value.

Library users have not always been approached as educated consumers. They have been forced to deal with reference publications which in successive issues too often update only a small percentage of the information contained in the original volume; they have been told that these sources represent the universe of available data in the particular field. Library indexing was begun as an aid to locally perceived user needs. Such prestigious publications as *Ulrich's Periodicals Directory* and *Granger's Index to Poetry* were begun as projects to enable the authors, themselves librarians, to serve their libraries' patrons in a more flexible manner than before. These and other similar projects were nearly always begun by librarians for the use of librarians.

The indexing function is inherently more adaptable than cataloging. Its flexibility makes it the ideal tool to retrieve information because it can be shaped to accommodate the terminology of a new field or a unique user group. Is this not what a computer is actually doing? Indexing can develop and change with its subject matter, as well as with user demand. In the language of computers, it is user-friendly; it is approachable and, in book form, very suitable for browsing, providing in this way the serendipity of research. From the user point of view, its use is also cost-effective. Clearly the pro-

Marietta Chicorel, President, American Library Publishing Company, Inc., 275 Central Park West, New York, NY 10024.

duction of indexes, which serves the unpredictable demands of users and the needs of librarians charged with identifying required and appropriate information, is a service activity, much as librarianship is a service profession.

In the future, indexing will be the most practical and cost-effective response to the increasingly sophisticated demands from users. As a result of the computer revolution, a crucial change in user viewpoint is going to involve the awareness that the answers to questions *can* be had; users will refuse to settle for empty gestures. A prototypical exchange between a "frontline" librarian and user will contain the implicit or explicit demand, "You're telling me that with all your computers and new technology you can't get me this information?"

Many myths cherished by librarians will have to be abandoned, including the one that if a librarian provides a patron with a source that *should* contain an answer to the patron's question, the librarian is held blameless even if it does not. The "educated consumer" will hold the library accountable for the quality of service that his or her tax dollar is paying for.

The situation in which librarians are likely to find themselves later on has come about at least in part as a consequence of the growth of the library publishing industry. In order to survive and fulfill the demand from users and librarians alike and in order to supply an effective alternative to computer retrieval, library publishers will have to produce sources which appeal to, and are useful to the "educated consumer."

From the standpoint of the publisher, indexing is a relatively high-cost production item. From user's perspective, the production of indexes that only present 10-20% of newly available information each year is inadequate, and hence such material is going to be unacceptable. Libraries wil not be able to afford such indulgence, especially as computer and data base services become more and more appealing and accepted.

But indexing will not change in nature: only in depth and breadth. It will become necessary for library publishers to provide the kind of resources for librarians that give users their answers. This is the objective of the user coming in to the library, of the librarians who are charged with serving this need, and, obviously, of the library publishers entrusted to produce the materials for both.

The challenge is for library publishers to provide the necessary resources to serve the greatest variety of user needs in the most advantageous manner.

BIBLIOGRAPHY

Anstine, Francesca A., Elisabeth B. Davis, Bernice Hulsizer, & Mitsuko Williams. "Data Analysis and Discussion." *Library Research,* 4 (Summer, 1982), pp. 147-59.

Battin, Patricia. "Developing university and research library professionals: A director's perspective." *American Libraries,* 14 (January, 1983), pp. 22-25.

Dahlin, Robert. "Electronic Publishing Reports." *Publishers Weekly,* 222 (Dec. 17, 1982), p. 50.

"The Future of the Publishing Industry: The Challenge of Technology." *CUNY Graduate School Magazine,* 1 (Spring, 1982), pp. 8-11.

Isaacson, Kathy. "Machine-Readable Information in the Library." *RQ,* 22 (Winter, 1982), pp. 164-70.

Morrison, Sylvia. "CPI Surveys—a Service to Subscribers." *Canadian Library Journal,* 38 (June 1981), pp. 167-169.

Shatzkin, Leonard. "'In Cold Type.' A Sampler of Excerpts from a New Book that Offers a Radical View of Publishing's Future." *Publishers Weekly,* 222 (July 16, 1982), pp. 32-36.

Shneour, Elie A. "A Look into the Book of the Future." *Publishers Weekly,* 223 (January 21, 1983), p. 48.

Toffler, Alvin. *The Third Wave.* New York: Bantam, 1980.

Binding:
From Basement to Boardroom

Phyllis Reeve, MA, MLS

ABSTRACT. Technological change, in conjunction with economic pressures, affects the details of library binding procedures and suggests alternatives to the expensive preservation of deteriorating collections. Concern for the physical condition of the collection must be made a part of all library planning.

Binding in the space age library takes advantage of new technologies and reflects changing attitudes towards the library building and its contents.

Computerized systems for serials and circulation control are maintaining binding records and generating instruction forms to replace card files and handwritten binding slips. Electronic publication and microforms are eliminating the need for binding many journals. The insidious computer has attacked from another direction also; standards of binding have been put in a new perspective by the pressure of on-line bibliographic searching on photocopying services. The one available copy within a network must be readily reproduced, without cracking its spine or losing information in the crease of a narrow margin.

The physical nature of the library's collection comes under increasing scrutiny as more is known about acid content and deteriorating paper. The mender's tools, glue pots and rolls of tape are suspect, and the search intensifies for more benign and chemically appropriate products. The library building itself, with its dust, heat and humidity, is identified as a prime enemy of books and non-book materials. Few libraries can afford a controlled environment or an on-going program of collection preservation, although the truth may

Phyllis Reeve, Assistant Acquisitions Librarian, University of British Columbia, Acquisitions Division, Library Processing Centre, 2206 East Mall, Vancouver, B. C., Canada V6T 1Z8.

be that no library can really afford not to have them. Perhaps a few major centers will undertake large-scale deacidification projects, such as the experiment conducted by the Library of Congress in conjunction with NASA, and reported in the Library of Congress *Information Bulletin* of November 12, 1982. Assured of expert, longterm preservation at such centres, smaller libraries could feel justified in cutting back on rebinding budgets.

However it is to be achieved, collection preservation must be made a priority in long-range planning. Binding decisions must be brought from the basement workroom into the boardroom. Planners need to make preservation a factor in all decisions affecting the library, from choice of equipment to methods of staff training. The ideal in the minds of library administrators should be a full program for the preservation of library materials, accomplished through continuous monitoring of the collection and its treatment by trained conservators, under ideal atmospheric conditions.

In the real world, even in the space age, this ideal can be only a touchstone to balance against the practical and the economically feasible. With increased funds of accurate information available to them, librarians can involve themselves in binding decisions as part of their concern for the building of a useful and accessible collection. Books so fragile that they must be protected from the touch of human hands can scarcely be described as "accessible." Basing their actions on knowledge of techniques, costs and available resources, librarians will consult with experts and demand specialized training for the technicians who bind or repair their books. They will, as a matter of course, familiarize themselves with such studies and recommendations as those offered by the Association of Research Libraries, the Library Binding Institute, the Special Libraries Association, and Columbia University. For concise words of practical wisdom, they will turn to handbooks like the helpful *Conservation Treatment Procedures* manual by Carolyn Clark Morrow, the National Library of Canada's *Guidelines for Preventive Conservation,* or the "kits" issued by the Systems and Procedures Exchange Center (SPEC) of the Association of Research Libraries/Office of Management Studies.

This new awareness does not necessarily imply an elaborate inhouse facility for mending, deacidification, and binding. It may, on the contrary, mean more use of outside technical expertise, or, as has been suggested, participation in regional preservation centers. Without an unexpected and sudden improvement in the standard quality of paper, many books will be discarded as soon as their contents can be microfilmed. The logical next step is to publish in microformat or on-line, and eliminate the paper and glue object that we now think of as a "book." It is all the same, difficult and unpleasant to believe that the arts and humanities will succumb completely to publication in such formats. We can assume, therefore, that books and bindings as we know them now will continue to exist for the foreseeable future.

Binding itself will retain its status as an art, perhaps increasing in prestige as it is used selectively and in accordance with other planned procedures. The elaborately tooled and gilded bindings of the Victorian era will not return; we are doomed to contemplation of humdrum standard buckram. What may be salvaged from the past is a knowledgeable concern for the pages between the covers, and a determination that the binding or other container does the best and most appropriate service for the bibliographical contents of a given work.

REFERENCES

Banks, Joyce M. *Guidelines for Preventive Conservation.* Ottawa: Committee on Conservation/Preservation of Library Materials, 1981.

Morrow, Carolyn Clark. *Conservation Treatment Procedures: a Manual of Step-by-step procedures for the maintenance and Repair of Library Materials.* Littleton, Colorado: Libraries Unlimited, Inc., 1982.

Preservation of Library Materials. Ed. Joyce R. Russell. New York: Special Libraries Association, 1980.

Systems and Procedures Exchange Center (SPEC). *Basic Preservation Procedures; Kit 70.* Washington, D.C.: Association of Research Libraries/Office of Management Studies, 1981.

———. *Planning for Preservation; Kit 66.* Washington, D.C.: Association of Research Libraries/Office of Management Studies, 1980.

———. *Preservation of Library Materials; Kit 35.* Washington, D.C.: Association of Research Libraries /Office of Management Studies, 1977.

New Technologies and the Future of Nonprint and Audio-Visual Services

Jean Walter Farrington

ABSTRACT. The transition from non-automated or semi-automated libraries to fully computerized service centers is described; and the use of non-print formats such as microforms, videodiscs, videotex, and teletext is projected.

It is generally accepted that the library of 20 years hence will be a very different place from today's library. How different remains to be seen. Whether one calls the coming phenomenon the "information age"[1] or the "paperless society,"[2] the new revolution comprised of computers and advanced telecommunications and easy electronic access to all kinds of data will alter greatly both the look of the library, and its functions as we now know them. In the words of one futurist, F. W. Lancaster:

> The library will be a center in which access to data bases and data banks will be possible and in which trained personnel will be available to assist the user in the exploitation of these resources. The library may also serve as a "printout center." Even if a user has a terminal capable of interrogating a wide range of data bases, he may not have a high-speed printer available to him.[3]

Already, there are the beginnings of an electronic publishing industry. To cite one example, the North-Holland Publishing Company is experimenting with publishing its journal of short communications, *Computer Compacts,* online as well as in paper.[4] Items sub-

---

Jean Walter Farrington, Acting Head, Circulation Department, Van Pelt Library, University of Pennsylvania, Philadelphia, PA 19104.

mitted to the online version are to be no more than 500 words or two screen displays long and will be targeted to an audience of computer professionals. A second example is the recently formed company, Comtex Scientific which has plans to offer more than 22 electronic journals. Initially, the company will make available online the progress reports scientists are required to file with their government funding agencies.[5] The potential market for online journals is a large one since it is estimated that about 70 percent of the almost 2 million scientists working in North America have access to a micro- or a mini-computer.

While the developments in computer technology and telecommunications are exciting, they are also somewhat scary. What will happen to traditional reference service as we know it? What will become of the definite (albeit sometimes blurry) lines between technical services and public services? What will happen to other technologies, such as microforms, slides, films, videocassettes, etc.? Will all these media forms be replaced by a combination of the "great computer in the sky," and the little desktop terminal in every office?

While some experts, like Lancaster, predict radical changes by the end of the century, most likely there will be a more gradual transition from today's non-automated or semi-automated libraries to the fully computerized service center he envisions. In the time between today and tomorrow, more attention will probably be given to non-print formats such as microforms, videodiscs, videotex, and teletext. Most certainly non-print or audio-visual service, to whatever extent it exists now in libraries, will be affected and changed as technology changes. Let us, therefore, look at three areas: 1) videotex/teletext and its possibilities for libraries, 2) current and future production of journals and how it affects collections and service, and 3) videodisc technology and its implications for information storage.

Although videotex and teletext have existed primarily outside the library, they may offer new ways for libraries to market their collections and services, both within the library walls and in patrons' homes. Defined as "the delivery of text and graphics from a computer through a wide variety of electronic systems, to a user's command,"[6] videotex and teletext usually use cable TV or telephone lines or a combination of the two. Videotex is interactive in that the user may communicate back to the computer; teletext is one-way communication only and is less expensive than videotex. The first real experiment with videotex in this country was OCLC's three-month prototype system called Channel 2000. It included a wide range of library and information sciences including selections from the *Academic American Encyclopedia.* A survey of users demonstrated that they were very pleased with the library services and spent considerable time browsing the encyclopedia.

The importance of videotex and teletext for non-print services is that these forms of communication may well reduce the need for certain items in the library. If the *Encyclopedia Britannica* were available on videotext, for example, a regional library collection may not need to have hard copy. Likewise, titles that currently are preserved on microform, such as journals like *Time* and *Newsweek,* might be available through videotex or teletext to someone's home or in the library instead of on microfilm. Using videotex in a library may be a first sign of the library's willingness to move beyond its walls. Videotex could also have an effect on how librarians fulfill their service role by giving them "the opportunity to switch from the limiting role of information instructor by creating original information based in the library's own resources and delivering it to the community directly through their television sets or home computers."[7] This could certainly come true for public libraries, and may well be the case for academic libraries as their functions and holdings are linked together in one online system and faculty have the ability to access the library holdings with their personal office computers. What is clear is that videotex/teletext are technologies which should not remain unexamined, for they offer the possibility of expanding library horizons.

The production and publishing of journals is another area in which technology is challenging the traditional methods. The high cost of paper is one reason publishers are considering other alternatives. Several years ago the simultaneous publication of a journal in hard copy and microfiche was news. Today, the news is that a few journals have already gone to an electronic format and others may soon do so. Articles by Hickey,[8] Lancaster et al., and Suprenant,[9] address such issues as the "microbook," the digital storage of both text and graphics, and the ultimate demise of the paper or microform journal with virtually all writing and editing and publishing done online. Copies for those who need them would be available on demand using high-speed printers.

Since journals frequently comprise 50-75% of many libraries' microform holdings, such a change in publishing would drastically affect this area of the library. Both bound periodical volumes and microfilm and microfiche would cease their drive to claim more floor and shelving space. Certainly existing microform holdings would continue to remain as microforms for a good long time, but the collection would "grow" in terms of subscriptions to online journals. There would be a resulting need for more computer terminals and, of course, good quality high-speed printers. The library's collections might almost cease growing in terms of physical pieces acquired. Subscriptions would give the library the right to access and make on-demand copies of certain titles. Individual journal titles not "held" by a particular library might be available through an online network for a per use fee. This possible reduction in the amount of physical material acquired would undoubtedly result in some restructuring of technical services operations. Taking the extreme view, Lancaster sounds the death knell for cataloging departments in all but the largest libraries, stating that their primary duties will be: "cataloging of local interest materials, cataloging of printed materials from foreign sources, and augmentation of subject access points for materials of special interest."[10] For large academic libraries whose collections are 40-50% non-English language materials, this death sentence is probably premature. Getting rid of cataloging backlogs and converting materials not currently in machine-readable form could well occupy catalogers and other technical services librarians for far more than twenty years!

On another front, the videodisc may well become a bridging technology between the paper and microform of today, and the terminals and computers of tomorrow. Videodisc is an exciting medium because of its storage density and its versatility of format. One 12 " videodisc can hold up to 54,000 frames per side for a total of 60 minutes' playing time and can accommodate a mixture of audio and visual material including photographs, moving pictures, and slides as well as text. The amount of material stored on one videodisc can be the equivalent of 54 books, each 250 pages long. Furthermore, optical videodiscs (those read by a laser) are impervious to heat and scratching, and suffer no adverse effects due to temperature variations. They also have the capability of being connected with a microcomputer to provide interactive instructional capabilities. The standard educational optical videodisc player systems already come equipped with a programmable microprocessor which makes it possible to randomly access any frame in the disc. As one might expect, the initial investment in a videodisc player system is not insignificant ($2,000-3,000), especially compared to the cost of a microfiche reader; and therefore, it is unlikely that videodisc technology will storm the library overnight. Nonetheless, for storage of documents or graphics at a local site, videodiscs can be invaluable. Drawbacks to videodisc technology today are several and include the scarcity of material currently on videodisc, the complex and expensive mastering and replication process, and the inability to re-use or update the material on a disc once it has been recorded. Finally, there are still problems with the quality of resolution for text which must be solved before the optical videodisc gains widespread acceptance. Under development is a digital optical disc which could be recorded on-site at a computer and whose storage capacity (10 billion characters) would far exceed current videodiscs. These digital discs, should they become marketable, might possibly compete seriously with online services.''[11]

Two examples of current use of videodiscs are Pergamon's Video PATSEARCH product and Arete's *Academic America Encyclopedia*. Video PATSEARCH is a combination of an online data base of U.S. patent summaries coupled with a videodisc system to store the patent drawings locally. Presently, the system consists of 8 videodiscs containing a total of 750,000 front-page patent drawings for the years 1971-1981. The library leases the hardware, consisting of a microcomputer, terminal, and videodisc player plus videodiscs, on a yearly basis. Since videodiscs are excellent for displaying graphics and provide for random access, this product makes use of the best features of both this and online computer technology. The second example is the *Academic American Encyclopedia*. Arete plans to transfer to videodisc some of the material now on magnetic tape which was used in the Channel 2000 videotex experiment. The videodisc will include a sampling of text articles, color illustrations, and sound and motion segments. Should Arete decide to take the next step, the entire 21 volume work with sound and motion sequences could be put on 3-4 discs. The advantage of this technology over simply an online encyclopedia is the ability to graphically illustrate concepts, such as the difference between Art Nouveau and Art Deco, and to show the forces which keep a cathedral from caving in.[12]

In the future, videodiscs might well be used for educational and training materials provided in the library as an adjunct to classroom instruction, or for library orientation packages which could be accessed from terminals throughout the library, or for other supporting documents or graphics tied to a remote data base.

It is quite evident that regardless of which technology prevails and how the evolutionary line proceeds, any and all of these new technological developments will change the patterns and face of nonprint/audio-visual services. Without question, access to information is being made more widely available to individuals without librarian intervention, as individuals acquire their own computers. This trend will only accelerate when libraries truly have online catalogs, and the professor no longer needs to leave his or her office to conduct a literature search, locate a book, and check it out. Libraries may indeed see less of their patrons, and yet provide more access to greater amounts of information. In addition, these new technological developments, electronic journals, online data bases, videotex and video and digital discs, do all raise the specter of fewer "physical" library acquisitions, less material to catalog, and hence, a change in job description for technical service librarians. The new technologies will certainly also change the nature of the reference librarian's job, but perhaps to a lesser degree. These are exciting times and exciting developments, and it will be a challenge to creatively accept and utilize them. Some imaginative reorientation and rethinking of today's library and library service will certainly be required.

REFERENCES

1. Wilson P. Dizard. "The Coming Information Age," *The Information Society* 1:91-111 (1981).

2. F. W. Lancaster. *Toward Paperless Information Systems,* New York, Academic Press, 1978.

3. Ibid, p.155-156.

4. *Outlook for Research Libraries,* November 1981.

5. William J. Broad. "Journals: Fearing the Electronic Future," *Science,* 216: 964-966 (28 May 1982).

6. John and Robin Adams. "Videotex and Teletext: New Roles for Librarians," *Wilson Library Bulletin,* November 1982, p.206.

7. Ibid, p.209.

8. Thomas Hickey. "The Journal in the Year 2000," *Wilson Library Bulletin,* November 1982, p.256-260.

9. Tom Suprenant. "Future Libraries," *Wilson Library Bulletin,* October 1982, p.152-153.

10. F. W. Lancaster et al. "The Changing Face of the Library: A Look at Libraries and Librarians in the Year 2001," *Collection Management,* 3:55-76 (Spring 1979).

11. Charles M. Goldstein. "Optical Disc Technology and Its Implications and Information Storage and Retrieval in the Eighties" [preprint of talk], NATO AGARD, Munich, Germany, September 1981.

12. F. L. Greenagel. "Arete—a 3000 Year-old Word for the Latest in Electronic Publishing, *Electronic Publishing Review,* v.1, no.3 (1981), 177-182.

Trends in Library and Information Service Organizations

Pauline F. Micciche

ABSTRACT. The line between technical and other library services and between library and nonlibrary information services will become increasingly blurred as the century progresses. Individuals will use home, local, regional, national, and international communications systems, and computer and information services as needed. Libraries will examine the offerings of a wide range of profit, not-for-profit, and governmental library and information service organizations—and carefully choose those that meet their specific needs.

To remain viable, today's computer library service organizations will package a greater variety and number of services into smaller and smaller bundles offered to a wider range of users, and a host of smaller companies will develop to serve these needs. Technical services personnel will increasingly be called on to generate specialized information for use in computerized (and other) systems and to coordinate the library's choice of services.

We live in interesting times—times of great change, difficulty, and opportunity. Over 10% of the workforce in the United States is unemployed and inflation is high, reducing the real dollar value of the income earned by those who are gainfully employed. Loss of income for citizens translates into diminished revenue and increased expenses for governments, fewer and smaller sales for business, and less income for not-for-profit institutions.

THE HOME COMPUTER AGE

More and more of the workforce are in service industries, and do not produce durable goods. Instead over 50% of them create, manipulate, or deliver information. (Another 29% work in non-

---

Pauline F. Micciche, Proposal Coordinator, OCLC Local Library Systems, OCLC, 6565 Frantz Road, Dublin, OH 43017.

information industry service occupations.) Computers and computer services make the development of personal and larger stores of information and their rapid exchange over long distances possible and affordable for more and more individuals and organizations. Computers also handle telecommunications and satellite communications associated with the rapid transfer of this data. In addition, more and more businesses are incorporating computers of various sizes into their operations, and using outside computerized information services. Eight-five percent of the U.S. customers of Videotex, a text information service using television technology, are businesses.

Microcomputers have begun to permeate the home. They are sold in department stores like Sears and discount book stores as well as ubiquitous computer specialty shops. They have been offered as premiums. A home builder in Naperville, Illinois, gave away an Apple II microcomputer to each home buyer; a furniture dealer in Columbus, Ohio, is offering a free Timex/Sinclair 1000 with each furniture purchase over $799. Personal microcomputers are even appearing as prizes in contests run by publishers and mail order companies. Atari shipped about six million videogame units, a specialized form of microcomputer, in 1982. Atari has about 75% of the market, making the total number sold in the United States about nine million.

This increased use of computers in homes and businesses has increased the need to know how to build, program, service, and use them and the services they provide. This need has led to their increased use at the college level, and the introduction of their use in schools below the college level.

One college has begun issuing a microcomputer to incoming freshmen, and at least three others have programs that require the use of one. (Schools below the college level have been able to purchase microcomputers, the kind advertised as personal or home computers with federal block grant funds. In addition, microcomputer and software manufacturers are developing "courseware," another name for computer assisted instruction packages, and are advertising special departments to handle their sale to schools. We now have four, instead of three R's, reading, writing, 'rithmetic, and RAM (random access computer memory)—and RAM helps teach the other three.

The personal or home computer is one durable good with increasing sales, a reverse of the current sales trend for other goods. Over three million microcomputers were sold in the United States in

1981, despite economic conditions. According to a survey of the subscribers to the Source (a computer service), the average age of the home computer user has risen three years between 1981 and 1982.

As more small business operators find uses for microcomputers and the new generation of computer literatures reaches adulthood, the average age of microcomputer uses can only increase.

Who will computer companies hire to work with these computers? Schools around the country have computer literacy instruction programs. OCLC has hosted sessions for some of these schools. Most public schools and at least twenty public libraries in Ohio have adult microcomputer literacy instruction programs. Low and moderate income families will not be left behind because public libraries in areas with families at all economic levels will have these programs. The Lorain (Ohio) Public Library will increase its program for low and moderate income patrons in 1983.

THE HOME NETWORK

Individuals use their home computers for entertainment, education, home management, financial management, and commercial services such as the Source and Compuserv. They soon discover local bulletin boards, the first step in the journey to the home network. A bulletin board provides a means for individuals to communicate with one another using their personal or home computers, a modem, and the telephone. They call another home computer (usually supported by another individual or group of individuals) to leave and pick up one another's messages (electronic mail), swap public-domain software, etc. There is even a computer bulletin board in Toronto for librarians called INFOPORT. Commercial services also offer electronic mail, interactive communication between subscribers, and access to private and commercial data bases.

LOCAL SYSTEMS

Cluster/One and PLAN 4000 (personal local-area network) are two commercially available systems that can link personal computers to one another. Cluster/One can link 65 Apple microcomputers together and PLAN up to 255 Apple II, Apple III, and IBM Personal

Computers. PLAN uses an interface device costing about $600 that plugs into each computer and coaxial cable. It also can provide a link to a mainframe computer, the kind used for large applications such as the OCLC Online Union Catalog and interactive television cable services. LINC (Local Interactive Network Communications), another local area network device, uses a telephone wire instead of coaxial cable to link computers. Its plug-in device transforms a Victor 4 microcomputer into a network station that can support up to sixteen other stations. The device itself costs about $500, and the software needed to use it between $300 and $500. Such elaborate linkages are generally used for business and professional applications, but could be used by cable and telephone companies to offer local or wider area networks.

As computers become as common in homes as television sets are today (in the United States almost every home has at least one, and many have two or more), patrons will want access to the library's information store and services via their home computers as well as in person.

To provide this access, libraries may be able to tap into cable and telephone company networks to service patrons with home computers. Because in-library service will still be available, those who cannot afford or are uninterested in using separate home computers or cable facilities, will still have access to this information at the local library.

The geometric growth of information sources and the decrease in funds to support library operations, have encouraged libraries to examine their need for local computerized library systems to handle the increased information needs of their patrons without increasing staff. More and more of their findings are positive. The Pike's Peak District Library (PPDL) began using the El Paso County computer for circulation in August, 1975, and acquired its own computer (named Maggie after a staff member) in 1978. In seven years PPDL was using Maggie for 32 different applications.

Local libraries are also finding a market for their application programs. PPDL offers Maggie; Virginia Polytechnic Institute, VTLS; and the Clinton-Essex-Franklin Library catalog card and label printing programs for the Apple II personal computer. Commercial software companies offer software for microcomputers: The Book Report(Licorice Software and Services) for school libraries; Library Circulations System that handles up to 18,000 items for schools, public libraries, corporations and institutions, and Film Rental System that handles 750 films per magnetic disk (both by Media Research Assoc.[sic], Inc.); and the E.P.I. Retrieval System for educational material (Database for Education, Inc.).

The local information stores and services these libraries provide will become hubs of computerized information exchange. Libraries will both provide local information and services and access to regional, national, and international networks, and the information these store or transfer.

REGIONAL SYSTEMS

Regional networks have expanded their services to include tape validation, subject search, consulting, physical delivery, cooperative purchasing, local online catalogs and reciprocal borrowing, and bibliographic services from only one or a few of them. For example, in 1980 PALINET and the Union Catalog of Pennsylvania added OCLC tape validation for its members through a contract with Baker and Taylor. Networks also offer consultative and evaluative services. PRLC (the Pittsburgh Regional Library Center) undertook to serve as coordinator and independent evaluator for WEBNET (a system operated by the Office of Communications Programs of the University of Pittsburgh School of Library and Information Science), which began as an online catalog providing interlibrary loan, cataloging, acquisitions, and subject searching in the fall of 1978. It now includes a circulation system being tested by two of the six participating libraries. SOLINET (the Southeastern Library Network) began operation of the LAMBDA system, a bibliographic data base with subject access, and the AMIGOS Bibliographic Council, Inc., had converted OCLC Subscription Service tapes to the DataPhase format, and had CLSI and AACR2 conversions in progress by September, 1982. CLASS (California Authority for Systems and Services) has contracted with commercial firms (Gaylord Brothers and the Computer System Group of Maryland among them) to allow them to market CLASS microcomputer systems. These relationships among not-for-profit regional networks and commercial firms help limit costs for participating libraries through the more favorable terms made possible by the larger volume involved, and give them a wider choice of services within a blanket contract.

NATIONAL AND INTERNATIONAL SYSTEMS

Commercial, not-for-profit, and governmental agencies will both vie with, and cooperate with one another to fill information needs directly for individuals or through other agencies such as libraries. The United States Internal Revenue Tele-Tax service providing recorded tax information on audio tapes on 140 topics such as filing requirements, deductions, and tax credits is available twenty-four hours a day, seven days a week, to individuals with touch-tone phones. Teletax uses a computer to select and start the tape chosen by callers, and record and evaluate their evaluations of the service's usefulness.

BRS, a commercial computerized search service, already offers individuals service during evening hours. Some retail booksellers have installed computerized book order systems for their retail outlets, maintaining up-to-date inventory and gathering special order and stock requests, among other functions. The home office will soon discover that establishing a toll-free number and accepting special orders directly from individuals with personal computers, has become less expensive than maintaining special order departments within each outlet and speeds cash flow. Library booksellers will provide similar services for libraries as well. These retail booksellers and library jobbers in turn will use similar systems to order directly from publishers.

New information services will develop, some services will remain national, and some will expand internationally or join with other national services to form international networks or organizations. The British Library anticipates expanding its online services to support a kingdom-wide UK Library Database System (UKLDS). By mid-1984, UKLDS is expected to consist of a common bibliographic and holdings database for the British Library, regional UK cooperatives (BLCMP, LASER, SCOLCAP, AND SWALCAP) and other participating libraries.

One national network that started as a regional network in Ohio (United States), the Online Computer Library Center (OCLC), has already become international. Its United Kingdom network (OCLC Europe) has established network nodes in London, Bristol, Colchester, Birmingham, Manchester, Newcastle, and Edinburgh, and services libraries in West Germany and Finland as well. Other OCLC international affiliates are in Canada, Mexico, and Australia. And at least one regional library service has become international.

This is AMIGOS, which has extended its services to libraries in Mexico.

CONCLUSIONS

The implications of all this for libraries, technical services departments within libraries, and library computer service organizations are complex. Libraries and their technical services departments will deal with new types of materials, and a variety of new services and equipment. Traditional technical and public services will cooperate ever more closely as procedural efficiency and political problems are resolved. The transition will not be easy—but it will come.

NEW TYPES OF MATERIALS

Many computer programs are expensive relative to the cost of the equipment, and are likely to remain so because of the people-intensive costs to develop, enhance, and maintain them. As more and more are developed, library patrons will seek an alternative to purchasing programs with limited life spans, such as computer games and courseware, and more expensive programs they use infrequently or which are frequently replaced by more versatile software. Libraries have already begun adding computer games and other software to their collections. Not long ago OCLC users discussed standards for inputting these new materials. The Copyright Clearance Center or an organization much like it will handle the copyright problems involved, as software producers find it to their advantage to obtain a large part of their profit from fees for use of library copies of the programs they release. This will put an additional burden on libraries and will lead to the need for automated reporting of the number of uses to the involved clearance center, using a feature such as the proposed OCLC direct transmission program (an enhancement planned for the centralized OCLC Online Acquisitions Subsystem). Bibliographic service organizations will provide the new formats developed by standards organizations for handling the bibliographic description of the new materials. Search services have already begun offering subject access to this material, and it is unlikely that bibliographic service organizations that do not now offer such access would consider adding it for these types of materials alone of sufficient benefit to their participants to offer it for the next three to five years. Those that already offer subject access will provide it routinely.

NEW SERVICES

It is impossible to predict all of the new information services that will develop in the next few years. Current technology suggests they will revolve around cable, telephone, and satellite communication modes. (There are already satellite transmission receivers, "dishes" small enough for home use on the market for $500 to $1000.) Recently offered services suggest that more and more of them will be offered directly to individuals, such as the Tele-Tax and BRS services, but that libraries can play an important role both as a producer and a supplier.

THE NEW LIBRARY

Individuals have, and will always obtain the information they need using the fastest, most efficient means available to them. To do that, they must know that these means exist. The library of the twenty-first century can, and will provide a variety of means. Its tools for providing these means will include personal service, local computerized systems, cooperation in regional, national, and international computerized systems, and the brokering of some commercial systems. Now is when libraries will develop their future role in humanity's exchange of information among individuals and groups. Now is indeed an interesting and challenging time for libraries and librarians. There are many signs that libraries and librarians are meeting the challenge aggressively.

Networking Trends:
Reflections on Their Effect
on Technical Services

Lenore S. Maruyama, MALS

ABSTRACT. Technical network developments in the areas of computer-to-computer links, electronic publishing, electronic mail, and microcomputers are described in terms of what is available now, or will be in the next five years, with some of the possible ramifications on technical services. In addition, five scenarios taken from another paper on "Libraries in the Year 2000" are quoted to provide a framework for what technical services might be like in the next twenty years.

INTRODUCTION

Wherever we are, it is but a stage on the way to somewhere else, and whatever we do, however well we do it, it is only a preparation to do something else that shall be different.

Robert Louis Stevenson wrote these words in the first half of the nineteenth century, but this statement aptly characterizes the situation facing the library profession in the last quarter of the twentieth century. Technological developments are taking place, or are being planned that may effect dramatic changes in library and information services in general, and in technical services in particular, and although the profession is valiantly trying to prepare for these changes, the technology is advancing so rapidly that often the requirements for its use are out-of-date before the planning process has begun.

Some of the developments involving networking are described

Lenore S. Maruyama is a free-lance writer and consultant, 4443 P Street, N.W., Washington D.C. 20007.

221

briefly in the following sections in terms of what is available now, and in the next five years and in the year 2000, with some of the possible ramifications on technical services. It should be noted that these sections are not intended to provide a complete inventory or state-of-the-art of the technology, or a complete inventory of changes that may take place in technical services but to convey a sense of what we may have to face in the future.

THE NEXT FIVE YEARS

The technological developments selected for this discussion include:

— Computer-to-computer links
— Electronic publishing
— Electronic mail
— Microcomputers

Computer-to-computer links involve transmission of data from one computer to another, with the recipient processing the data to meet the requirements of his own system. Three types of computer-to-computer links are emerging, or have emerged in the library field. The first type connects a mainframe computer to other mainframe computers and is exemplified by the Linked Systems Project involving the Washington Library Network, the Research Libraries Information Network, and the Library of Congress. The participants are developing a telecommunications interface that will provide computer-to-computer links among their systems, and the first application of these links will be to support the exchange of machine-readable name authority records sometime in 1984. Expansion of these links to other systems and to other applications, e.g., machine-readable bibliographic records, is contemplated for later phases of the project.

The second could be a prototype: the Irving Communications Network which is attempting to link the systems of five libraries in the Denver metropolitan area for transmission of data among them.[1] Two of the libraries are using DataPhase systems, two, CL Systems, Inc., and the fifth, a system running on UNIVAC equipment. The major categories of library functions to be implemented for the network include the following capabilities, in order of priority: circulation, patron inquiry, bibliographic inquiry, acquisition of materials, administrative information, statistics, interlibrary loan, cataloging, reference and information, and security. Because similar conditions exist in virtually every metropolitan area (incompatible systems, different political jurisdictions, and cooperative agreements, such as reciprocal borrowing), the progress of this project is being watched closely.

The third type involves a link from a mainframe computer to a microcomputer or minicomputer. This capability has been developed primarily by commercial vendors and has gained wide acceptability because it allows libraries to have the best of two worlds: access to the cataloging data bases maintained by OCLC, the Research Libraries Information Network, or the University of Toronto Library Automation Systems, and the ability to incorporate the cataloging records into their local systems without expensive (or extensive) rekeying. Although this link was originally established to obtain machine-readable records for stand-alone circulation systems, one vendor has introduced, in addition to the link itself, modules to input records when necessary, and to provide online serials check-in and acquisitions.

Electronic publishing and electronic mail are not new concepts, but new applications related to library and information services are being introduced rapidly. Since there are so many overlapping technical and logical components of the two systems, it appears necessary to distinguish between the two. For the purposes of this article, electronic publishing is viewed as a passive system that permits a user at one location to "read" text transmitted from another location. Electronic mail is considered an interactive system that permits a user at one location to respond to a "letter" transmitted from another location. Even these definitions are not entirely accurate since the text (e.g., a journal article) is usually transmitted following a request from the user, but the distinction between passive and interactive does provide a starting point for this discussion.

Recent developments in the area of electronic publishing include expansion to textual materials with broader subject coverage (the early offerings had been concentrated in the legal field and articles from newspapers), the growth of nonbibliographic machine-readable data bases, and introduction of optical disks as a storage medium and laser scanning for input. The ADONIS project, for example, will be using laser scanning and optical disks to create high quality textual and graphic displays for the scientific, technical, and medical journals it will produce.[2] Electronic mail is being used heavily for transmitting interlibrary loan requests and purchase orders, but library professionals have also begun to use electronic mail for queries that could range from reference-type questions to questions about cataloging rules or the MARC formats or to communiques among officers of professional associations.

The microcomputer, of course, is synonomous with the "computer" selected as *Time* magazine's Man of the Year. In addition to the library functions that can be performed on a microcomputer, the integration of the personal computer with the college and university curriculum at institutions such as Carnegie-Mellon University (Pittsburgh, PA.), Stevens Institute of Technology (Hoboken, NY), or Clarkson College of Technology (Potsdam, NY) have even greater implications. Clarkson, for example, has not only made the library a part of an integrated information support system for instructional, research, and administrative activities but also incorporated with it the campus computing center.[3]

What effects might these developments have on technical services?

Greater Emphasis on Subject Analysis and Classification as Well as Summaries

Assuming that the process of obtaining machine-readable bibliographic and authority records will be much more efficient and rapid in the future through the existing mechanisms as well as the computer-to-computer links, libraries must start thinking about the requirements that will be placed on them by users who can access their files from terminals that are not located in the libraries themselves. Access by classification numbers and subjects will become increasingly important, and it would seem that libraries would have to ensure that *all* materials are provided with at least minimal subject analysis. Retrospective conversion projects, in general, should concentrate on capturing data that would be used to access a record, particularly subject headings and classification numbers.

More summaries should also be provided so that the user can determine with a greater degree of accuracy if a particular title meets his needs. Summaries will become more important in library applications (e.g., for items like microcomputer software) but will be even more important when accessing journals through an electronic publishing service like ADONIS where the cost of the full-text service will probably be sufficiently high that a user cannot afford to get too many inappropriate items.

Process of Resolving Cataloging or Format Problems to be Expedited

Problem-solving in areas related to cataloging or the MARC formats can be greatly expedited by the use of electronic mail. Questions can be formulated more precisely, and a record of the response can be kept. More importantly, the problems of geographic locations and time zones are eliminated—both the sender and the recipient can initiate the message or pick up the message at times that are convenient for them. And, the game of telephone tag is eliminated. Electronic mail, when compared with the regular mail service, could provide turn-around time in less than twenty-four hours. Such a system, of course, requires that the responding institution, whether it be another library, a network service center, a bibliographic utility, or the Library of Congress, have the appropriate hardware to handle this process efficiently.

Different and Unfamiliar Items to be Placed Under Bibliographic Control

Although it is still likely that printed books and serials will constitute the major portion of any library's collection, the number of nonprint materials to be placed under bibliographic control will increase substantially. As one example, the dramatic surge in the sales of microcomputers has brought many libraries something new to catalog: microcomputer software. Next year, it might be video disks. Nonprint materials can no longer be ignored or left to the "media" specialists because they have become too pervasive in our everyday life. If a library decides to acquire these materials, their existence in the collection should be noted as is done for any printed materials. Also, the problem of controlling ephemeral material, such as brochures or pamphlets that are needed only for limited periods, could be resolved by creating machine-readable records for local use through the stand-alone systems, and adding these records to a circulation system to assist in keeping track of usage. The process of weeding these special collections should then be facilitated greatly. (Adding records for such materials to a large network bibliographic file would not be recommended on the assumption that these records would have to be deleted within six months or a year.)

THE YEAR 2000

Although prepared for an entirely different purpose, Susan Crook's article "Libraries in the Year 2000" presented several scenarios for prospective library and information services that provide a useful sequel to the discussion in the previous section.[4] Portions of each scenario are quoted below to set the context for the discussion of possible developments in technical services in the year 2000.

> PRINTED TEXT SERVICE WITHOUT BOOKS—The Classics Reading Company. . .provides the equivalent of circulation services for current and retrospective books. (It could provide the same service for journals. . .this role is not considered in the discussion. . .) The Company owns no physical books; it provides book text via broadcast or cable delivery. . . . The. . .Company was also established on the premise that different users had different information using needs and styles. . . The. . .Company's initial target was, therefore, users accustomed to controlling equipment and services to meet their own information needs—users who would be willing to read text delivered via their home television screens. . . .Over-the-air broadcast is used for transmission. . .For newer publications, produced for printing in machine-readable form, video discs are used for storage; for older publications, microfiche is employed, with a laser scanner to convert the text to electronic form. . . .to provide texts of books printed before photocomposition-produced masters were available, the firm contracts with a not-for-profit library service company, which obtains texts from a wide range of libraries and creates fiche in a common facility. . . .Materials include texts of books on disc or microfiche. The company offers the combination of current, retrospective, and out-of-print titles, because its principals believe the return on older titles justifies establishing the arrangements to acquire them. Users are anyone within reach of the facility's transmissions who is equipped with a buffered decoder to receive the transmission and a television or other display unit.

PUBLIC REFERENCE SERVICE—Reference Questions USA. . . is a publicly-supported entity providing answers nationwide by mail or telephone. It provides the reference functions offered today in public and academic libraries at the desk staffed by professionals and screened from directional questions by an information desk. It provides only limited services to users such as today's humanities researchers, who need direct or indirect browsing access to extensive files of text. . . . It was meant to enable libraries wishing to concentrate on serving unique regional and local needs to offload classic and increasingly electronic-based reference services. Users would initially be referred to the central facility by their local libraries. Eventually users would become familiar enough with the service that they would access it directly themselves. . . . Reference Questions USA serves all 50 states from a site in Kansas. . . . The facility's staff is 150 trained librarians; the facility is staffed and equipped to provide multilingual services. Its services are accessible via an 800 telephone number. Public entities subscribe to receive services on the part of citizens. Replies are provided by telephone or mail at no charge as part of the service. . . . an audio tape cassette will be made at an extra charge paid by the end user. . . . Reference Questions USA utilizes physical and electronic bibliographic and full text sources. Its collection and agreements with online bibliographic full text and numeric data sources give it resources similar to central and subject reference, document, pamphlet, and technical report collections, as well as some maps, of a large public library. . . . It loans no materials and performs no custodial or bibliographic functions for any users besides its own staff. . . . In general, . . . it serves public libraries' traditional users. . .

COMMUNITY CULTURE CENTER—Metropolis Public Library. . . resembles today's public libraries in their locally-oriented services. The phrase community culture center denotes the fact that it evolves between 1982 and the year 2000 by linking itself to social trends and political issues important to the Metropolis local population and government. . . . Its programs and its buildings evidence its many linkages to the local population's needs. . . . It is located in the downtown site built in the 1970s. . . . Those branches and sites continuing to have sizable residential or commercial populations were closed or reopened on the basis of the character of local needs and support. The central location. . .is equipped to create video discs containing material of local interest and occasionally to create collections of material of short-term interest to local groups; to store and distribute products of local public interest cable channels; to create local output and distribute government "documents" and to distribute program information from federal agencies on an on-demand basis; to serve as an output center to produce fine quality hard copy of materials published electronically—for example, illustrations to accompany the text of electronically published scientific articles; to create machine readable copies of master document copies for loan or nominal sale in tape form for home use—in a limited number of standard formats and when legal requirements for duplication are met. . . .Categories of information. . .in the collection. . .include community-specific materials and services as deemed important by groups which supported the need for continued library services during the last two decades. . . . ; information still published in print form—including children's books, mass magazines, trade magazines, fiction, and some nonfiction. . . . ; computer and print files of local information including local history, adult education course offerings, local theater, government offices, clubs and organizations, referral information for human welfare agencies.

COLLEGE/UNIVERSITY INFORMATION SERVICE— Redbrick University Library. . .is the terminal-filled information production and dissemination center of its campus. It is the undergraduate library portion of 1982's academic library. Manuscript and archival collections and extensive retrospective print collections are administered for the University by the Humanities Research Institute. . . .Redbrick University's Library/Information Services offers facilities (administered but not housed together) for computer-aided instruction; computer conferencing; internal cable; sharing of text within private academic networks and use of local, regional, and national information sharing networks; distribution of information over internal systems from centrally located media; and assistance in the creation of learning materials using video disc. . . .Redbricks's information resources come in all formats—print, microform, mass market magazines and trade journals, magnetic and video tapes, and video disc. Electronic data bases are the medium absorbing most materials budget. The Library/Information Center also contains an extensive collection of commercial and internally developed applications software.

RESEARCH SERVICES—The Humanities Research Institute. . .is a loose confederation of research libraries. . . . Therefore, like today's research libraries Institute members serve on-site and remote, personal and institutional members. Unlike today's research libraries, however, the members of the institute wear only one hat—they serve only research users. (There could be a similar institute of libraries in the fields of medicine or science and technology. This scenario does not discuss such an institution. . . .) Institutional members. . . for the most part still occupy their 1980s locations. Their facilities tend to house collections including full size print originals of most sources. Tape or fiche copies are retained of all documents duplicated for local or remote users, although no overall effort is made to convert print materials for electronic storage. Federal support has underwritten equipment for transmission of documents among institute members. Private donations have been used to acquire laser printers and video disc recorders for a handful of members with extensive manuscript collections and large endowments. . . . There is wide variation among institute members' collections as well as among services available to users of the collections. Federal funds are available to provide small public service staffs to members opening substantial portions of their collections to citizens with serious interest in those collections. Institute members have the option, however, of relying on federal assistance only for technical support—for example, in the area of preservation, and in turn, need offer no browsing facilities. . .Services. . . may include texts of works. . .(fiche or original or both), and entire subject collections to afford readers browsing facilities; special fee-based services supported by requisite staff capability, to provide on-demand analysis and duplication utilizing capital equipment for copying and text analysis; and bibliographic access supplemented by some sophisticated electronic aids. (Institute policy has been to encourage members to offer on-demand analysis services rather than to prospectively provide access at fine levels of detail to collections which are, for the most part, not in machine readable form.)

Accompanying these scenarios is an appendix describing library functions in the light of the technology and market developments in the year 2000.[5] Crooks implies that although these (traditional) functions will remain, the methods we use to perform them will change as well as the people who will perform them. In the acquisitions area, for example, the wide-scale availability of electronic full text services would mean that libraries would be narrowing the range of subject material being acquired; for cataloging, the availability of the full text services will probably mean that the vendors (rather than the libraries) would have to prepare indexes and summaries to access the text.

The three aspects of technical services that were mentioned in the previous section (greater emphasis on subject analysis and classification as well as summaries, process of resolving cataloging or format problems to be expedited, and different and unfamiliar items to be put under bibliographic control) would still have to be in place in the year 2000 for the scenarios to work. The "how" and the "who," of course, remain to be worked out.

CONCLUSIONS

Although comparing the trends in technical services in two separate timeframes in this manner may appear to be comparing apples with kiwi fruit, it does focus on one fact. The five scenarios for the year 2000 assume that goals and objectives for the particular institution are in place. At present, the existence of such goals and objectives seems to be the exception rather than the rule. Technical services will have to respond to the needs of the library, which in turn has to meet the needs of either its parent institution or its constituents.

What about cost? Since the points mentioned above involve intellectual effort of varying degrees of complexity, implementing them requires personnel. Staff costs are escalating, so that it would be unrealistic to think that additional personnel could be (or even should be) hired to perform these functions. Here again, the planning process is essential to determine not only the goals and objectives but the strategies for implementation and the priorities for implementation. Most of the technology is in place to support these efforts, but first, one must know what it is we want to do.

One final point concerning the networking technology. Although it may be much easier to exchange machine-readable records in the future through telecommunication links, the files of records will become even larger, thereby making global changes to these files much more difficult. The lead time needed to make changes because of the size of the files and the complexity of the programs to process these records becomes increasingly longer as well. While this does not mean that changes cannot be made, it does mean that virtually all changes have to be analyzed in terms of their expected benefit and the cost of effecting them.

NOTES

1. Boulder Public Library Foundation and the Irving Libraries. *Preliminary Design Proposal for Detailed System Design.* (Prepared) by National Link Corporation. (Feb. 22, 1982) p. 3.

2. Sponsors of the ADONIS project include Academic Press, Blackwell Scientific Publications, Elsevier Science Publishers, Pergamon Press, Springer Verlag, and John Wiley, who together publish about 1,500 journals. *ADONIS—A New Concept to Solve an Old Problem.* Text of the presentation made by Cuadra Associates, Ltd. and Berul Associates, Ltd. during market research investigations, Jan.-March 1982. Distributed (not presented) to the Network Advisory Committee, March 10, 1982. . . 11 p.

3. Robert A. Plane. "Merging a Library and a Computing Center." *Perspectives in Computing,* 2: 14-21 (October 1982).

4. Susan H. Crooks. "Libraries in the Year 2000." In *Document Delivery—Background Papers Commissioned by the Network Advisory Committee.* (Washington: Library of Congress, 1982).

5. *Ibid.,* p. 20-24.

Electronic Document Delivery:
Current European Developments

Peter W. Lea, MLS, ALA, MIInfSc

ABSTRACT. A number of experimental projects are currently being undertaken in Europe, involving various public and private organizations. Three of the major projects are *ADONIS, HERMES,* and *ARTEMIS.* These are described with a recently published study on the concept. The implications for the future of both libraries and the traditional published journal are discussed.

Members of the information community who regularly scan their professional literature for papers on electronic publishing and related topics, may have noticed frequent references recently made in European journals to a group of classical Greek deities. A fleeting question may have crossed the mind of the casual browser as to what the gods of hunting, music, poetry, and other worthy but rather dilettante arts have to do with the contemporary, dynamic communications world. The answer lies in what may be one of the most important and significant developments to take place in information transfer since books were first unchained; that is the electronic document delivery systems.

ADONIS, HERMES, and *ARTEMIS* are some of the proposed schemes connected with the electronic transmission of the complete text (including graphics) of documents to a library or individual end user. The journal articles would be stored on a high density storage medium such as digital optical discs. They would be retrieved on demand and transmitted via the telecommunication networks to receiving centres where they would be reproduced on fast laser printers. A number of variations of this type of system could include facsimile transmission and teletex services.

Peter W. Lea is Senior Lecturer at the Department of Library and Information Studies, Ormond Building, Manchester Polytechnic, Lower Ormond Street, Manchester, M15 6BX, England.

A number of factors are influencing the rapid and positive developments of the concept in Europe:

1. The existing, and fast evolving technology for capturing, storing, transmitting, and receiving documents is currently both adequate and economically viable, according to preliminary studies.
2. Publishers see the new systems offering an alternative and increasingly lucrative source of revenue, particularly in a climate of declining library subscriptions of some journals. Related to this, is the much aired criticism of the prolific photocopying activities of certain national libraries which many publishers claim, without much supporting evidence, to be the cause of the decline. Electronic document delivery systems would enable them to monitor and control the supply of documents.
3. The growth of use of on-line bibliographical retrieval services suggests that there will be a corresponding growth in demand of original documents.
4. It is claimed that there is a strong market need for electronic document delivery services, that are fast, reliable, of high quality and able to provide a high satisfaction rate.
5. Intra-governmental support and encouragement is being provided by such organizations as Department 13 of the Commission of the European Communities (C.E.C.).
6. Other advantages that such schemes could offer publishers are the creation of new products and packages of information to potential new markets, which could be identified precisely from the files of users.

There can be no doubt that economic considerations offer the greatest incentives to change, and these together with availability of sophisticated telecommunication networks and information systems suggest that there is every likelihood that during the next few years some of the systems currently being evaluated will come to fruition.

It may seem curious that the main initiative for the implementation of electronic document delivery has come from Europe rather than from the United States. Although there exists in the United States a strongly technologically oriented information society, it appears that the future of document fulfillment there will follow a pattern of labour intensive services via traditional postal channels. The alternative European approach has been stimulated by the existence of a major international organization, the C.E.C., supporting the innovations, the networks to carry the services, and the desire of European based major international publishers to have some control over the system of document delivery, which is dominated at present by the public sector, exemplified by the British Library Lending Division.

The proposed system which has received most attention and so far the greatest capital investment is ADONIS, which has been formed by a consortium of major scientific technical and medical publishers including Elsevier, Blackwell, Pergamon, and Springer. In the past year the consortium has undertaken discussions in Europe, the U.S.A., and Japan with other publishers and governmental agencies including large document fulfillment centres such as the British Library Lending Division, with a view to setting up a world-wide electronic document supply system. Market research and independent systems analyses suggest that such a system would be economically viable, and ADONIS is planned to be operational in 1984. A chief executive has been appointed, and the centre will be based near London. The aim of ADONIS will be to supply articles on demand from a 3500-5000 journal data base with a five year back-file supplied by 200 publishers. The journals will be stored on optical video discs from original printed versions, and transmitted to local centres where they will be printed and supplied for a fee. It is hoped that the target of 1 to 1.5 million requests per year will be achieved. These figures should provide a service at reasonably competitive rates; greater use will bring operating costs down.

The concept which appears to have created the greatest amount of documentation recently is ARTEMIS (Automatic Retrieval of Text from Europe's Multinational Information Service). The name and the proposed system were conceived by the management consultants Arthur D. Little, who were commissioned by the Directorate General XIII (DG XIII) of the Commission for the European Communities. Two major reports on the concept have been published describing the technology and investigating the feasibility of the systems[1] and disseminating the results of a workshop where equipment was demonstrated and the ARTEMIS proposal was discussed.[2]

The results of the study suggest that present technology could provide the facilities to transmit by facsimile and teletex documents stored at a database to local centers. It was also felt that by using the existing Euronet/Diane network overnight with large volumes of documents, the service could be financially quite attractive compared to present costs of conventional document delivery services.

Proposals to take part in pilot experiments have been invited by the C.E.C. It is expected that several hundred initial declarations will be made, which will be cut to ten or twelve official proposals by May 1983. The C.E.C. would partly fund the experiment and act as a "marriage broker" in bringing together organizations to form a consortium.

A timely, if rather expensive, report has been published recently which unusually has not been graced with the name of a Greek god. *Electronic Document Delivery* is a study undertaken by PIRA, the UK research association for printing and related industries.[3] It examines the relationship between user needs and the various technological options for document delivery.

Future plans include increasing scientific technical and medical coverage, expanding beyond those subjects into other areas and adapting the service to specialized market requirements.

HERMES is a demonstration project being carried out by the (British) National Physical Laboratory, and the Printing Industry Research Association (P.I.R.A.) for the U.K. Department of Industry.

The aims of the project are:

1. To stimulate product development of retrieval software, computer systems, storage techniques, telecommunications and terminals.
2. To provide a foundation for document delivery services if found to be economic.
3. To demonstrate the various technologies in use and promote awareness of them.

The project, which is to be conducted in four phases, is based on the recently adopted C.C.I.T.T. standard for teletex. Teletex is a new telecommunication service in which office information can be transmitted between communicating word processors. It has a number of advantages over conventional telex systems in that a wider range of characters can be transmitted, it is faster and therefore cheaper than telex and possesses an automatic memory for correspondence. The phases, the first of which began in 1982, will examine parts of a proposed configuration that will develop from fairly basic electronic mail services to a public service phase which could integrate teletex with digital facsimile transmission to enable graphics to be transmitted with text. Possible application of HERMES could include the dissemination of contents pages of scientific technical and medical journals, statutes, patents, standard specifications, and a possible link with the ADONIS service where contents pages and full text could be available. If the HERMES project proves to be successful, it is hoped that some form of system will be publicly available within the next few years.

Over 500 replies from librarians, information scientists, and managers in various libraries provided a number of encouraging points for any organization concerned or interested in electronic document delivery. The most popular features of a proposed new service would be that a comprehensive range of documents would be available from a single source; there would be immediate viewing on a terminal; ordering would be easy, and favourable comments were made on the probable pricing structure. Publishers showed a reasonable interest in electronic document delivery; many were either already involved in the use of new technology or were planning to be so within five years. Generally, PIRA found that user needs could be met by current technology, at a reasonable price, a finding that confirmed the results of other studies. A consortium would be needed to provide a service and provide the range of documents required, and there is a willingness amongst publishers to actually set up such systems.

A seminar held in London towards the end of 1982 examined the implications for libraries and information centres of electronic document delivery systems. Existing methods of obtaining documents were described such as those provided by the British Library Lending Division and database producers via inter-library lending schemes in Europe.

The publishers described their systems and suggested a number of advantages both to the user community and themselves. It is claimed that a better and wider service could be provided to the market, whilst greater control could be achieved over library photocopying and copyright.

Issues raised by the library community illustrated some of the concern, and in some cases scepticism, regarding certain proposed changes and their apparent advantages. These were related to capital investment costs, particularly for those libraries where document delivery is not a prime function, and running costs could be considerably higher than those forecast by the publishers. Moreover, as the technology to be used for the systems is at an experimental stage, worries were expressed about the possibility of its quickly becoming obsolete.

The long-term implications of electronic delivery gave rise to some fears about the future of both the traditionally published journal and libraries. Already there exists a trend towards the supply of single articles and although current plans are to create the single copy desired by the user from an original printed journal, it does not need a great deal of imagination to envisage the time when it would become totally uneconomic to produce the original printed journal, and on-demand publishing from a totally electronic data store might become the common form of publishing of low-use titles. Linked with this development could appear a tendency to by-pass the library and go directly to the electronic document delivery service, a situation which clearly vindicates many of the gloomy forecasts made during the 1970s of the future, or lack of it, for libraries. Furthermore, once costs and control are predominantly in the hands of the private sector, and single copy provision becomes the norm, what will happen to the economics of the publishing system? Currently, large profits are still being made from high demand publications, and these could in turn subsidise electronically transmitted copies of articles. How long could this state continue before the balance of demand and use tilts so far as to cause the publishers to increase prices of the electronic services to counteract any falling income, as is happening already with on-line bibliographical retrieval services?

Typically a member of the often forgotten majority, the user community, has very simple needs. The user wants a service that can provide a reasonably prompt (within one week) supply of papers from a single source at a price that the user's library, parent organisation, or the user himself or herself does not find prohibitive. The user does not particularly need an ultra rapid service. He or she certainly does not wish to apply to a range of access points for needed documents, nor to see any change in the present financial arrangements where, for example, the local academic library bears the costs of the document request service for faculty members. It is essential that these basic, yet important, points are kept to the forefront when changes are considered.

Commercial publishers are cooperating in these new ventures for virtually the first time on any large scale, which suggests the importance they are placing on the new schemes for disseminating information. It is essential that the current discussions continue between the private sector and the public sector represented by libraries, and that cooperation develops between these two major groups of the information community to the benefit of the third major group, the users of information.

REFERENCES

1. *Electronic Document Delivery I. The Artemis Concept for Document Digitalisation and Teletransmission.* (Oxford: Learned Information Ltd., 1981)

2. *Electronic Document Delivery II. Proceedings of a workshop and exhibition organized by the C.E.C. Directorate General Information Market and Innotation.* (Oxford: Learned Information Ltd., 1981)

3. *Electronic Document Delivery: a Study of the Relationships between Users Needs and Technology Options.* (Leatherhead, UK: International Publishing Research Centre (P.I.R.A.) for the Publishers Association and C.E.C. 1982), 2 vols.

Publishers in Electronicsland

Naomi B. Pascal

ABSTRACT. Most book publishers today are looking at the new technologies primarily as means of producing conventional volumes more efficiently. Publishers of educational and reference materials, however, are developing new formats that require library adaptations in storage, cataloguing, dissemination, and record keeping, and new definitions of such terms as "acquisition," "shelving," and "circulation." Many issues involving copyright, fair use, and the First Amendment are still to be settled.

Last November, according to the December 1982 issue of the Newsletter of the Association of American Publishers (AAP), an author named Burke Campbell "pushed a button on his terminal and immediately 'published' his nineteen-chapter novel entitled *The Blind Pharaoh,* on-line. The 25,000 subscribers to The Source [a commercial data-base retrieval service] were, from that time on, able to type the command level word 'Novel' on their individual terminals and receive the entire novel either displayed on their screens or printed on their individual printers. . . . Campbell wrote his novel on-line, edited it on-line, and published it on-line in Toronto. He is compensated each time a reader accesses any part of the novel." The charges to the readers varied with their reading speeds, but "the average price to read the novel was $2.80 in connect time charges."

It would be interesting to know what principle of selection was involved in linking Mr. Campbell with The Source. It is evident, however, that in this case the traditional functions of the book publisher—editing, design, production, promotion, warehousing, shipping, and billing—have been either eliminated or transformed. The fact that the "book" described is identified as a novel is especially noteworthy, since it has become customary to respond to those who

Naomi B. Pascal is Editor-in-Chief of the University of Washington Press, Seattle, WA 98105.

241

forecast the imminent demise of the conventional book in the electronic age by saying, "You wouldn't want to curl up in a hammock with a cathode ray tube."

On the whole, I would say that publishers (I am speaking of book publishers rather than newspaper, magazine, or technical report publishers) have lagged behind libraries in making full use of the new technologies. While libraries have been forging ahead, developing computer-linked networks and information search-and-retrieval systems, until quite recently the applications to publishing were peripheral. Publishing houses, like other businesses, use computers to streamline their business operations. And computerized typesetting has been firmly established for some time. For most book publishers today, the emphasis is on learning to make the best possible use of the word processor. This means acquiring the equipment and the ability to handle a tape or floppy disc submitted by an author (and more and more authors are buying their own word processors, or at least have access to one), to edit it, perhaps to insert production codes, and to transmit it to a phototypesetter. The end result, however, is still envisioned as a volume printed and bound, and the technology involved in producing it will not be apparent to the library, bookstore, or individual who purchases it.

It is for publishers of educational materials and reference works that the technological possibilities appear to be most intoxicating. An article in the January 7, 1983, issue of *Publishers Weekly,* the trade journal of the publishing industry, on the venerable Boston-based publisher Houghton Mifflin, emphasizes that company's commitment to electronics and to computerized educational materials, with plans under way for the development of "courseware" in cooperation with curriculum-planning agencies. In addition, the well-known Roger Tory Peterson bird guides have been put on videodiscs, which the publisher expects will eventually be distributed by bookstores alongside the actual field guides. Libraries, surely, may also expect to make either format available to their clients. In an experiment carried out last year by the Online Computer Library Center (OCLC), the entire twenty-one volume *Academic American Encyclopedia,* published by Arete, was put on-line and is thus accessible to two hundred computer-equipped customers. This and other aspects of the technological revolution as it affects publishing are discussed in a useful "Publishers Weekly Special Report" entitled *Electronics and Publishing,* published by R. R. Bowker Company.

Not all publishers, of course, are interested in electronic capabilities, and some have deliberately chosen to continue their exclusive dedication to the traditional book. The question has been raised, moreover, as to what role a publisher can or ought to play, given the ease with which information can now be transmitted directly from the creator to the consumer (who no longer even has to go to a library to use a computer but can afford to purchase his or her own). To this argument it can be answered that, in view of the enormous capacities of data banks and videodiscs, which will accept uncritically and indiscriminately vast quantities of information, the publisher's exercise of editorial judgment in selecting and arranging material is more important than ever. Although it is not clear how many of the nonbook but book-related products developed by publishers will find a place in bookstores, it seems to me that libraries will inevitably be even more deeply involved than they are at present in acquiring, cataloguing, and making available to their users (either in person or via computer) materials in a great variety of formats.

Libraries will also undoubtedly find it necessary to keep extensive records of all such transactions in order to protect the rights of authors and their publishers. Authors in Great Britain, joining those in Germany, the Scandinavian countries, Australia, and New Zealand, have recently begun to receive some payment when their books are borrowed from public libraries. For materials that exist only in an electronic format, some means of compensating authors and publishers on the basis of use will have to be devised to supplement the present system based on number of copies sold. The distinction between publishing and broadcasting may also become blurred, and questions relating to the First Amendment, such as "whether books, magazines and newspapers, historically unregulated, will shift into the legal realm of broadcasting when electronically delivered" (*AAP Newsletter,* October 1982), require continued consideration. Since even the comparatively uncomplicated question of copyright infringement through academic copying has not yet been settled—witness AAP's recent suit against New York University, nine professors, and a photocopying center—it seems likely that solutions to these new problems will not easily be reached.

Those of us who were brought up on books, and who have been working with them throughout our adult lives, can be assured, I think, that they are not about to become obsolete. And, despite *The Blind Pharaoh,* for any work of the mind or the imagination that is intended to be read straight through, not merely accessed in a search for bits of information, a book remains a singularly convenient, attractive, and inexpensive artifact. But the extreme youth of today's inventors and entrepreneurs of computer hardware and software, as profiled in *Time* magazine's "Machine of the Year" issue of 3 January 1983, and the impressive evidence that schoolchildren take to computers with an alacrity that only a few show when first exposed to books, can lead to some sober thoughts about the future. The generation gap appears even in the comic strips, where the comparatively mature *Doonesbury* character who wants to purchase a word processor is referred to "consumer-compatible lifeware" when what he seeks is a salesclerk he can understand, while the eternally infantile Dondi gleefully and nonchalantly engages in computer warfare with a corrupt school principal.

One further challenge to libraries in the electronic age was expressed in an article in the *New York Times* (2 January 1983), entitled "Campus Computers Reshape Social Life and Work Habits." Describing the use of computers at universities for everything from replacing live lecturers in the classroom to playing Cupid through electronic mail, the author observes, "Computer centers are replacing libraries as the focus of much academic and social activity."

Electronic Publications and Their Implications for Libraries

F. W. Lancaster, FLA

ABSTRACT. Future growth in the number and diversity of electronic publications, along with new capabilities that these publications bring with them, may eventually lead to the replacement of print on paper and the demise of the library as we now know it.

The term "electronic publication" can be interpreted to mean any information source published in electronic (i.e., machine-readable) form. This would include sources *distributed* on magnetic tape and on such media as videodisk as well as sources not really distributed at all but only *accessible* (e.g., through terminals, including home computers and domestic television sets).

Electronic publications were born, no more than 20 years ago, when computers were first applied to the printing of conventional publications. When a machine-readable data base was prepared in order to print, say, *Index Medicus,* the machine-readable version could itself be distributed. It was the electronic equivalent of the familiar print-on-paper product; it was an electronic publication.

Many publications now exist in this "dual mode," i.e., a print-on-paper version that has an electronic equivalent. However, many "electronic only" publications (i.e., those that have no print-on-paper counterparts) have also emerged.

As we all know, the first electronic publications were mostly secondary publications, data bases of bibliographic records equivalent to printed indexing or abstracting services. Several hundred of these can now be accessed online in various parts of the world.

The user community has expanded rapidly as the scope of electronic publications has widened in two ways:

F. W. Lancaster, Graduate School of Library and Information Science, University of Illinois at Urbana-Champaign, 410 David Kinley Hall, 1407 W. Gregory Drive, Urbana, IL 61801.

245

1. Expansion of subject matter from science and technology (at first) to the social sciences, humanities, and sources of "general interest."
2. Increasing diversity in the type of publication available: bibliographic, numeric, directory, full text (of newspapers, journal articles, encyclopedias, and so on).

This diversity has led to an ever-increasing array of possible uses: retrospective literature searching, current awareness (SDI), question-answering, and, most recently, document delivery. Moreover, electronic sources are becoming accessible in more and more ways, including access through home computers and interactive television.

It seems reasonable to suppose that these trends will continue at a greatly accelerating pace, and that electronic publications will increase in accessibility as print on paper declines in accessibility. Furthermore, the cost of publishing in electronic form can be expected to fall rapidly relative to the cost of publishing as print on paper. For all practical purposes, electronic publications will eventually supplant print on paper (Lancaster)[1], and perhaps more rapidly than most observers seem willing to accept.

Ironically, it is probably correct to say that no "true" electronic publications have yet appeared. By this I mean that those electronic publications that now exist have been designed to "look like" print on paper. A page of such a publication, displayed on a screen, is virtually the same as a page in a printed book. Electronic publications will come into their own when they are designed, ab initio, to capitalize on the true capabilities that electronics can provide: a reorganizable, dynamic text and dynamic illustrations, including electronic "models." The true electronic publication will allow the user to interact with it in a way that print on paper cannot do. We have reached the limits of what can be achieved with print on paper as a communication device. In contrast, the surface of electronic communication has hardly yet been scratched!!

Clearly, these developments have profound and far-reaching implications for libraries. Indeed, they threaten the very existence of the library as a viable institution.

Perhaps most obviously, the existence of information sources that are *accessed* through computer and telecommunications technologies, rather than *distributed* as physical artifacts, changes our entire notion of what constitutes a library. Obviously, the distinction between what a library "owns" and what it does not own is beginning to become quite artificial. In a sense we can say that the "collection" of a library consists of anything that can be accessed by, or on behalf of its users, whether the materials are accessible by being physically present in the library or not.

As our notion of "collection" changes, so must our notion of what constitutes the catalog of a library. It hardly makes sense to include in the catalog only those publications that are physically present in the library, and to exclude those other publications that are routinely accessed online on behalf of users. Indeed, if we carry this to its logical conclusion, and if the future does lie with electronic publication rather than with print on paper, all collections of all libraries eventually become the same. The "collection" of *every* library will be *everything* that can be accessed. This also raises the question of who should be responsible for cataloging electronic sources that, in a sense, "belong" equally to all potential users, to say nothing of the question of *how* they should be cataloged.

The "disembodiment" process implied in these developments leads one to believe that the library may soon be bypassed: any material needed can be accessed by anyone who needs it from some form of terminal in the office or in the home. The role of the librarian—as an information consultant—may last much longer than that of the library. But even the information service function of the librarian may be made redundant through the development of "user-cordial" interfaces and "intelligent" systems. Food for thought?

REFERENCE NOTE

1. Lancaster, F. W. *Libraries and Librarians in an Age of Electronics.* Arlington, Va., Information Resources Press, 1982.

Beyond Online Ordering:
Future Trends in Subscription
Agency Services

Philip E. N. Greene III

ABSTRACT. This paper predicts some of the general trends that can be expected from subscription service agencies during the next twenty years. Predominant needs in serials work are identified, and current and possible future services to meet these needs are discussed. The impact these service changes will have on acquisitions operations is also addressed.

The "Amazing Randi" is a well known magician who, while entertaining his audiences with feats of magic, offers $10,000 to any of his contemporaries who can perform a "real" feat of magic. To date, he has not been separated from his money. His point, quite simply, is that all magic is an illusion.

In a real sense, forecasting the future of subscription agency services and their impact on acquisitions work is a feat of magic that can be challenged with every statement. However, based on today's situation, it is possible to make some reasonable projections.

The value of serial publications as a source of timely research and reference information will assuredly continue to grow. And, in line with the trends of the past few years, this will require increasing levels of fiscal and physical control if collections are to serve patrons adequately. Twenty years ago, no library dreamed of spending 50% of their total acquisitions budget on serials. But with an estimated 20,000 new titles appearing each year, this 50% has become standard operating procedure for many libraries.

In the future, 50% of the budget may not get the job done. We have all been made well aware of the diverse and frustrating nature

Philip E. N. Greene III, is Vice President and General Manager, EBSCO Subscription Services, EBSCO Building, Red Bank, NJ 07701.

of library funding problems. Today's 50% share of a budget often turns out to be equal to yesterday's 25% share. How much will acquisitions departments actually be able to spend ten or twenty years from now? The present economic situation also reveals a continuing rise in costs per title. Assuming yearly inflation of 10%, compounded annually, a title which costs $100 today will cost $259 in 1992. If the inflation rate happens to be 15%, the journal will be $403 in 1992, an increase of 303%.

A little over a decade ago, most agencies were simply clearing houses for library subscriptions. However, the trends toward decreasing budgets and increasing usage, costs, and numbers of titles, have resulted in a multitude of special services and reports. Agencies have gone beyond being an extension of library purchasing functions, to become an integral part of the management plan in many acquisitions, technical services, and serials departments. These increased levels of sophistication in service were the result of finding out what librarians wanted. Likewise, future services will be shaped by the needs we discover from meeting and corresponding with library professionals.

The general needs of the coming years seem to be fairly well established. Greater skill in serials collection management is needed, as are increases in cooperation and resource sharing. Clearly, these needs are already being addressed. For example, the EBSCO "Historical Price Analysis" breaks down the inflationary factor of serials for a three-year period, in effect creating a collection-specific price index. And EBSCO's Missing Copy Bank is a unique combination of resource sharing and cooperation between libraries and our agency which is available online, or through a regional customer service representative.

The future promises additional methods for meeting the collection and cost control needs of the library community, most notably through the use of automation. As advances in programming, telecommunications, and artificial intelligence are made, improved agency services will undoubtedly follow.

An agency's ability to interface with libraries and publishers in an electronic world will be of great importance. Agencies will strive to increase electronic communications with publishers in order to meet all their clients' needs, including ordering, billing, payment, and claiming. Better management services will also be developed, such as improved forecasting abilities, highly sophisticated online accounting functions, bibliographic support programs, and other customized services. Additional cooperative efforts, and the expansion of data communication networks, like the EBSCONET system, will in all probability lead to more widespread union listing, interlibrary loan, and document delivery activities.

New equipment configurations will appear with functions divided between online and in-house systems. Agencies will step in to supply needed data and direction for clients to use in conjunction with their mini- and microcomputer systems. While a direct interface between the library and the agency will be important, it is probable that a good deal of in-house processing will be done over the next ten years.

Larger, full service agencies will continue to broaden and expand their services in the future. Eventually, this should result in integrated systems for acquisitions work that will include complete subscription services, standing orders/continuations, approval plans, book ordering and delivery, and full accounting services.

EBSCO's participation in areas such as electronic publishing is not yet clearly defined. What is obvious is that we will be involved to at least some degree. Considering the communication networks we have already established with our clients and some publishers, we may well become involved in the delivery of electronic text.

The future of subscription agencies will ultimately depend on their ability to anticipate library needs, and to support the necessary research to make their electronic interfaces useable, practical, and cost effective. Of course, this will require the continued investment of funds by agencies for research and development.

What effects will these future trends in service have on acquisitions work? For those librarians who use the tools available to them, it will mean steady increases in efficiency. Hopefully, the resulting savings in time and money will somehow compensate for the rashes of cutbacks in staff and materials. As more sophisticated services and competitive prices develop, acquisition librarians will become more discriminating customers. Their expertise will increase, and they will learn to work more closely with vendors of all types, rather than merely reacting to existing services. User services should also improve as librarians find additional time to assist patrons, and to make online union lists, indexing, and other automated tools available. The overall result of improved services during the next twenty years will be to make acquisitions work less complicated, less time consuming, and less expensive.

It is, and will continue to be, the function of subscription agencies to provide cost effective services that help ensure serials expenditures are as productive as possible for libraries. And crucial to this function will be the agency's ability to work with libraries on a basis of partnership. Every day brings new needs and problems to our clients. The next ten to twenty years will be full of challenges that will demand a heightened sensitivity to their requirements. As we evolve to help meet and anticipate these technical service challenges of the future, subscription agencies will become an even more viable and important factor in the management of libraries.

Vendor Services in the Information Age

Rebecca T. Lenzini

ABSTRACT. In the next ten years, libraries will look to vendors for more and greater services than in past decades. The vendor will assume a role as member on the library's technical services team and will provide vital operational support, which will enable the library to better serve the end user, with reduced library staff.

The relationship between vendor and library will be interactive, evolving from buyer/seller to team approach. The end user will increasingly influence both library and vendor decision-making as the information chain tightens.

What was fundamentally true in the past of the role of the vendor in relation to library services will remain true in the coming ten years, and will serve as the foundation upon which we build other services that, in the end, will change the very nature of this relationship. The vendor will continue to serve as the advocate of the library, facilitating the dissemination and management of information and forming a meaningful middleground. However, the vendor will assume an even more vital role in the operation and management of the library, which will by then be characterized by fewer employees but more and better public service.

Both libraries and vendors have long shared the position of middleman in the chain of information transfer, which begins with the creator of information, continues through the publisher and then vendor, to the library and finally to the user, who may well be the creator. This chain, always important in our eyes, is now becoming critical for everyone, since . . . "although we continue to think we live in an industrial society, we have in fact changed to an economy based on the creation and distribution of information."[1] This quotation is taken from the nation's number one non-fiction bestseller, *Megatrends,* an analysis of the major forces that will change our lives over the next ten years.

Rebecca T. Lenzini, Manager, Customer Services, F. W. Faxon, Company, Inc., 15 Southwest Park, Westwood, MA 02090.

We are no longer part of a minority. Says Naisbitt, author of *Megatrends,* "The overwhelming majority of service workers are actually engaged in the creation, processing and distribution of information."[2]

The next ten years will bring changes specifically related to the business conducted between libraries and library vendors. It will also bring shared changes since both institutions are part of the information chain, and must evolve with it as we move fully into the information age. Let us first consider those changes which will affect the current relationship between library and library vendor.

Already one can witness the coming evolution within the library from specialist to generalist as the lines between technical services and public services begin to fade. The development of library computer systems broke down many existing barriers as the mutual concerns of public and technical services towards automation fostered (or, in some cases, forced) direct communication between the two. Happily, during this design and implementation process, it seems that technical services has gained a new-found respect within the library industry. Similar effects are already being felt by vendors like Faxon, who have moved into the world of online services and find ourselves no longer dealing solely with one specialist or even one level of staff within the library. We now confer with serialists, heads of technical services or public services, reference librarians and bibliographers, all of whom are concerned about the application of automation.

Automation continues to support the move toward generalization as computing systems absorb more and more of the control over detail that is vital to the library's effective operation. Two by-products of this generalization affect the vendor: first, a need for full services and a broader range of services from vendors as the library attempts to transfer even more record keeping and detail away from the practicing generalist; second, the increasing need for the vendor to replace the specialists the library can no longer afford to support on a full-time basis.

Libraries are already presented with the challenge of providing more and better service with fewer staff, a situation which demands that the library be efficiently managed and organized. In order to accomplish this goal, economic realities of the past few years have meant that libraries must look to vendors for more and greater services than in the past decades. This trend will not only continue, it will grow substantially in the coming years.

Tailoring of services will become more important for the vendor, who will utilize existing data resources as well as research and development personnel, and large computing facilities to create the specific products requested by individual libraries or even by individual users within an institution. As vendors develop and offer this wider range of services, libraries will find it more cost effective and efficient to utilize the services of fewer and fewer vendors.

During the next ten years, the vendor will in fact become a member of the library's technical services team. The vendor will successfully assume a larger role in the library's operational and management work, while providing the practicing professional with tools such as statistical analyses, report generators, and text editing, available locally at the library's terminal. The vendor will no longer be viewed as a secondary provider of information but will indeed be a main source, and the relationship between library and vendor will be truly interactive.

For our part, the next five to ten years mandate that we listen harder than ever to the requests and demands of the library. As the relationship between vendor and library continues to tighten, the library will accept a greater role in the vendor's decision-making process. It will no longer simply be a situation where the library purchases a product that the vendor has developed. Rather, the library as user will be interactively involved in the design, the implementation, and even the success of the vendor product, as the buyer/seller gives way to the team approach.

Many scholars have speculated on the nature of the information chain as it continues to evolve. Naisbitt points out that the "information float,"[3] of which we have all been a part, is collapsing, thanks to automation and to the telecommunications satellite. The age of full text is already upon us, and it seems clear that a greater proportion of journals and journal articles will be available only electronically. Packaging in the form of the journal will still occur, though the content will no longer be dictated but rather will be selected. In an age wide open to choices, selectivity will become even more critical. Vendors will help with these tasks, too, forming again the role of the effective middleman or consultant.

As the chain of information tightens, the end user becomes more important and exercises greater control over information selection. The library, having shifted its operational burdens to automated systems and to vendors, will give increased emphasis to public service directed primarily to the end user. In five or ten years, users will find that most of the information they seek can be obtained without entering the library, though much of it may be provided by library operated systems. The end user thus becomes a critical factor influencing the services library vendors provide.

It also seems clear that the need for print will continue for a least the next ten years. Naisbitt identifies "high tech/high touch"[1] as one megatrend. That is to say, the coldness of technology produces in us the need for human contact, a heightened need in fact. Print is "high touch" and as such will continue to exist. Libraries are also "high touch" by definition because they bring together people. The electronic age and the print age will co-exist, and the library is likely to continue, wearing several hats, for the next decade.

The familiar points of the information chain described earlier in this paper are clearly being drawn more tightly together. In this evolution, some links in the chain will become stronger and more vital, while others will be virtually squeezed out. Naisbitt suggests that "reconceptualization"[2] is vital for survival beyond the short term. Both libraries and library vendors have begun the effort to re-establish ourselves as information providers, and we will continue over the next decade to work together toward this end.

REFERENCE NOTES

1. Naisbitt, John. *Megatrends; Ten New Directions Transforming Our Lives* (New York, NY: Warner Books, 1982), 1.
2. Ibid., 14.
3. Ibid., 22. "Information float" is defined by Naisbitt as being the amount of time that information spends in the information channel. Information in the mail for four or five days, or awaiting publication for three to six months is in the information float. Automation, full-text retrieval, and online mailboxing will eliminate, or at least help collapse this information float, according to Naisbitt.
4. Ibid., 39.
5. Ibid., 85.

Selections from a Dictionary
of Libinfosci Terms

Norman D. Stevens

ABSTRACT. Some reflections on the future are presented from the perspective of what took place earlier on. These reflections are cast in the form of excerpts from a dictionary of library and information terms published in the year 2050.

INTRODUCTION

The following entries have been carefully selected from the April 1, 2050, edition of the World Library Association's *Dictionary of Libinfosci Terms* for the interesting and illuminating historical perspective which they provide on aspects of the technical services operations of American libraries in the late 20th century. The full text of the dictionary is available to all members of the Association through Unitermserv.

Acquisitions: An obsolete term for both a set of procedures and a functional unit commonly found in libraries through the end of the 20th century. The procedures typically involved unduly complicated techniques for identifying material which the library wished to add to its collections, sending a request to a supplier, receiving and recording the material, processing payment, and sending the material along to others for further arcane and complex procedural handling. The functional unit was a body of staff with specific responsibility for handling those complex functions in isolation from the remainder of the library staff. The procedures and the functional unit largely disappeared with the advent in the early 21st century of automatic universal accessibility to new forms of publication.

Bar coding: An extremely primitive machine readable technique used for a limited period of time in the late 20th century as a means

Norman D. Stevens, University Librarian, University of Connecticut Library, Storrs, CT 06238.

of attempting to link, in the individual library, bibliographic records to an individual item, and borrowers to a locally maintained patron address file. Bar coding, along with similar primitive techniques such as magnetic stripes and optical character recognition, were replaced by the adoption in 2015 of the universal linked identification system (unlides) for both materials and individuals.

Binding: A technique that libraries were forced to use for many years to place material that publishers and other suppliers had produced either in a non-durable format or in isolated but related pieces, or both, into a self-contained durable container which provided some physical protection from the ravages of readers who had direct physical access to library materials.

Catalog: Originally a peculiar piece of library furniture consisting of a large case, most often wooden, containing a series of long rectangular drawers designed to hold catalog cards (usually 3″ × 5″) containing the bibliographic information about the holdings of a library. The cards were generally arranged in alphabetical order by author, title, and/or subject, with labels on the individual drawers indicating the contents of that drawer. The term was subsequently used, for a limited period of time, to designate any file containing information about the contents of a library that was designed to serve the public. Since approximately 2020, the information formerly contained in a catalog has been available in most libinfocenters through access to universal bibliographic records (unbirs).

Cataloging: An obsolete term for both a set of especially arcane procedures and a functional unit that dominated library practice in the 20th century. The procedures, which were taught in highly specialized courses in library schools, and which were governed by incomprehensible rules adopted by library associations, involved the most complex techniques imaginable for providing for the individual library what it felt were the necessary bibliographic records needed to differentiate items in its collections. The quality of local cataloging was often a source of pride so that, despite the advent of shared systems such as OCLC in the last half of the 20th century, cataloging procedures tended to continue to have a local flavor for a number of years thereafter. The functional unit known as the Cataloging Department, was most often located in a remote part of the library building, isolated from other staff and from users. That unit, which generally was the largest single body of library staff, spent large amounts of time providing exact and precise bibliographic records that were difficult to interpret, and were of limited use. The procedures and the functional unit eventually disappeared with the advent in the early 21st century of automatic universal bibliographic identifiers (aunibids) in all publications.

Library: An obsolete term used for many years to describe the predecessors of contemporary libinfocenters. The term may best be used to describe those organizations whose primary emphasis was on the collection of vast quantities of little used material, at the local level on which they spent not only large quantities of physical space but also inordinate amounts of staff time and financial resources, predominantly in the mechanical and non-intellectual processes (q.v., technical services) related to the physical handling of that material.

OCLC: An organization, founded in the late 1960s as the Ohio College Library Center, that represented one of the first successful efforts to centralize the storage and manipulation of bibliographic records in an effort to assist libraries to reduce the rate of rise in the costs of technical services. It ultimately failed because of its commitment to a highly centralized physical organization and because, despite its many innovative features, it and its users remained wedded to many of the traditional concepts and methods of processing library materials. The advent of universal bibliographic records (unbirs) on a decentralized basis in 2015, and their rapid acceptance by libinfoceners, brought about the final demise of OCLC, then popularly known as the Old Concepts of Library Cataloging, in 2018.

Processing: An obsolete term used to describe the many complicated steps that had to be undertaken in individual libraries in the 20th century as they made individual physical units containing information, directly accessible to users. Processing involved a number of techniques, many of which are now known only by name, such as binding, bookplating, checkpointing, labelling, pocketing, and spine marking.

Serials: An obsolete term for a publication format in which a large number of information content pieces (incops) were packaged together with a generic title that often bore no direct relationship to the content, that changed frequently for no good reason, and caused serious problems for libraries that had to handle such items. The term was often also used to describe those functional units in libraries responsible for handling these materials which required specialized knowledge and techniques. Fortunately those materials are of concern now only to those few highly specialized libinfocenters that are responsible for collecting, storing, preserving, and making available older materials in printed formats. Serials as such went out of existence by 2009.

Technical Services: An obsolete term used to describe the largest component of most library staffs in the 20th century. That component of the staff was entirely devoted to arcane and mysterious processes involved in selecting, acquiring, cataloging, processing, and otherwise making available to library users, physical material containing information content pieces (incops). The processes were complicated, expensive, and time-consuming, and generally served to severely limit direct service to users, both by producing records that were difficult to understand and interpret, even by other library staff, and by consuming from 75-80% of the library's financial and personnel resources. The advent in the early 21st century of new forms of publication and of new techniques for providing universal records and universal access to information content made the organizational structure obsolete. That change in organizational structure, more than any other single factor, is generally credited as being responsible for the dramatic improvement in the quality of library service that has occurred in the first half of the 21st century.

Subject Index

AACR2
  catalog record degradation 62
  online focus 118,119
  public catalog access 14-15
  uniform titles 145
Abbreviated title 144-145
Academic libraries
  access to materials 100-102
  automated systems 100-106
  cataloging 133-134
  collection development 107,108
  cooperative systems 100-104
  data base searches 100
  delivery procedures 102,103-104
  effectiveness 107-108
  functions 83-84,107-108
  preservation activities 108
  projected developments 228-229
  resources 100
  serials 150-153
Acquisitions
  automation 16-17,21-22
    budgetary constraints 26
  government documents 185,187-188
  monographs 88-89
  serials 89-91
    budget 249-250
  serials
  problems 89-91
  staff, 89
Acquisitions librarians, changing role 35
ADONIS 150-151,223-224,233,235,237
A.L.A. Catalog Rules 117
AMIGOS 217,219
Archival collections, 80,114
ARTEMIS 10,233,235
Artificial intelligence 13-14
Authority control
  automatic indexing 38-39
  online catalogs 20,113,119,120,
    121-127

  traditional basis 122-123
  Universal Entries 124-216
  user-oriented 124-126
  subject headings 62-63
  union catalogs 173,175
Automated systems
  academic libraries 100-106
  computer-to-computer links 222-223
  decentralized vs. centralized 39,54-56
  Dortmunder Bibliotheksystem(Dobis)
    52-54
  integrated 26,40-41,111-112
  interconnection 56-57,58,101,222-223
  international 218-219
  local 215-217
  national 218
  regional 217
Automation
  deleterious effects 61-63
  economics 39-42
  libraries, effect on 31-36,114-115
  limitations 12-17
  management, effect on 29
  resistance to 42
  staffing, effect on 32

Bar coding 91,257-258
Bibliographic checking 97
Bibliographic control
  automated 17
    limitations 28
  electronic publications 86
  nonprint materials 219-225
Bibliographic records
  centralized systems 55
  degradation 62
  MARC 70,139,140,143-147,225
  serial union lists 164-165
Bibliographic uniformity 48
Bibliographic utilities
  competition among 26,87-88

self-employed 6,112
Librarianship, changing nature of 75-77
Libraries
  automation gap 61-62
  cooperation among 88
  demographics 15
  economic constraints 87
  technological changes 5-10
  undercapitalization 86
Library education 69-70
Library of Congress
  authority files 20,119
  bibliographic utilities interface 118
  serial cataloging 146
  serial records 144
  subject headings 63-70
LINX 10,90

MARC format 70,139,140,143-147,225
MEDLARS 111
Microcomputers
  current trends 114-115
  bibliographic data base interconnection
    58
  government document processing 188
  impact 213-215
  potential use 57-58
  in small libraries 58
Microforms
  government documents 192-193
  serials 209-210
Micrographics 27
Monographs
  acquisition 88-89
  series 43

National Level Bibliographic Record
  (NLBR) 126
National library network 88,92
Networking 221-231
New Serial Titles 163
Newspapers, electronic 15,156
Nonprint materials, bibliographic control
  219,225

OCLC (On-line College Library Center)
  alternative records 91
  future trends 10
  government documents processing 182,
    183-186,188,189,196

intersystem connection 20
library cooperation 117
serials check-in system 39
Online public access catalog(OPAC) 8
Optical disc storage 9
Order transmission, online access 21

PALINET 217
Paper deacidification 92,204
Paris Principles 122
PATSEARCH 211
PERLINE 10
PIRA 236,237
Preservation 21,26-27,92,108,203-205
Printed materials, electronic publications
  vs. 8,9,14,19-20,37-38,80,87
Professional staff 32-34
Public libraries 15,107
Public relations 77
Public services 29-30,34,58-59,69,
  133,254

RLG (Research Libraries Group) 195
RLIN (Research Libraries Information
  Network)
  acquisitions system 39
  future trends 10
  government documents processing 182
  intersystem connections 20
  library cooperation 117
  OCLC merger 70
Record keeping 95-98
Reference books, online 15-16
Reference librarians 42-43
Reference service 227
Research libraries 92,229-230
Resource sharing, failure 26
Retrospective conversion 21,194,195,224
Robotics 7,12
Royalties 80
Rules for Descriptive Cataloging 117

Security systems 22
Serials
  abbreviated titles 144-145
  acquisitions 89-91
    budget 249-250
    problems 89-91
  automated systems 22,119
  cataloging 143-147,164